WildFly Performance Tuning

Develop high-performing server applications using the widely successful WildFly platform

Arnold Johansson

Anders Welén

BIRMINGHAM - MUMBAI

WildFly Performance Tuning

First published: June 2014

Production reference: 1190614

Published by Packt Publishing Ltd.
Livery Place
35 Livery Street
Birmingham B3 2PB, UK.

ISBN 978-1-78398-056-7

www.packtpub.com

Cover image by Bartosz Chucherko (chucherko@gmx.com)

Credits

Authors
Arnold Johansson
Anders Welén

Reviewers
Ricardo Arguello
Robin Morero
Christopher Ritchie
Kylin Soong

Commissioning Editor
Ashwin Nair

Acquisition Editor
Rebecca Pedley

Content Development Editor
Anila Vincent

Technical Editors
Kapil Hemnani
Manal Pednekar
Faisal Siddiqui

Copy Editors
Roshni Banerjee
Sayanee Mukherjee
Karuna Narayanan
Stuti Srivastava

Project Coordinator
Aaron. S. Lazar

Proofreaders
Simran Bhogal
Stephen Copestake
Lindsey Thomas

Indexers
Mehreen Deshmukh
Tejal Soni

Production Coordinator
Nilesh R. Mohite

Cover Work
Nilesh R. Mohite

About the Authors

Arnold Johansson is a versatile information technologist with a true passion for improving people, businesses, and organizations using "good tech".

As an early adapter of the Java language and its growing ecosystem, he is an outspoken proponent of secure Java Enterprise solutions and real Open Source software.

After nearly two decades as an IT consultant in many levels and verticals, Arnold now focuses on leading organizations on an architectural stable and efficient path of excellence.

> Mother and Father, thank you for everything!

Anders Welén embraced the object-oriented techniques of the Java language early in life, and later evolved to Java Enterprise specifications. As a true believer and evangelist of Open Source, he naturally discovered the JBoss Application Server, which led to years of providing expert consultation, training, and support for the JBoss and Java EE infrastructures.

As a result, Anders has seen a lot of both good and bad architectures, software solutions, and projects, most of which were a struggle from time to time due to performance problems.

Whenever Anders, through presentations, consultation, training, and (in this case) a book, sees that what he's trying to explain is getting through and the audience is picking up on it and adopting it for their own challenges, it gives him a warm feeling inside.

To my parents, Stig and Birgitta, for teaching me to be curious.
To my love, Lotta, for her support while I was writing this book.

And finally, to the French language lessons in school, as I chose, and therefore discovered, Computer Science to avoid them.

About the Reviewers

Ricardo Arguello is a software architect with more than 15 years of experience. He has worked on enterprise applications and distributed architectures for most of his career. He has collaborated as a JBoss.org committer in the past and is now part of the Fedora Project as a packager of WildFly dependencies. He loves to give talks on the need to become active Open Source collaborators rather than be passive users of the technology.

Ricardo is the founder and owner of Soporte Libre, an Ecuadorian company devoted to providing onsite technical support for enterprise clients using mission-critical applications that run on Open Source. With almost 10 years' experience in delivering middleware solutions and infrastructure platforms based on Linux, Soporte Libre has become one of the most important Open Source businesses in Ecuador.

Robin Morero is a full stack developer/architect based in Gothenburg, Sweden. He has a background in the telecom industry and in product development. He is experienced in middleware, e-commerce, BSS, BRM, CRM products, and custom development.

Christopher Ritchie is a Sun-certified programmer with over 10 years' software experience. Having worked in both the UK and South African markets, he has worked on a variety of software applications, ranging from online gaming to telecoms and Internet banking.

He currently works as a software architect at his company in South Africa. He has a keen interest in the JBoss Application Server (now WildFly) and is an advocate of Java EE technologies. You can get to know more about him by visiting his website at www.chris-ritchie.com.

Kylin Soong has six years' experience in working with JBoss and WildFly, including developing and maintaining proficiency in Java programming, JEE environment (JBoss/WildFly) development, knowledge of middleware architecture, and performance tuning.

www.PacktPub.com

Support files, eBooks, discount offers, and more

You might want to visit www.PacktPub.com for support files and downloads related to your book.

Did you know that Packt offers eBook versions of every book published, with PDF and ePub files available? You can upgrade to the eBook version at www.PacktPub.com and, as a print book customer, you are entitled to a discount on the eBook copy. Get in touch with us at service@packtpub.com for more details.

At www.PacktPub.com, you can also read a collection of free technical articles, sign up for a range of free newsletters and receive exclusive discounts and offers on Packt books and eBooks.

http://PacktLib.PacktPub.com

Do you need instant solutions to your IT questions? PacktLib is Packt's online digital book library. Here, you can access, read, and search across Packt's entire library of books.

Why subscribe?

- Fully searchable across every book published by Packt
- Copy-and-paste, print, and bookmark content
- On-demand and accessible via web browsers

Free access for Packt account holders

If you have an account with Packt at www.PacktPub.com, you can use this to access PacktLib today and view nine entirely free books. Simply use your login credentials for immediate access.

Table of Contents

Preface

Buying a new suit isn't easy. Hopefully, you know why you need one. There might be a certain occasion, such as a wedding or party, or perhaps you just need to look sharper at work. Whatever the reason, there are likely to be some inherent requirements. Cloth, colors, patterns, the cut and the placement as well as the number of buttons are examples of factors that will all depend on environment and time of usage. The thoughtful buyer will take all of these factors, and possibly more, into consideration before making a selection.

Getting something cheap can be acceptable and cost-effective in the short run. For longer commitments, however, it will certainly be more financially viable (and probably more aesthetically preferable) to get the quality of a well-designed, tailored fit, especially as this might even be customizable as your needs (size) change.

Should you need to sit a lot in your precious garment, it would be wise to double up with at least an extra pair of pants. When wear and tear, or some other reason, makes you drop a pair, it is good to quickly have another on standby.

Get the requirements sorted, find the right design, try it out, and tune it to fit new needs when needed. If you find a wrinkle, make sure to iron it out and try it on again. That is what you must do during the lifecycle of a suit and an IT system alike.

Let's go and get dressed for success with WildFly!

What this book covers

Chapter 1, The Science of Performance Tuning, talks about what performance tuning is all about and how it can be applied within an organization.

Chapter 2, Tools of the Tuning Trade, introduces some useful Open Source tools to use when performance tuning anything covered in this book.

Chapter 3, *Tuning the Java Virtual Machine*, covers what the engine of Java is and how to tune it as well as all other Java-based applications.

Chapter 4, *Tuning WildFly*, explains what can be tuned in the WildFly Application Server.

Chapter 5, *EJB Tuning in WildFly*, talks about how Enterprise JavaBeans can be tuned.

Chapter 6, *Tuning the Persistence Layer*, covers how to design an effective database as well as how to tune JPA and queries.

Chapter 7, *Tuning the Web Container in WildFly*, explores Undertow — the blazingly fast, new web container in WildFly — and discusses how it can be tuned to become even better.

Chapter 8, *Tuning Web Applications and Services*, covers numerous tuning tricks and tips surrounding the web applications and services based on Java EE.

Chapter 9, *JMS and HornetQ*, explains how JMS works and can be tuned in HornetQ, the JMS provider of WildFly.

Chapter 10, *WildFly Clustering*, explores tuning in a clustered WildFly, HornetQ, and Java EE components.

What you need for this book

As a base, it is recommended that you start out with the following platforms and tools:

- Java SE 7
- WildFly 8.x (8.0.0.Final is used in the book)
- VisualVM
- Apache JMeter

More tools have been introduced within the book, but they are considered optional depending on what you are interested in exploring and tuning.

Who this book is for

This book is for anyone interested in what performance tuning is all about and how to do it using Java technologies, the WildFly Application Server, and other Open Source software.

The first chapter should be considered a compulsory read for anyone working anywhere near any form of IT, project and business managers included!

Chapter 2, *Tools of the Tuning Trade*, and *Chapter 3*, *Tuning the Java Virtual Machine*, are very useful for anyone working with Java technologies.

From *Chapter 4*, *Tuning WildFly*, and forward, the content in this book turns toward developers and architects that need to tune WildFly and the different layers of the Java EE stack.

The final chapter is for those who (think they) need to cluster, and tune their clustered environment.

In general, you will probably need to be a seasoned developer or software architect in order to take in everything from this book. However, the book has been designed so that you, as a reader, can target the area you are interested in, or have a need for, at the moment. The book will grow with you, and you with the book.

Conventions

In this book, you will find a number of styles of text that distinguish between different kinds of information. Here are some examples of these styles, and an explanation of their meaning.

Code words in text are shown as follows: "As the JVM runs out of memory, an OutOfMemoryError error will occur."

A block of code or configuration is set as follows:

```
@MessageDriven(activationConfig = {
  @ActivationConfigProperty(propertyName = "destinationType",
    propertyValue = "javax.jms.Queue"),
  @ActivationConfigProperty(propertyName = "destination",
    propertyValue = "queue/testQueue"),
    @ActivationConfigProperty(propertyName = "maxSession",
    propertyValue = "20"),
  @ActivationConfigProperty(propertyName = "acknowledgeMode",
    propertyValue = "Auto-acknowledge") })
public class TestMDB implements MessageListener {
  public void onMessage(Message message) {
  . . .
    }
}
```

When we wish to draw your attention to a particular part of a code block, the relevant lines or items are set in bold:

```
remote.cluster.ejb.clusternode.selector=RRSelector
```

Any command-line input or output is written as follows:

```
/subsystem=ejb3/strict-max-bean-instance-pool=mdb-strict-max-pool:read-attribute(name=max-pool-size)
```

New terms and **important words** are shown in bold. Words that you see on the screen, in menus or dialog boxes for example, appear in the text like this: "Unfortunately, **Management Console** only provides a configuration view on this pool and not any runtime information."

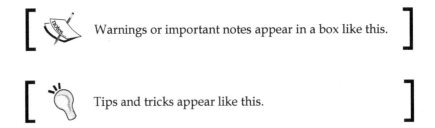

> Warnings or important notes appear in a box like this.

> Tips and tricks appear like this.

Reader feedback

Feedback from our readers is always welcome. Let us know what you think about this book—what you liked or may have disliked. Reader feedback is important for us to develop titles that you really get the most out of.

To send us general feedback, simply send an e-mail to feedback@packtpub.com, and mention the book title via the subject of your message.

If there is a topic that you have expertise in and you are interested in either writing or contributing to a book, see our author guide on www.packtpub.com/authors.

Customer support

Now that you are the proud owner of a Packt book, we have a number of things to help you to get the most from your purchase.

Errata

Although we have taken every care to ensure the accuracy of our content, mistakes do happen. If you find a mistake in one of our books—maybe a mistake in the text or the code—we would be grateful if you would report this to us. By doing so, you can save other readers from frustration and help us improve subsequent versions of this book. If you find any errata, please report them by visiting `http://www.packtpub.com/submit-errata`, selecting your book, clicking on the **errata submission form** link, and entering the details of your errata. Once your errata are verified, your submission will be accepted and the errata will be uploaded on our website, or added to any list of existing errata, under the Errata section of that title. Any existing errata can be viewed by selecting your title from `http://www.packtpub.com/support`.

Piracy

Piracy of copyright material on the Internet is an ongoing problem across all media. At Packt, we take the protection of our copyright and licenses very seriously. If you come across any illegal copies of our works, in any form, on the Internet, please provide us with the location address or website name immediately so that we can pursue a remedy.

Please contact us at `copyright@packtpub.com` with a link to the suspected pirated material.

We appreciate your help in protecting our authors, and our ability to bring you valuable content.

Questions

You can contact us at `questions@packtpub.com` if you are having a problem with any aspect of the book, and we will do our best to address it.

1
The Science of Performance Tuning

There are many definitions of science. However, the most common definition is the systematic gathering and organization of knowledge. This refers to knowledge that, apart from its original purpose, can be used for further explorations of even more, and possibly further detailed, knowledge. Gaining new knowledge often involves validating theorems or ideas through experiments and tests. When a test has been validated or falsified, some things can be changed, or tuned, and the test can be performed again in order to gather more knowledge about what is going on in certain environments or situations.

As we will see, this approach of searching for knowledge in science is directly transferable to the improvement of performance in IT systems. In our opinion, performance testing and tuning is a science that is possibly spiced with some gut feeling (which is often based on experience, so we would say knowledge possibly sprung from science).

In this chapter, we will kick off by defining some key terminologies and measures of performance. After that, we will turn our focus to the process of performance tuning and its place in the software development process and the software life cycle. This will include its iterative behavior and talking about when, where, and how performance tuning should be done in an enterprise stack.

Performance

In the world of **Information Technology (IT)**, performance is often used as a generic term of measure. This measure can be experienced somewhat differently depending on the role an individual has.

A user of a certain application will think more or less favorably of the application depending on how fast it responds, or flows, from his or her individual perspective and interactions. For a developer, an administrator, or someone else with a more technical insight of the application, performance can mean several things, so it will need to be defined and quantified in more detail. These expert roles will primarily need to distinguish between **response time**, **throughput**, and **resource utilization efficiency**.

Response time

Response time is normally measured in seconds (and is often defined with some prefix, such as milli or nano) and relates to the sum of time it takes to send a request to an operation, the execution time of the operation in a specific environment, and the time taken to respond to the requester that the operation has completed. The request, the execution of the operation, and the response are collectively called a **roundtrip**: a there-and-back-again trip.

A typical example, (depicted in the following diagram), is a user who has filled out a form on a web page. When the user sends the form by clicking on the **Submit** button and sends the data in the form, the timer starts ticking. As the data is received by a server, the data populates a JavaBean in a Java Servlet. From the servlet, subsequent calls to other components such as other servlets and EJBs will occur. Some data will then be persisted in a database. Other data can be retrieved from the same or other databases, and everything will be transformed into a new set of data in the shape of an HTML page that is sent back to the browser of the end user. As this response of data materializes at the user's end, the timer is stopped and the response time of the roundtrip can be revealed:

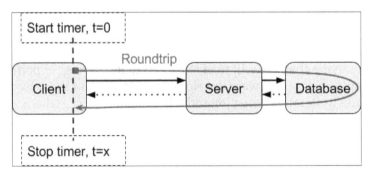

The response time, starting at t=0 and ending at t=x, and the roundtrip for a use case in a system.

Deciding what, or how much, should be included in a use case for measuring the response time, will vary on the test or problem at hand.

The total response time for the roundtrip of a system can be defined as the total time it takes to execute a call from an end user through all layers of the network and code to a database or legacy system, and all the way back again. This is an important and common value that is often used in **service level agreements (SLA)**. However, it provides a far from complete picture of the performance and health of a system. It is important to have a set of use cases with the measured response time from various points in the system that covers its common and most vital functionality and components. These will be extremely helpful during tuning and when changes or problems occur.

> It is important to remember that the roundtrip in a use case must be constant, in terms of start and stop points, between measurements. Changing the definition will render the measurements useless as they must be comparable!

So, what can affect the response time? In short, any change might affect the response time in a positive or negative way. Changes that you can perform as a technician in the software, hardware, and related infrastructure—code, configuration, hardware, network topology, and so on—of a system, will have their effect and not seldom other than you might expect.

With all these things static, there might still be changes that can make the response time vary. Here, we're mostly concerned with the load on the system. As the load of the system increases, its response times will eventually rise as the system throughput decreases.

When an application performs work, that work is often triggered by external or internal clients. This will require resources, such as CPU, volatile memory, network, and persistent storage. The level of this utilization is the load of the system. Load can be measured for one or several of these resources.

Take, for example, an increasing number of users and the interactions they do in a system. The increase in system transactions could eventually exhaust available connections of a pool. The excess of transactions would need to be queued for released resources or even timeout. This then turns into a bottleneck, where the system isn't able to handle the increasing number of transactions quickly enough.

Throughput

The load a system can manage is coupled to the measure of the system throughput. Throughput is generically measured in transactions per given time unit, where a transaction can be a task or operation, or even a set of operations that act as one.

The time unit is often measured in seconds but can be significantly smaller (milli, nano) or bigger (minutes, hours, and so forth). Commonly, throughput is denoted as **transaction per second** (TPS).

Here, a transaction or operation can be of any size such as a small computational function or a big business case spanning over several components or systems. The size is not of importance but the amount of operations is.

An alternative measure of throughput that is often used is the amount of data transferred per second, such as bytes per second. Just like an SLA often has one or more stated response times for a set of use cases, throughput normally also has TPS values for the system as a whole and possibly, some for subsystems/components that are important from a business perspective.

From a technical or IT-operations perspective, it is equally important to know what throughput certain systems or subsystems regularly have, and at what levels these might start to have problems and failures. These will be important indicators for when upgrades are in order.

With a focus on Java EE, it is important to remember that the Java EE specification, and therefore, most application servers that implement it, were designed for overall throughput and not guarantees about response times.

Utilization efficiency

Low response times and a high measure of throughput is normally what anyone wants from a system, as this will help in keeping customers happy and the business thriving. If money is of no concern, it might not be a big deal from a technical perspective to have a lot of hardware and using more resources than needed, as long as business is booming.

This poor efficiency will, however invoke unnecessary costs, be it to the environment, the employment force, development time, system management, administration, and so on. Sooner or later, a business that wants to be or stay profitable must have an efficient organization that can rely on cost-efficient IT departments and systems. This includes utilizing available resources in the most efficient way while keeping the customers happy. It's a balancing act that business and IT departments must do together.

Having a bit less computational force, memory, and IT staff available might (among many things) cause higher response times and worse throughput. Consequently, software must be more efficient on available hardware. To make the software efficient, we need to test and improve its performance.

Scalability

A system needs to be able to handle an increasing load in order for the business to stay attractive to customers. The response times need to be kept down for each individual user and the total throughput needs to increase as the amount of transactions increase. We say that the system needs to scale to the load, and scalability is the capability that the system needs in order to increase total throughput.

When a system needs to be scaled, there are two major disciplines that can be followed: **vertical scaling** and **horizontal scaling**. Vertical scaling (or scaling up), as shown in the following diagram, involves adding more hardware resources, such as processor cores and memory, to an existing computer. This was the prevalent way to scale in the days of the mainframes but is used to some extent even today as virtualization has gained momentum:

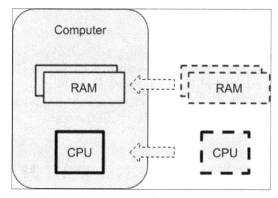

Vertical scaling involves adding more resources to
an existing computer.

Horizontal scaling (or scaling out) involves adding more computers that are connected through a network. A simple example of horizontal scaling is shown in the following diagram. This has been the concept of most computer topologies for several years and has gained enormous momentum with cloud services and big data:

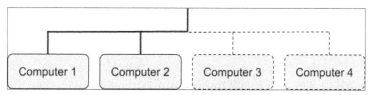

Horizontal scaling involves adding more computers to a networked collective
of computers, such as a cluster.

In general, adding more resources to a single computer becomes more expensive than adding more computers at some point. The single computer will be of low volume and will often be very specialized, as it needs to have an advanced and expensive architecture to handle a lot of processors and memory, whereas the many cheap computers can be simple, off-the-shelf products. The single computer will be a *better* computer standing next to any of the cheap ones, but at some point, the grand number of cheap computers will collectively be cheaper, faster, and thereby, better than the expensive one.

In the extreme, having just one computer can be hazardous as it will be a single point of failure. Using one computer will, however, be easier from an administrative point of view. There will only be one place to make changes or configurations. It will also be easier from a developer's point of view, as the programming model won't have to deal with many of the more complex scenarios that a distributed model can require.

As with all things, there are pros and cons with the two different types of scaling. There are also several factors that bridge the gap between them. The single computer in the vertical scaling scenario is seldom a single one. It is most common to have at least one backup server. In the horizontal-scaling scenario, the programming model has been simplified thanks to modern enterprise frameworks and the topology of computers can be adapted to let each cheap server in the network work on its own without the need (and complexity) to know about the rest.

Performance tuning anti-patterns

To tune the performance of a system means to improve one or more of its measures of performance. The question is how, when, and where should it be done? This is an area of great underestimation and major misconception. In the subsections that follow, we'll give you some examples of common mistakes and problems. Try to avoid them, or help out by correcting them, whenever and wherever you can.

The one-off

For many not-so-developed or understaffed organizations, performance testing with some possible tuning is more or less a one-off, something done just before an application is shipped out to production.

By only performing the testing and tuning at this point, the amount of work, if done properly, is much higher and much more complex than if it was done iteratively during the development of the application.

Naturally, an organization must keep within its financial limits, but doing performance testing just before a release is very hazardous. What will happen if an application turns out to not live up to the expected and necessary measures in production? It would clearly be very bad for business.

The wrong team

Very often, performance testing and tuning is run by staff that lacks the knowledge of how this testing and tuning should be performed. Getting the right individuals, in terms of competence, on board in the testing and tuning team is crucial. This can vary but normally involves **quality assurance (QA)** staff, experienced performance testers, and technical staff, such as architects and developers that have actually been involved in creating the system under test.

The lack of mandate

Even though the quality value of a system's performance has grown to be relatively recognized in most organizations today, there are still places where staff responsible for performance-related tests and tuning lack the voice or mandate to enforce proper quality tall-gates.

The clever developer

As passionate developers, we like to be clever. Making our code run smoothly is satisfying, and the performance improvements we make can give us a feel-good boost and self-confidence. That is great, but it's often not very meaningful to just (over)optimize our own functions or components. As developers, we won't know for sure how much or what parts of our code will actually be executed in such an amount that it will need performance tuning. In the long run, it can even hamper the performance as our optimizations might cause problems in other places of the system as a whole.

So, performance tuning is something that an organization as a whole should take seriously. It should be done iteratively and handled by a competent team with complementing skills, experiences, and mandate. As it's such an important factor for today's businesses, it should have a given place in any organizational process map.

Software development and quality assurance

Back in the days, when software development started to be structured and development teams grew, the waterfall methodology ruled. Today, that methodology has mostly been replaced by agile counterparts that include highly iterative approaches to the work. What has changed is the iterative and shortcut behavior among the tasks involved along with their iterative frequency. It is not uncommon to perform several iterations per day in modern development teams.

No matter what the methodology is, we perform some kind of analysis (requirement, architectural) in software development from which design and implementation phases follow. After, and often during the implementation phase, unit tests are run.

The unit test should be on a functional level, verifying the smallest building blocks in code, such as specific functions or methods within a class. These tests are normally run by the individual developer and are also advantageous to automate in order to run during daily/nightly builds.

Higher levels of tests include the following:

- **System tests**: These tests are used to verify a system as whole
- **Integration tests**: These tests are used to verify integration points between two or more components or systems
- **Acceptance tests**: These tests are used for the final verification by the product owner before or during the deployment in a production environment

Most of these tests should be automated and run with live data as soon as possible. Note that both combinations and other variants of tests can exist in different organizations depending on various needs, organizational, or other inherited reasons.

All these types of tests are commonly part of a well-run business' QA process, but they are also heavily entwined in the software development process as the knowledge and cooperation from both IT and QA staff are required. This is all good, but what about performance tests and performance tuning?

Naturally, performance testing should be included as a compulsory step in the software development process and the results thereof should simultaneously be an integral part of the QA process. The ownership might be arguable, but the important thing is that it gets done, and gets done well. The exact location of when to do performance testing will, however, need a bit more discussion.

Software development with performance focus

Let's first revisit the major steps of the software development process in more detail with a healthy focus on performance and some quality. Remember that these steps are run iteratively, with possible shortcuts, and sometimes, with very short iterations!

Some organizations may also define the process a bit differently, with some steps included in other processes such as the requirement and QA processes. The following diagram shows us a common version of the software development process from which we will discuss its different phases. We will, however, not talk about the acceptance testing and deployment phases in the process, as they normally won't have any direct impact on performance tuning.

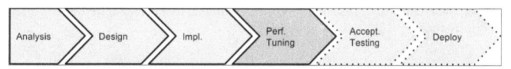

A generic version of the software development process with performance tuning.

Analysis

Creating high-quality software should always begin with some thorough requirement analysis. This is often very focused on the business functions and their values, but it is also very important to pay attention to the architecture of the software itself and its required performance.

It is important to identify a set of situations that will occur in the system and turn them into structured scenarios or use cases. These use cases need to be measurable and their values need to be assessed from both business and technical perspectives. Not all use cases need to have their performance assessed, but for those that need to, deciding what types of benchmarks to use are important.

Some common performance-related questions that should be answered during the analysis phase are:

- How many concurrent users should the system as a whole be able to serve and what minimum response times are required in different situations?
- What levels of different software, hardware, and network resources must the various parts of the system have at their disposal in order to run smoothly?
- Which information and level of audit is needed in different scenarios to uphold legislative, business, or operation requirements?

From the preceding questions, it should be clear that the software requirements span not only the business-related functionality but also nonfunctional requirements, such as security and logging, as well as estimates of hardware and network resources. All of of these can, and will, affect performance.

Design

Everything related to the software structure, and the software itself, is structured here and defined in more detail. The overall architecture should be set for all major components. Tiers of both hardware and software are detailed to fit and adhere to the architecture and various requirements. Databases and data structures at different levels are to be designed wherever possible. The efficiency of candidate algorithms and libraries should be evaluated.

In short, the architectural decisions and design details must constantly be weighted in performance.

Implementation

If the previous steps have been performed properly, implementing the software source code with standard configurations of the system can be quite straightforward. There should be information and decisions about what use cases and functions should be paid special attention in terms of performance. Utilizing known best practices and experiences (such as the ones mentioned in this book) should also be in a developer's toolbox.

 Try to not do to any overzealous tuning here though, as it might be useless and possibly even counterproductive for the system in large and not very cost-efficient.

After, and during, the implementation phase, there should be some testing performed. Normally, the amount of testing increases as the software gets closer to production. Unit testing should be performed pretty much all the time and is actually tightly merged with coding in the implementation phase. However, system and integration testing will not be that useful until the software reaches some minimal level of testing maturity.

Performance testing and tuning

The new kids on the block in the software development cycle are performance testing, and its crafty cousin, tuning. Performance testing and tuning can be performed in pretty much every iteration during the software development of the system. There must be some reasonable need for it though, and it should be performed in a controlled environment with competent staff.

A performance test within a development iteration might focus on individual functions or components of the software being developed in order to verify that design decisions are sound. These isolated tests can however, never replace a complete and more realistic system-wide performance test.

Doing more complete performance tests on the entire system won't normally be useful until the later iterations of development. Naturally, it should be performed before deploying the system into production. However, remember to leave plenty of time to correct any faults or unreached requirements, so test earlier rather than later. Don't wait until the last iteration to do all the performance testing and tuning.

As it is often pretty much impossible to immediately live up to all requirements and foresee all factors that might affect a system, the performance tuning process must explore how different factors (configuration, environment, load, and so on) influence the different use cases of a system. Furthermore, factors are quite likely to evolve over time.

In order to structurally handle all these variables and variances while delivering a system that effectively lives up to requirements, performance tuning is (currently) best turned into a cyclical and iterative process in itself.

The iterative performance-tuning process

The tuning of a system involves testing in order to find bottlenecks in the system and eliminate them by tuning the system and related components.

Test cases and iteration

Before performance tuning actually starts, it must be determined what test-cases, or rather indicators, to focus on. This set of indicators might stay static, but after some work (iterations), it is also common that some that are deemed not to be as fruitful as expected are simply removed. Similarly, some new ones might be added over time, both to follow the evolution of the system as well as to widen or deepen our understanding of it. All this is done to improve its efficiency.

It is important that the bulk of test cases are kept between test iterations and even between product releases. This is done in order to be able to compare results and see how different changes affect the system. All these results will build into a knowledge base that can help when tuning and making predictions to both the system at hand and others in similar cases and environments.

The result of a performance test case is normally a measure of the response time, throughput, or utilization efficiency of one or more components. These components may be of any size or complexity. If the components are subcomponents of a larger application or system, the set of test cases often overlap—some covering the entire system and some covering the various subcomponents.

Setting the baseline

The first time a test is to be performed, there might not be much real data to lean on. The requirements should give, or at least indicate, some hard numbers. These values are called a **baseline**.

Running tests and collecting data

With the baseline set, tests are set up and run. As the tests execute, data must be collected. For some, only the end result might matter, but for most, tests getting data during the entire test run and from various points of measure will give a more detailed picture of the health of the tested systems, possible bottlenecks, and tuning points to explore.

Analyzing the data

Analyzing the data might involve several people and tools, each with some area, or areas, of specialty. The collective input and analysis from all these people and resources will normally be your best guide to what to make of the test data, as in, what to tune and in what order.

Tuning and retesting

After the analysis is done, the system will be tuned and the baseline will possibly be refined, and more retests will follow. Each of these retests will explore a possible tuning alternative.

 It is vital that only one individual thing is changed from one test till its retest. Change more than one thing and you won't know for sure what caused any new effects that are seen. Also, consider that several changes might neutralize or hide their individual effects.

Remember that not only direct code or configuration changes to a system require a performance test. Any and all changes to a system or its environment actually make the system an aspirant for performance tuning. Also, note that not all changes require performance tuning to be performed.

As you can imagine, following all tuning possibilities and always doing complete retests could easily spin out of control. It would result in infinite branches of tuning and tests—a situation that would be uncontrollable for any organization. It is, therefore, important to choose carefully between the various possibilities using knowledge, experience, and some healthy common sense. The tuning leads should be followed one by one, normally starting with the one identified to give the most effect (improved performance or reduction of bottleneck).

The performance-tuning process is normally complete when all requirements are satisfied or when enough of an improvement has been reached (normally defined by the product owner or architect in charge). The tuning process is an iterative process that is realized by the major steps shown in the following diagram.

Apart from resolving bottlenecks and living up to requirements, it is equally important to not over-optimize a system. First, it is not cost efficient. If no one has asked for that extra performance—in terms of business or architectural/operational requirements—it should simply not be done. Second, over-optimizing some things (such as very minor bottlenecks) in a system can very easily, turn its balance off, thus creating new problems elsewhere.

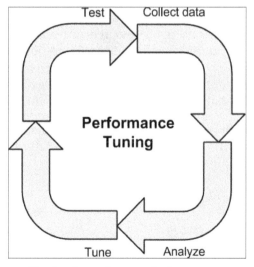

The iterative performance-tuning process.

Test data

Possibly one of the hardest areas of the software development and QA processes is related to having / finding / creating useful test data. Really good test data should have the following properties:

- It should be realistic and have the same properties as real live data
- It should not expose real user data or other sensitive information
- It should have coverage for all test cases
- It should be useful for both positive and negative tests

For tuning during load testing, the test data should also exist in large quantities.

As one can imagine, it requires a lot of work, and it can be very expensive to have a full set of up-to-date test data with all these properties available, especially, as the data and its properties can be more or less dynamic and change over time.

We highly encourage all efforts to use test data with the preceding properties. As always, it will be a balancing act between the available resources of an organization such as financial strength, people, and getting things done.

For load testing, the test data is normally generated more or less from scratch or taken from real production data. It is important that the data is complete enough for the relevant test scenarios. The test data does not, however, need to be as complete as for functional testing. Volume, is more important.

Documentation

Throughout the performance-tuning process, it is important to have a stable and complete documentation routine in order. For each iteration, at a minimum, all test cases with traceable system configuration setups and measurement results should be documented and saved. This will add to the knowledge base of the organization, especially if it is made available to various departments of the organization.

It can then be a force to efficiently compare data of old releases with over time or to make good estimates of hardware procurement or other resources. Never forget the mantra of performance tuning:

> *Test, tune one thing at time and test again.*

The environment of performance tests

It has been mentioned that performance testing and tuning should be performed in a controlled environment. In a perfect world, this means an environment that is free of disturbance, production-like, and unchanged between tests.

Using the following three rules of thumb for your test environment, you will be as close to achieving the perfect environment as you can for your performance tests:

- **No disturbances**: The tests should not be disturbed by other events, such as the executions of batches, backups, unrelated network traffic, or similar factors, to ensure that measurements relates only to the system under test. In a production environment, there is likely to be external disturbances, but the origins of these are hopefully known, and the systems that generate them should have gone through separate performance tests. Simulations in performance tests of what happens to a system at the same time as an external disturbance runs might be useful for some situations, but it is seldom an exact science and is not recommended in general.

- **Production-like**: The test environment should also be as similar to the production environment as possible in terms of test data, configuration, resources, services, hardware, and network capabilities in order to have results that would actually be worth something as the system is deployed into the real production environment. To have a full-blown copy of the production environment available for performance testing is not always possible due to various reasons. When the test environment isn't quite up to level with its production counterpart, it is important to be aware of the differences and to be able to extrapolate any test results. Just be very careful to trust any estimates you make about the results in a different environment.

- **Unchanged**: The test environment must stay equal between iterations of the same test and preferably for all tests. This intertest equality of the environment is needed in order to make reliable comparisons of the results from repeated tests. The exception to this, naturally, is when some part of the environment itself is required to change as part of tuning. Then, only one thing per test run can change and it must be thoroughly documented.

The software life cycle

After a system has successfully gone through the last phases of software development (including performance testing, tuning, and acceptance testing), it will be deployed in production where its hopefully long and successful life will begin for real.

Upgrades

Over its lifetime, the system will most likely need to be upgraded for one reason or another. Upgrading might involve changes to the hardware, code, and configuration. Before this upgraded system is put into production, it should be as thoroughly tested as it was when it was first released in order to ensure that it will meet old, and any new, requirements. Naturally, this includes performance testing and tuning, when needed.

Metrics

During its life in production, a lot of things about the system will be of interest to the business, QA, and the different IT departments. Some important questions that need to be addressed among the different instances could be:

- **Business**: What use cases are actually utilized and to what grade? For what reasons are important functions not used? Are they avoided due to poor response times, perhaps? Does the system and its components really give the expected **Return of investment** (**ROI**) or can there be optimizations made?

- **QA and IT**: Are the error rates under control? Is the hardware utilization actually in alignment with what is estimated or is there need for more or less of something? What about the response times and usage of components, caches, and other software resources? What is the health of the system at any given time?

Information to answer these questions and more can quite easily be answered by the system itself. Some information might be available for extraction directly out of the box from the system or from underlying resources, while others might need to be enabled by configuration or by more or less advanced instrumentation in code.

The information is often extracted/collected by logging or monitoring through a protocol such as SNMP (mostly used by hardware and operating system services) or by using an API such as the **Java Management Extension** (**JMX**) API.

WildFly exposes information about quite a few resources through JMX, and instrumenting your application code to expose values using JMX is very easy and powerful. JMX can also be used externally from a system to give it instructions such as clearing a cache, starting/stopping a service, and so on.

Quantifiable information from and about a system, regardless of how it is retrieved, is called **metric**. The various metrics can be useful for a single situation such as a monitoring alert for something going wrong. However, it is also important to collect metrics over time as a proof of living up to SLA and be able to do various analysis related to the business, quality, or technology.

Performance testing and tuning is one of the areas that can benefit hugely from having metrics available. It is, for example, very valuable during the design, or modification, of test cases and setting realistic baselines.

Tuning an enterprise stack

Tuning can be broadly divided into different categories based on the different layers of an enterprise IT environment. This environment is often called an enterprise stack and consists of the layers shown in the following diagram. We will now turn our attention to these layers one by one and discuss what tuning means and consists of in each of them, starting from the bottom:

Layers of an enterprise stack.

Network

Network tuning typically involves the configuration of various network equipment such as firewalls, routers, and network interfaces, but can also include verifying the use of the correct type of cables and connectors. This type of tuning is often initially missed during performance tuning, but in today's communication-heavy solutions, it is absolutely vital to have a network that runs smoothly and at its highest performance. Network tuning is also highly related to, and thus overlaps, hardware and OS tuning.

Hardware

Hardware tuning includes selecting the right hardware components—CPU, memory, discs, and so on—for a given system and its requirements. Shortage of memory will increase I/O operations. Slow disks might make databases and entire systems crawl.

Data encryption and other computing-heavy functions will require a relatively large amount of CPU. Often, the solution can be to just to add more or better hardware, but it is equally important that the hardware is well-balanced and plays well together.

Operating System

Operating System (OS) tuning is closely related to network and hardware tuning as it defines how the OS and hardware/network will cooperate and what restrictions will be enforced. For example, CPU time slicing, I/O behavior, and network access.

Through the OS, a lot of information can also be retrieved regarding the health of not only the OS itself, but also of the hardware and network.

Java Virtual Machine

Java Virtual Machine (JVM) tuning involves configuring the memory levels and the garbage collector of the JVM. Although modern JVMs are considerably more intelligent, effective, and advanced compared to older versions, they often still need a bit of love and application-specific tuning. Tuning a JVM can drastically improve the performance of the application that is being executed in the JVM. This tuning is, however, quite volatile as things can easily go wrong and create new bottlenecks and even worsen performance unless used in a very controlled way. More about this will be covered in detail in *Chapter 3, Tuning the Java Virtual Machine*.

Middleware

Middleware tuning includes adjusting various configuration parameters of the platform called **middleware**. This is done in order to make the platform and its services more optimized for the applications and its components that run within it. A middleware platform is often realized as an advanced application server; for example, WildFly. Others might be simpler and won't include as many services; for example, a web container like Apache Tomcat.

Some parameters and services of the middleware can be utilized by all applications, while others can be application specific. For WildFly, some configuration and services include thread pools, connection pools for EJBs, JMS (queues/topics) and databases, EJB component lifecycle management, and much more. All these configurations have default values that might be just fine, but they also might be tweaked in order to achieve magnitudes of improved performance. Middleware is arguably where most configuration-related tuning can be made in the stack, but more of this will be discussed in chapters to come.

Application

Application tuning is first and foremost achieved by making a thoughtful design and writing good, efficient code. This also involves selecting the best algorithms and libraries for your specific application. If the original design proves to be insufficient, and other tuning types won't solve the problem, the design or code might need to be redone completely or at least be improved in some way.

This can, for example, involve changing an entire platform, framework, or programming model, or it can involve just improving a specific function or pattern. It could also involve making better use of APIs or available resources. For example, by using the `StringBuffer` or `StringBuilder` classes instead of `String` or by improving the speed of database calls by using indexes. Application tuning, in terms of initial design and implementation of a system, is often not directly seen as tuning. However, creating a tuned application is, without a doubt, the most important type of tuning you can do. Think about it. If you make poor design decisions or write poor code, it will be really hard, if not impossible, to fix that by just tuning the hardware or JVM. It would also be quite expensive – both in terms of time and money – to make large design and code changes to a system.

As we have seen from the preceding text above and in the following diagram, tuning can be performed pretty much everywhere in the stack, and tuning in one place can and will affect things in all locations. Thus, having a broad and open-minded view about possible ripple effects of singular changes will aid you in making the best decisions.

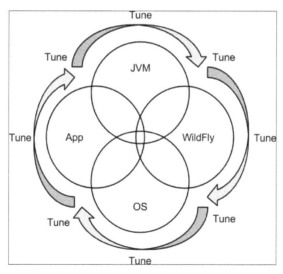

Iterative tuning in the enterprise stack. Tuning is everywhere and everything depends on many direct and indirect relations. Here, WildFly is depicting the middleware. Also hardware- and network-tuning is included in the OS tuning.

Summary

In this chapter, we made the connection and discussed performance tuning as a science. We defined performance as measures and listed some of the most important ones used in IT—response time, throughput, and utilization efficiency.

We learned that the performance-tuning process is highly iterative, and that it is vital to only tune one thing at a time between tests. Here, we also specified the main place of the tuning process within the software development process and listed some common tuning anti-patterns.

Good quality test data and production-like environments are fundamental cornerstones of testing in general and for performance testing, this is no exception; it's quite the opposite!

After going through metrics and their inherent value made available during the life cycle of a piece of software, we finally talked about the tuning possibilities available in all the layers of a complete enterprise stack. This is a stack that encompasses many software layers (such as an application or system, the middleware, and the operating system) as well as hardware and network equipment.

To put the theories of this chapter into practice, we will need a powerful set of supporting tools. Moving on, this is exactly what we will be looking at in the next chapter.

2
Tools of the Tuning Trade

In order to practically and efficiently tune a system, you will need the support of some good tools that cover the different aspects of performance tuning. In this chapter, we will focus on the following:

- The following key features of performance tuning:
    - Profiling
    - Monitoring
    - Load generation

- Some theory behind these features
- How the features are being implemented in a few well-known tools
- Making sure that the tools and WildFly get along
- Some common use cases that the tools provide support for

There are some great performance-tuning tools on the market from various different vendors, but as we're following the Open Source philosophy in this book, all the tools we will use here come from the open source ecosystem. If you use tools from vendors other than the ones mentioned here, don't worry! This is natural and is something that we as authors come across time and again when assisting various organizations. As long as your toolset is complete in terms of the necessary functionality, this is what really counts.

Even though you might not have used the tools we present here, we won't go into much detail about any installation or basic setup procedures, at least, not unless they are explicitly needed for a vital feature. We'll leave these instructions to the documentation available on each of the tool's site. If these don't fulfil your needs, there are also numerous online resources such as community forums and blogs that are full of useful hints and valuable tips.

If you didn't know it earlier, performance tuning is a very multifaceted investigative hands-on job, and to be truly efficient, you will need good tools to support your work.

The key features of performance tuning

Some of the tools in the tuning area have started out with support for one thing or, perhaps, for a few things such as memory analysis or load testing. Over time, however, quite a few of them have evolved in their own right or with the aid of plugins to often have multiple functions. They also often cover several areas in the tuning field.

So, what kind of support do we expect from a set of tuning tools? When looking at the enterprise stack, it becomes clear that we need different types of tools depending on the different layers of the stack:

- For the Java-based layers of the stack—the JVM, middleware, and application—you'll first and foremost need to perform performance and memory profiling.

- For the network, hardware, and OS layers, you will mainly need to monitor various resources such as CPU, memory, and network throughput.

- On top of these, you also need to be able to put the system and its various components under the defined levels of stress or load. This involves having support for different protocols, data sets, APIs, and so on.

Profiling

In general, **profiling** a software system involves analyzing the behavior and performance usage of resources that are involved, as the system executes. This analysis is most often performed to find points of optimization and for the removal of bottlenecks in the system. Profiling is also commonly, but not necessarily, performed under various levels of load on the system.

Profiling is a very powerful function for investigating and helping resolve suspected bottlenecks. Profiling can also be very complex, and the wrong interpretations may lead to disastrous results. It should, therefore, only be performed in stable environments, preferably, by staff that has shown an aptitude for it.

Profiling in production

Conducting profiling during software development and in the performance-tuning phase is quite normal. Then, you're normally confined to your personal development environment such as your desktop/laptop or some test environment where the effects that the actual profiling has on the system's performance often can be ignored. Profiling can involve adding more code to an existing codebase by instrumentation and by taking various types of snapshots or dumps of system resources; it can slow down the profiled system considerably.

However, there may be a scenario where you might need to profile a system in its production environment. Here, a different set of rules normally applies. Regular business operations should normally not be disturbed unless total crisis has occurred. Arguably, if you need to do profiling in production, your business has some deep problems that can often be traced to poor performance testing and QA. No matter what the underlying reason is though, it is not unusual for this situation to occur.

When profiling in a production environment, it is vital to be prepared. You need to get in and do your tests quickly, efficiently, and correctly so that you get out fast without disturbing the business that the system supports. This means that before entering the production environment, you'll need to figure out very closely the area within the system in which the problem could be. You'd also need to have a plan for what and how to measure, to some minimal level, in order to both have all the information you need and still not afflict (too much) disturbance on the business operations.

Profiling a JVM

When we talk about profiling a Java-based system, we are actually talking about profiling what is going on within an executing JVM. Profiling a JVM focuses on the following two areas:

- **Performance profiling**: This type of profiling involves analyzing the Java classes and their allocations. The class instances and executing methods are, for example, measured in terms of the level of memory usage, object sizes, and execution times.

- **Memory profiling**: For memory profiling, the focus lies on the information about how the different memory areas are utilized and what happens when the **garbage collector** (**GC**) runs. We'll discuss the JVM, its cornerstones, and tuning possibilities in a lot more detail in an upcoming chapter.

Profiling and sampling

In the Java universe, profiling technically involves instrumenting the Java bytecode in order to make accurate calculations of execution down to the method level. Instrumenting the Java bytecode is a time-consuming operation that is performed for all code in the JVM when profiling starts. The amount of instrumented bytecode can, however, be limited by defining what should be included or excluded, thereby speeding up the instrumentation time in profiling. Depending on tool support, theses definitions can be done on package, class, or method level. As the profiling terminates, the bytecode is normally restored.

Sampling is a kind of lightweight profiling. Instead of physically instrumenting the Java bytecode as done in profiling, sampling relies on analyzing the stack traces and thread dumps that are taken at regular time intervals. These intervals can be defined, for example to 10 per second.

So, what approach should you use? As always, the answer is that it depends on your situation. Here, it depends on how well you know your system, how well you know what to focus on in the system, and what you need or want to optimize within the system. The following table summarizes some key features as well as the pros and cons of profiling versus sampling in general terms:

	Profiling	Sampling
Data input comes from	Instrumented bytecode	Collected dumps
Data input interval is set per	Object entry	Time interval
The startup time is	Slow (due to bytecode instrumentation)	Fast (immediate)
The runtime performance is	Good	Good
The accuracy of measures is	High to exact	Good

If you're in a situation where you need to browse relatively quickly through various parts of the system in order to narrow down where a problem is located, it is convenient to use the sampler. As the sampler starts up quickly and can give you a fairly good picture of how things are looking, it will help you find something to focus on more closely.

When you have found or at least limited your focus area with sampling, you'll probably need to find out, with reliable accuracy, what is causing the problem. In this case, profiling is most likely to be your weapon of choice.

VisualVM

A very useful and free JVM profiler is **VisualVM**. At the time of writing this book, this tool normally comes bundled when you download and install the **Java Development Kit** (**JDK**) from the Oracle Java site (http://www.oracle.com/technetwork/java/javase). In this distribution, the tool is located in $JAVA_HOME/bin and named jvisualvm.sh (for UNIX-based environments) or jvisualvm.bat (for Windows).

As an alternative, you can download it from its own site (http://visualvm.java.net). This is where you'll find the unbranded bleeding-edge version.

The core of VisualVM is shared by the NetBeans IDE (https://netbeans.org). So, if you use the NetBeans profiler, you'll be using a lot of the functionality that is the same as those found in VisualVM, but with differentiating workflows. There's also a launcher plugin of VisualVM for the Eclipse IDE (http://eclipse.org) available at https://visualvm.java.net/eclipse-launcher.html.

All examples in this book are based on the current version, VisualVM 1.3.6, and it has been run in the standalone mode, that is, not as part of an IDE in any way.

Standard features

VisualVM is one of those tools that has evolved into supporting several interesting areas related to tuning. In general and out-of-the-box, VisualVM normally provides the following five major features that are visualized in different views in the UI:

- **Overview**: A non-interactive information view over the various JVM core information containing arguments, properties, and some monitoring.

- **Monitor**: Heap dumps and full GCs can be ordered. Also, live graphs are on display for the following components:
    - CPU usage and GC activity
    - Heap or PermGen memory usage with counter values of the size used and maximum size for both memory areas
    - Classes with counter values for loaded, unloaded, and shared loaded/unloaded
    - Threads with counter values for live, daemon, started, and peak

- **Threads**: Thread dumps can be taken and the threads (active or finished) of the JVM are visualized in different formats (timeline, table, and details).

- **Profiler**: The profiler supports both profiling of performance (CPU) and memory.

- **Sampler**: The sampler has a setup and functionality that is similar to the profiler. Lately, development has however been focused on the sampler, and it has received more information about PermGen and threads in comparison to the profiler, for example.

In the following screenshot, we see the user interface of VisualVM. Here, it displays the **Monitor** view when connected to a local JVM running a WildFly instance just after startup. As we can see from the graphs, there is currently no CPU or GC activity; the heap is quite stable as are the classes loaded and the live threads. This tells us that there is no or close to no activity causing any load on the server.

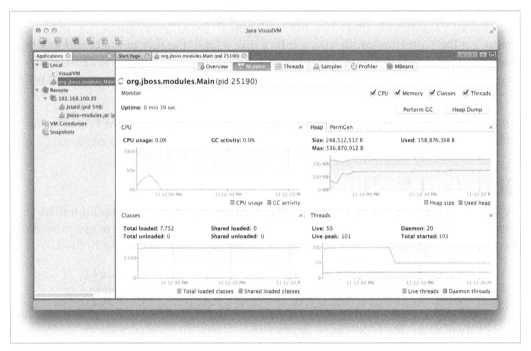

VisualVM displaying the Monitor view when connected to a JVM running a WildFly instance under close to no load

The features of plugins

On top of these standard features, a lot more can be added to VisualVM through plugins. These are installed by navigating to the **Tools | Plugins**. After a plugin has been installed, VisualVM might need to be restarted for the plugin to work.

Some useful plugins worth mentioning are as follows:

- **VisualGC**: This is a plugin that gives a graphical overview of the memory area dynamics.

- **VisualVM-JConsole**: This is really the JConsole tool, and thereby, this plugin in turn has a rich and useful ecosystem of plugins.

- **VisualVM-MBean**: This is an MBean browser. This is actually the JConsole MBean plugin that integrates directly into VisualVM.

- **The Tracer**: This plugin allows for a powerful correlation and analysis of data collected by probes.

Connecting to a JVM

When VisualVM is started, it can connect to the local and remote JVMs. On these, it can perform monitoring and various other performance-tuning activities as mentioned earlier.

Local JVM

As VisualVM is started, all the JVMs currently running on the same computer or host will directly be listed under the **Local** node on the **Applications** tab on the left-hand side. This includes the JVM of the VisualVM application itself. Whenever a JVM is started or terminated on the local computer, it will automatically and directly show up or disappear, respectively, from the node.

Remote JVM

It requires a more manual approach to add a JVM residing on another computer on the network.

On the remote host

First, on the remote computer, the JVM Stat Daemon, jstatd, must be started. This tool comes with the Java distribution and resides in $JAVA_HOME/bin. When it is started, it will make all the JVMs on that computer accessible from our VisualVM instance through the use of **Remote Method Invocation (RMI)**. Using this service is very advantageous, as it does not require any changes such as reconfiguration of the remote JVMs or the applications executing in them.

Now, jstatd won't work out-of-the-box due to the default security settings of the Java sandbox. Hence, it's necessary to grant jstatd some more permission. We'll do this by creating a file named jstatd.all.policy with the following content:

```
grant codebase "file:${java.home}/../lib/tools.jar" {
  permission java.security.AllPermission;
};
```

The daemon is then started (here, from the same directory in which the file is located) with the following command:

```
jstatd -J-Djava.security.policy=jstatd.all.policy
```

On the monitoring host

Now, to actually connect to the remote JVM from VisualVM, select **Add Remote Host** from the top menu, the toolbar icons, or the context menu. In the dialog that comes up (as shown in the following screenshot), state the hostname or IP address of the remote computer. The communication will use the RMI protocol and run on the default port 1099. Firewall configurations should be adapted accordingly, or the port number in the advanced settings of the dialog can be changed to anything that will suit your specific environment:

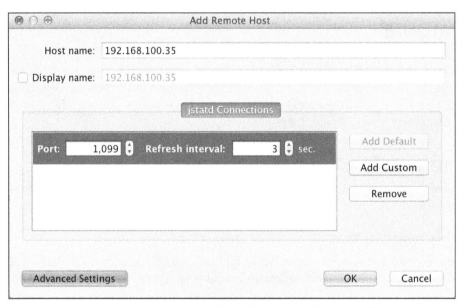

The Add Remote Host dialog window with expanded Advanced Settings

Now, when connected, the computer and all its JVMs will show up in a tree-node structure below the **Remote** node on the **Applications** tab on the left-hand side in the VisualVM UI. Any new JVMs starting up or terminating on the remote node will automatically turn up or disappear, respectively, in VisualVM, thanks to `jstatd`.

Monitoring a JVM

A local WildFly JVM instance will appear as the `org.jboss.modules.Main` node in the tree in the **Applications** tab, while a remote instance will appear as the `jboss-modules.jar` node.

Once a connection to a JVM has been made, you should get accustomed to the variety of information available in the different views (**Overview**, **Monitor**, **Threads**, and so on) for the JVM in the tool. Just browsing the live feeds and graphs of how the JVM behaves in terms of threads, CPU, memory, and so on can paint a pretty good picture. Starting out with this will make you comfortable with both the tool and the basic behavior and data flow from the specific application in the JVM that you really are interested in.

To dig a bit deeper into your system and really start to analyze system behavior, you should start profiling or sampling. Both profiling and sampling have support for CPU and memory-based profiling/sampling. They are available from the **Profiler** or **Sampler** views.

We mentioned that profiling takes a relatively long time to set up due to the instrumentation of bytecode that has to be performed before any actual analyzing can take place. It will, therefore, benefit the profiling startup time as well as the turnaround time of your work to limit the Java packages (containing classes) to profile and thereby to instrument. Setting what packages to include or exclude for profiling is performed in the **CPU settings** tab that is displayed when selecting the **Settings** checkbox in the **Profiler** view as seen in the following screenshot. The same location is available for the **Sampler** view.

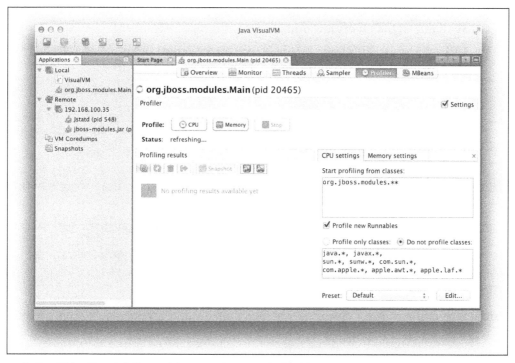

In the CPU settings tab (lower-right corner in screenshot) of the Profiler, the packages to profile or not can be defined, among other things

Note also that these settings can't be changed during profiling/ sampling but must be set prior to a profiling/sampling session.

Limiting the set of Java packages to profile or sample will also make some of the visualized data more manageable and allow you to focus on the specific code that is of interest for you, such as the code of your application.

By default, standard Java packages with code such as `java.*` and `javax.*` are excluded from profiling/sampling. Removing large packages of code that you trust or that you can't or won't care about, should also be added to this list. Think code from third parties such as frameworks and middleware.

Features

VisualVM provides lots of functions that are useful in finding bottlenecks and tuning a system.

The tool can take various snapshots and dumps that can be viewed directly or saved for further analysis. These include:

- **Application snapshot**: This includes core JVM information that is otherwise available in the **Overview** and **Monitor** views of VisualVM
- **CPU snapshot**: This snapshot lists the call tree runtime usage on package/ class/method level and hotspots within the nodes of the tree
- **Memory snapshot**: This snapshot show bytes, objects allocated, and generations per class or type
- **Thread dump**: This contains a variety of information of each thread such as address, state, and priority, to mention a few
- **Heap dump**: This contains loads of useful information such as core JVM information as in the **Overview** view, class and instances usage levels with attributes and references, and threads at dump time
- **VM Core dump**: This includes a heap and thread dump as described earlier

Between comparable snapshots such as memory snapshots, comparisons can be calculated. These can be very useful when investigating memory usage during suspected memory leaks, for example.

During ongoing profiling/sampling, various deltas and GCs can also be performed.

Test scenarios

When monitoring a system, it is always important to know the kind of operations that are performed. Without this knowledge, you won't really know for sure what you are looking at. Hence, having a well-designed set of test cases and scenarios whose behavior you know about will help speed up the tuning process and improve the quality of the system.

A JMX connection to WildFly

Setting up a JMX connection is necessary in order to be able to perform the sampling of a remote JVM.

Before we describe how to set up a JMX connection, we will, however, need to discuss some requirements of both WildFly and VisualVM.

Local or remote WildFly server

If WildFly and VisualVM reside on the same host, the connection will work with the default configuration of the application server. For a remote WildFly, this does not apply. As WildFly, by default, is secured to not expose its management interface other than locally (`localhost`/`127.0.0.1`), the application server must be reconfigured and restarted before a remote JMX connection can be made.

To accept remote connections, the WildFly management interface can be configured in several ways. The three most common ways are listed as follows:

- From the CLI (all on one line and without spaces or newlines):

    ```
    /interface=management:write-attribute(
    name=inet-address,value=
    "${jboss.bind.address.management:192.168.100.35}")
    ```

- In the WildFly configuration file (replace the existing IP address):

    ```
    <interface name="management">
        <inet-address value=
            "${jboss.bind.address.management:192.168.100.35}"/>
    </interface>
    ```

- From the command line (or in the script from) where WildFly is started:

    ```
    $WILDFLY_HOME/bin/standalone.sh
      -Djboss.bind.address.management=192.168.100.35
    ```

Here, the IP address, 192.168.100.35, is used as an example address belonging to the remote server. Make sure that you amend it to the IP address of your server. Also, these examples assume that your server is running in the standalone mode, utilizing the standalone.xml configuration file.

Setting up VisualVM

WildFly relies heavily on various remoting protocols for remote access, and for JMX, this is no exception. For a JMX client such as VisualVM in this case, it must use the http-remoting-jmx protocol to connect to a WildFly server instance. In order to do this, the client must have the classes implementing this protocol in its CLASSPATH. The classes are available as various artifacts or JAR files packaged in the WildFly modules. Getting hold of the correct set of these artifacts can be cumbersome, but luckily, there is a very convenient JAR file named jboss-client.jar, which is available in the WildFly distribution. The content of the JAR file supports everything a client needs to make JMX connections (and more) to WildFly server instances.

VisualVM should be started with jboss-client.jar in its CLASSPATH by executing the following command (assuming you have $JAVA_HOME/bin in your $PATH):

```
jvisualvm -cp:a $WILDFLY_HOME/bin/client/jboss-client.jar
```

Connection in VisualVM

When WildFly and VisualVM have been configured and started as described earlier, a remote JMX connection can finally be set up. By selecting **Add JMX Connection** from one of the multiple menu options available in VisualVM, a pop up, as shown in the following screenshot, will appear. By submitting a connection URL with the possible credentials here, the connection will be set up.

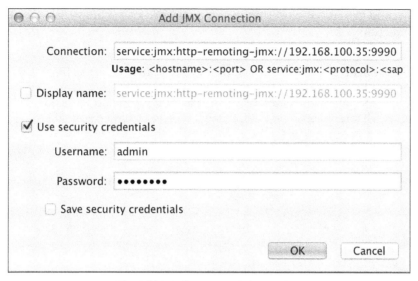

The Add JMX Connection dialog window

As the preceding screenshot shows, the connection URL will need to support the `http-remoting-jmx` protocol we mentioned earlier. WildFly accepts the connection for this protocol on its default management interface port, 9990. As the connection runs over the management interface, the credentials of an existing WildFly management user will also need to be provided. The management user is created by the WildFly tool, `add-user.sh`, located in `$WILDFLY_HOME/bin`.

The generic form of the complete URL is as follows:

```
service:jmx:http-remoting-jmx://<host>:<port>
```

So, in our example, we would add the URL as follows:

```
service:jmx:http-remoting-jmx://192.168.100.35:9990
```

Next, we would provide the username and password of a management user to set up a JMX connection.

> In the previous incarnation of the application server as JBoss AS7, the `remoting-jmx` protocol was used on the default port, 4447. As the WildFly architecture is now focused on port reduction, it multiplexes, with HTTP upgrade, several protocols over just two ports: 8080 for the application interface and 9990 for the management interface, on which `http-remoting-jmx` is located.

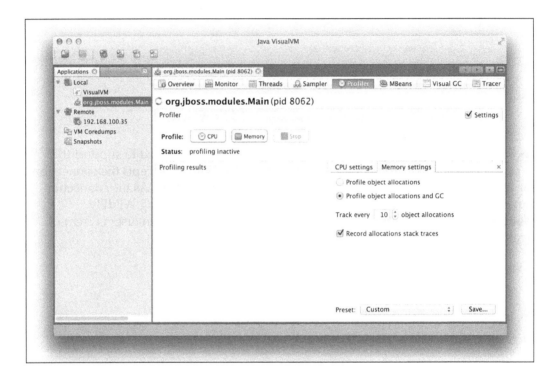

Monitoring

Keeping track of how your system reacts to different types of influences is imperative when you're testing it, tuning it, and over time in production. The measured values are extremely useful for both technical and business trend analysis as well as for comparing the performance between releases. When done correctly, these trends and comparisons can save your organization a lot of headache and enable it to quickly predict and adapt to upcoming problems.

There are explicit tools that monitor specific features and services, and there are others that give a more collective view of system health and performance. As we have seen, tools such as VisualVM can provide us with a multitude of information from various layers in the enterprise stack. It will give you the basic information about the hardware in terms of CPU usage, and as expected, it will provide a lot of information about the JVM as well as the middleware and the execution of inherent applications within the JVM.

A system that, for example, is instrumented with MBeans at strategic positions can give some extremely interesting and valuable information. This information can become even more valuable and easily accessible from an analyst view if it can be visually represented by graphs or other such techniques. This is often possible in the management system available in most organizations.

OS tools

All major operating systems come with a more or less standard set of tools that can extract and sometimes visualize important pieces of performance-related information from the network, hardware, and the OS itself. Here, we will mention a few of the most useful grouped by the OS that they come bundled with.

Unix and Linux

In UNIX and Linux-based operating systems, there are a lot of useful tools available as shell-executable commands. These tools will assist in monitoring system activities. The most common one might be the `top` command, which will give an interactive and real-time feed of processor activity and memory usage. Its output can be adapted to most needs, so it is, as it always is with UNIX-based commands, a good idea to read through its main pages. A basic output from `top` in Linux can look similar to the following example (the output has been limited to a few lines, as it normally is very long):

```
> top

Tasks: 230 total, 1 running, 229 sleeping, 0 stopped, 0 zombie
%Cpu(s):12,6us, 1,4sy, 0,0ni, 13,4id, 72,6wa, 0,0hi, 0,0si, 0,0st
KiB Mem:3940844 total, 3356556 used, 584288 free, 162736 buffers
KiB Swap:2094076 total, 0 used, 2094076 free, 1675992 cached

PID  USER PR NI  VIRT    RES    SHR  S  %CPU  %MEM   TIME+ CMD
1777 dude 20 0 3070664 152888 16732 S 39,55 3,880 0:05.55 java
1597 dude 20 0  566232  40480 28084 S 2,659 1,027 0:01.67 konsole
1487 root 20 0  312336  97100 75408 S 1,994 2,464 2:00.16 Xorg
2626 dude 20 0 1554320 487648 51172 S 0,997 12,37 5:44.11 firefox
4825 dude 20 0 3112452 191628 78820 S 0,332 4,863 0:25.17 sof.bin
```

 Using the following `top` command will give us thread-level information within the given process ID (such as the WildFly process):

```
top -H -p <PID>
```

Another useful and adaptive command is `vmstat`. As the name implies, this tool reports virtual memory statistics. It shows the amount of virtual memory, CPU, and paging activity. This is extremely useful when discovering bottlenecks caused by your applications or by the system hardware.

To monitor the virtual memory activity on your system, it's best to use `vmstat` with a delay. A delay is the number of seconds between updates if you don't supply a delay, it just reports the averages since the last boot). 5 seconds is the recommended delay interval.

A sample of vmstat run on Linux, with a 5-second delay will look something similar to the following example (after 12 seconds):

```
> vmstat 5
 r  b swpd   free  buff  cache si so bi  bo   in  cs us sy id wa st
 1  0    0 687372 15124 171676  0  0 48   35 248 377  3  1 94  2  0
 2  0    0 566708 15144 171768  0  0  0  489 409 973 65  5 30  0  0
 0  1    0 385368 15188 171808  0  0 50  223 993 702 59  3 36  1  0
 0  0    0 399252 15188 171872  0  0  0    1 659 943  2  0 97  0  0
 0  0    0 374908 15200 171816  0  0  0   48 592 714  2  0 97  1  0
 0  0    0 375756 15200 171740  0  0  0  390 501 657  1  0 98  1  0
```

To get a good overview of the status of the TCP-stack, interfaces, connections, I/O, and much more, netstat is very useful. For example, to list the status of all the sockets, you will use the -a flag as shown in the following example (the output has been limited to a few lines as the normal output can be quite long). The -n flag instructs netstat to present all the values as numeric. In the following output, the ports that WildFly listens (the LISTEN status) to are listed. In the following snippet, you can also see some HTTP clients that have connected (the ESTABL status) to WildFly:

```
> netstat -an
Active Internet connections (servers and established)
Proto Recv-Q Send-Q Local Address        Foreign Address      State
tcp        0      0 0.0.0.0:4949         0.0.0.0:*            LISTEN
tcp        0      0 0.0.0.0:22           0.0.0.0:*            LISTEN
tcp        0      0 127.0.0.1:631        0.0.0.0:*            LISTEN
tcp        0      0 127.0.0.1:25         0.0.0.0:*            LISTEN
tcp        0      0 0.0.0.0:17500        0.0.0.0:*            LISTEN
tcp        0      0 0.0.0.0:5666         0.0.0.0:*            LISTEN
tcp        0      0 192.168.1.9:5445     0.0.0.0:*            LISTEN
tcp        0      0 127.0.0.1:9990       0.0.0.0:*            LISTEN
tcp        0      0 127.0.0.1:3528       0.0.0.0:*            LISTEN
tcp        0      0 192.168.1.9:5455     0.0.0.0:*            LISTEN
tcp        0      0 127.0.0.1:9999       0.0.0.0:*            LISTEN
tcp        0      0 192.168.1.9:8080     0.0.0.0:*            LISTEN
tcp        0   2553 192.168.1.9:8080     192.168.1.12:40204   ESTABL
tcp        0   2553 192.168.1.9:8080     192.168.1.12:40203   ESTABL
tcp        0   2553 192.168.1.9:8080     192.168.1.12:40207   ESTABL
tcp        0   2553 192.168.1.9:8080     192.168.1.12:40201   ESTABL
tcp        0   2553 192.168.1.9:8080     192.168.1.12:40209   ESTABL
tcp        0   2553 192.168.1.9:8080     192.168.1.12:40205   ESTABL
tcp        0   2553 192.168.1.9:8080     192.168.1.12:40202   ESTABL
```

Using the tools mentioned in this section, you can investigate and validate when problems occur with too high or too low CPU usage, resource contention, and high disk utilization. Let's look at these problems a bit closer.

Low CPU utilization

If the computer has a low level of CPU usage or if the CPU(s) even stands idle, you are not using your infrastructure to its optimal level of performance. It might be that you simply have too much hardware in comparison to your needs. Acquiring the right amount of hardware is an important and valuable ROI-factor for business. So, having reliable performance estimates and tests to reveal how much hardware your system needs is very valuable.

If your system has low CPU utilization in conjunction to the following three symptoms, you should become suspicious:

- Normal network activity and I/O with high idle times across all CPUs
- As the system load rises, the idle time of the CPUs does not decrease
- As the system load increases, response times degrade too quickly

If you are experiencing any of these symptoms, it's likely that your application server is waiting for some resources to be freed. A fundamental instrument in finding the source of the problem is the JVM thread dump of the application server, which can easily be obtained from the VisualVM's **Monitor** view.

For example, let us assume that you have many threads with the following stack trace:

```
"Thread-1" prio=6 tid=0x01b66c00 nid=0xef0 waiting for monitor
        java.lang.Thread.State: BLOCKED (on object monitor)
            at DL$Thread2.run(DL.java:62)
            - waiting to lock <0x234ba128> (a java.lang.Object)
            - locked <0x239ba130> (a java.lang.Object)
```

These are all waiting for the same lock to be released. By searching for the lock in the stack trace, you might be able to figure out the problem. What you find could be a deadlock between the threads. The following is an example of a stack trace that creates a deadlock with the preceding example:

```
"Thread-0" prio=6 tid=0x01b66000 nid=0xefc waiting for monitor entr
        java.lang.Thread.State: BLOCKED (on object monitor)
            at DL$Thread1.run(DL.java:37)
            - waiting to lock <0x234ba130> (a java.lang.Object)
            - locked <0x234ba128> (a java.lang.Object)
```

The jstack and jstat command-line utilities (located in the $JAVA_HOME/bin directory) available from the JDK distribution are alternative tools to the graphical VisualVM.

High CPU utilization

One of the most pervasive myths among IT technicians in operations is that high CPU usage is an obvious indicator of a system bottleneck. In reality, the truth can be quite different.

By using a tool such as vmstat, it is quite easy to get more information that can reveal if there really is a bottleneck. If, for example, the CPU(s) are busy, say, with a high load of around 90 percent, it is important to regard what platform you are using and to have a look at how the CPU time is distributed. A UNIX system with equal distribution of the CPU time in regards to the user and system time for example, 45 percent user time and 45 percent system time, can be regarded as quite normal and actually a good use of the available infrastructure.

The real reason to be concerned about arises when the run queue of vmstat displays a value higher than the total amount of CPUs (or cores in today's multicore CPUs) that are available for the computer.

As this behavior starts to occur, it is a good idea to investigate the CPU distribution. If the system value is considerably higher than the user value, it can be a strong indicator that there are a lot of system calls being performed.

This can happen if you are executing lots of input/output, sockets, or timestamp creation. You should find out, along with your performance tools, the modules that cause excessive or inefficient input/output. One potential candidate is, for example, a class that gives out lots of unbuffered input/output. Replacing it with a buffered one could reduce the problem greatly.

If vmstat indicates that the problems can be referred to WildFly, it is a good idea to take a look at the JVM threads and collect a thread dump with, for example, VisualVM or jstack.

High resource contention

A special case of abnormal CPU utilization—low or high—is when only one or a few CPUs experience a peak of usage. This scenario is usually caused by the fact that your system uses a single thread to manage some resources. Your checklist should include garbage collection configuration at the top of the list (see *Chapter 3, Tuning the Java Virtual Machine*, for an in-depth discussion about it). If garbage collection is correctly configured, you should then verify whether you have any contention in getting access to other resources, for example, single-threaded object caches.

Using a tool such as mpstat, which indicates a thread's spin on mutex values, you will get a measure of whether there is a kernel contention (if a thread can't acquire a lock, it spins) or not. If a suspicion of contention exists, further investigation should make use of a thread dump. If a pattern of locks exists, as shown in the following code snippet where the threads wait for a queue, the evidence is quite clear:

```
"WorkerThread-8"..in Object.wait()..locked <0xf14213c8>(a Queue)
"WorkerThread-9"..in Object.wait()..locked <0xf14213c8>(a Queue)
"WorkerThread-8"..in Object.wait()..locked <0xf14213c8>(a Queue)
```

In order to resolve this problem, you should introduce additional shared resources. This can be done by distributing the cache through a larger set of JVMs using, for example, clustering.

High disk utilization

Excessive disk utilization is a frequent bottleneck for enterprise applications. The iostat command is commonly used by system administrators to review I/O statistics. If you get high levels of service time or a busy disk with constantly high read/write values, it is time to investigate the possible root causes of the problem. Some possible causes of excessive disk utilization in WildFly are as follows:

- Excessive application logging
- Transaction recovery logging
- Stateful Session Bean Passivation
- Poorly tuned persistent storage of queue and topic messages in the **Enterprise Management System** (**EMS**) (HornetQ)
- Poorly configured database cache

Apart from looking at the implementations of your applications and the tuning of WildFly with its subsystems, it is highly important to have control over which services that are using which disks. The speed of the disks and their controllers and drivers are important factors to investigate; they are also fairly common sources of the problem.

OS X

As Apple OS X is a UNIX-based operating system (POSIX compliant and with a BSD base), most standard UNIX tools are available here as well. Here, the command for looking at virtual memory statistics is named `vm_stat`. It has a different output from the UNIX `vmstat`, focusing on various values of memory pages.

In OS X, there is also a very useful and versatile GUI application named **Activity Monitor**. As can be seen from its user interface in the following screenshot, this tool supports the monitoring of live data as well as statistics from CPU, memory, hard disks, network, and even energy consumption per application and process. It can also sample processes, create memory and thread dumps, and run a complete and advanced system diagnostics for use after analysis.

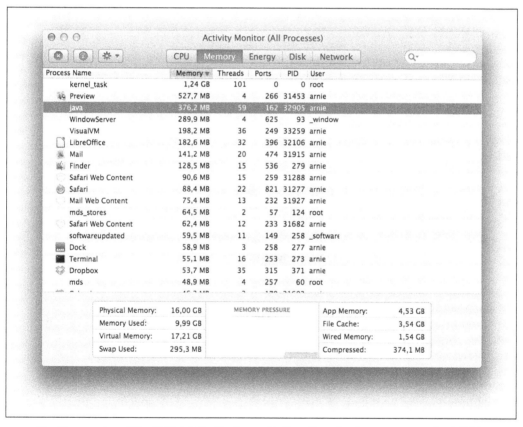

The Memory view of the OS X Activity Monitor application. Here, the Java process running WildFly has been selected. From the top menu, the main features and view are shown—CPU, Memory, Energy, Disk, and Network.

Windows

In Microsoft Windows, **Windows Task Manager** will give you a quick overview of the processes and CPU. For more information, the **Performance Monitor** is a very useful GUI application that will provide data and graphical representations of various resources available in the Windows system. Several tools based on the command-line available in UNIX, such as netstat, are also available in Windows, often with different parameters.

WildFly tools

A set of useful tools come with the WildFly distribution. Although they are not dedicated performance-tuning tools, they do have some related value, especially for monitoring. We will go through a few of them here. We will start out with the administrative tools that somewhat overlap. They are as follows:

- The Command Line Interface
- The WildFly Management Console
- The JBoss DMR API

We will then finish off with the special version of JConsole that comes bundled with WildFly.

The Command-line Interface

The **Command-line Interface** (**CLI**) is exactly what it says it is, a command-line interface tool to administer WildFly from a terminal. It is started with the jboss-cli.sh command (for UNIX-based environments) or jboss-cli.bat (for Windows) and will give direct access to the configuration of running WildFly instances. As it uses the management socket, it can access remote WildFly instances if the management interface is configured to bind to an external interface instead of the default, localhost default. This can easily be achieved by starting WildFly with the system property, jboss.bind.address.management, set to the appropriate IP address as we did when we created the remote JMX connection from VisualVM earlier.

The commands can be issued in the noninteractive mode by specifying them on the command line (here, from $WILDFLY_HOME/bin/) as follows:

```
./jboss-cli.sh --controller=127.0.0.1:9990 --connect "/
subsystem=datasources/data-source=ExampleDS:read-
attribute(name=connection-url)"
```

The CLI answer comes in the JSON format, making it relatively easy to incorporate a command in scripts and so on. In the preceding example, the `--controller` parameter allows you to specify the host to connect to by an IP address or hostname. The `--connect` parameter tells the CLI to actually connect to the server. More information about the parameters can be found using the following command:

```
./jboss-cli.sh --help
```

The CLI also supports batch processing. This means that it is possible to execute commands in the noninteractive mode by reading them from a text file. In the following example, the commands in the `myCommands.cli` file will be executed by the CLI:

```
./jboss-cli.sh --controller=127.0.0.1:9990 --connect --file=myCommands.cli
```

Using the CLI to retrieve various configuration and metric values of pools, threads, and application-specific variables is very valuable over time to see system trends and for living up to SLAs. It is also very useful for quickly getting specific values during daily operations and performance tuning.

The WildFly Management Console

The **WildFly Management Console** or **HAL** as it also is called is a web-based administrative interface. Apart from being bundled with WildFly, it can also be separately downloaded from `http://jbossas.github.io/console`, where the most bleeding-edge version can be found. As new functionality is continuously added to the console, it is a good idea to have a look here and see if there are any features you might need that are not available in the console of your WildFly distribution.

As WildFly is started, the console is accessible from the `http://localhost:9990/console/App.html` URL. Before accessing the console, you will, however, need to create a management user. This is easily performed by running the `add-user` tool from the `$WILDFLY_HOME/bin` directory.

As a part of the Management Console, a HTTP REST API is exposed. It's used internally by the console itself but can also be called directly. In the following example, the cURL tool (`http://curl.haxx.se/`) is used to generate the HTTP request that connects to and authenticates with the WildFly management interface. From here information about the ExampleDS datasource is retrieved.

```
curl --digest -L -D - http://localhost:9990/management --header
"Content-Type: application/json" -d '{"operation":"read-attribute",
"name":"connection-url", "address":["subsystem","datasources","data-
source","ExampleDS"], "json.pretty":1}' -u admin:admin
```

This can easily be integrated into various systems that support REST if needed. Similar to CLI, the console is very useful for daily operations and gives a very good overview of the system settings. It is continuously evolved with a growing fauna of functionality.

JBoss DMR

Another entry for the management of WildFly is the JBoss Dynamic Model Representation API (`https://github.com/jbossas/jboss-dmr`). This API can be used to write your own proprietary management tools to WildFly. Its details are, however, beyond the scope of this book.

JConsole

The `jconsole` tool is included in the Oracle Java distribution, but a special version is also bundled with WildFly. The differences are that the WildFly version has a plugin for the integrated use of the CLI and a `CLASSPATH` set for allowing the various remoting protocols out of the box. Remember that we set the `CLASSPATH` and `http-remoting-jmx` protocol for VisualVM to be able to create JMX connections to WildFly.

JConsole is a good tool for performing various types of monitoring. It is very similar to VisualVM, but among other things, it lacks the power of profiling. It does, however, have a rich set of plugins that we recommend you to try out, especially as they can be run in the JConsole plugin for VisualVM and thereby create a very multifaceted and powerful toolkit.

Generating load

There are very few applications that don't behave differently when they come under load. To be able to investigate how the system will react when put under expected or even extreme load, we use load generators.

It's nearly impossible to mimic all the different use cases and their individual usage. Therefore, the load tests are often limited to 10 or 20 selected use cases. Some of them should be the most common ones, and some known or suspected trouble makers.

It's often tempting to limit the tests to read-only ones to minimize the trouble of setting up a database with a known state before each execution. This may be okay in some cases, but be prepared to add read-write tests at some stage before entering production in order to reach acceptable levels of QoS.

Extensive load testing may be limited by the chosen load-generator software and the operating system, network, and so on in such a way that it can't generate the load needed. The solution is to add more distributable "slave" instances of the load generator. This can create new problems around the orchestration and synchronization of the nodes. It is, however, a vital feature that needs to be available for test cases where large loads must be produced to mimic real scenarios. It is equally important that these slave instances of the load generator report the results back to a "master" and that this can present the results in some useful and accumulated way.

There are a lot of tools on the market, but here, we limit ourselves to introduce the one we most often find in use: **Apache JMeter**.

Apache JMeter

Apache JMeter is an open source Java desktop application for load testing. It is available for download from the Apache website (`http://jmeter.apache.org`). In the examples of this book, we'll be using Version 2.10.

JMeter was originally designed for testing web applications but has since expanded to support other protocols. The supported protocols that may be of interest for a Java EE environment are as follows:

- HTTP(S)
- SOAP
- FTP
- JDBC
- JMS
- SMTP(S)
- POP3(S)
- IMAP(S)

The extensible core of JMeter provides a functionality that simplifies the process of supporting new protocols and operations. JMeter uses multithreading to produce load. This is used when simulating multiple callers. Besides call generation, it also provides functionalities for response validations, data analysis, and an easy-to-use GUI.

 If any product-specific JARs such as JDBC drivers or JMS-client libraries are needed, they are simply dropped into the $JMETER_HOME/lib/ext directory, which will add them to the CLASSPATH.

Building a basic test plan

When starting JMeter using $JMETER_HOME/bin/jmeter.sh (for UNIX systems) or jmeter.bat (for Windows), the application will appear with the **Test Plan** screen, as shown in the following screenshot:

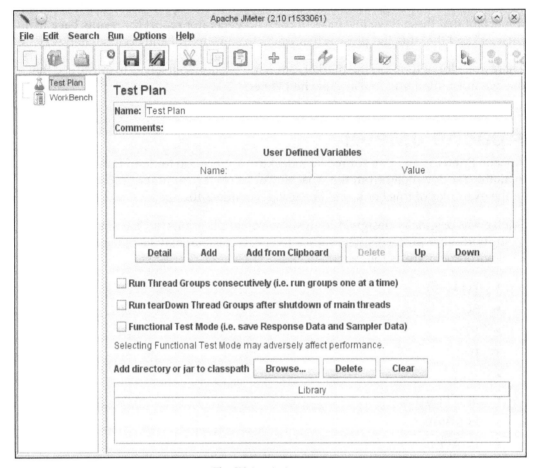

The JMeter startup page

The **Test Plan** is a container for running tests. The **WorkBench** functions as a temporary workspace to store the test elements. When you are ready to test what you have designed in **WorkBench**, you can copy or move the elements into **Test Plan**. To get an understanding of how JMeter works, let's create a simple test case by performing the following steps:

1. Define a thread group by right-clicking on **Test Plan** and navigating to **Add | Thread Group**. This is the main component of the test plan and will contain some subcomponents, as shown in the following screenshot:

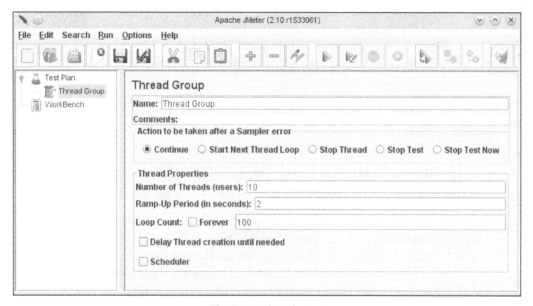

The JMeter thread group

The fields in the **Thread Group view** will allow a user to define the following:

- **Number of Threads (users)**: This refers to the number of users
- **Ramp-Up Period (in seconds)**: This refers to how long it takes to ramp-up to the full number of threads chosen
- **Loop Count**: This refers to the number of times to execute the test

 If you enable the **Scheduler** field in the lower part of the GUI, you will be able to define a startup time and a stopping time for your test, which can thus be deferred to a later time.

2. Add a sampler. In this example, we want to sample a web server, so we right-click on **Thread Group**, as seen in the left pane in the following screenshot, and navigate to **Add | Sampler | HTTP Request**:

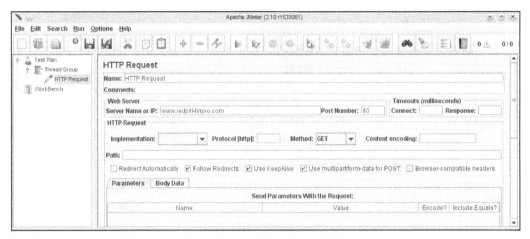

Part of a JMeter sampler example

In the **Web Server** section, you specify the server address, and in the **HTTP Request** section, you specify the path to the web page that should be tested.

3. Finally, we add a listener, which is responsible for displaying the statistical information about the sampler's result. There are several variants available, and for this example, we choose **Aggregate Report** by right-clicking on **Thread Group** and navigating to **Add | Listener | Aggregate Report**:

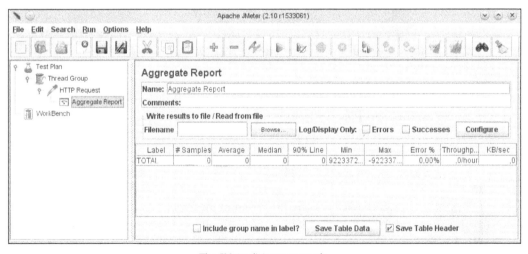

The JMeter listener example

Before running the test, JMeter requires that we save the test plan. Click on the **Save Test Plan** button from the **File** menu, and then, from the **Run** menu, select **Run**. The following screenshot shows how your **Aggregate Report** panel should look at the end of a profiler session. If you have selected to run a benchmark forever, you need to manually stop the run by selecting **Stop** from the **Run** menu.

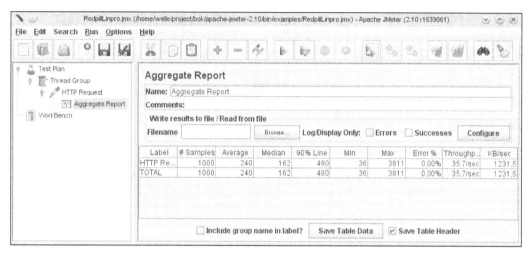

JMeter Aggregate Report result

Improving the test plan

By default, JMeter sends one request immediately after the other without any delay. This could potentially saturate the server and also produce a test that is not close to a real-world scenario. As a matter of fact, user requests are usually separated by a variable amount of time, which can be thought of as constant or following a statistical pattern such as a Gaussian curve.

In order to introduce a delay between requests, you can introduce timers in your test plan. Navigate to **Add | Timer** from the **Thread Group** context menu and select one of the available timers.

JMeter also supports more or less advanced validations that can be placed on the samplers results in the form of **assertions**. These are added just like other components we've shown in this chapter and can be used for XML validations, value checking, and so on.

If you have a web application that uses HTTP GET, it may be possible to use an Apache Web Server Access log file as an input to the specialized `AccessLogSampler` to feed the test case with a realistic real-world scenario.

Recording a web session using the JMeter HTTP proxy

With the notions you have learned until this point, you are able to create a simple web load test. In theory, you could build a more complex one by including a set of HTTP requests, each one targeted at a different URL and carrying the appropriate parameters. In practice, this would require quite a lot of time and would also be prone to human error (ironically, you would end up testing the composition of the test too!). Luckily, there's a handy option that allows us to use JMeter as proxy server, thus recording every request made to the application. A proxy server can be added by right-clicking on **Workbench** and navigating to **Add | Non Test Elements | HTTP(S) Test Script Recorder**. As shown in the following diagram, the **JMeter Proxy Server** sits in between the **Client** (browser) and **Web Server**:

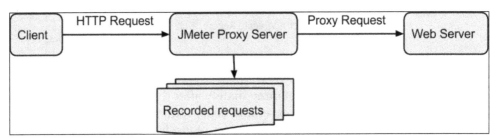

An overview of the JMeter proxy system

Now, you need to configure your browser so that the proxy server will actually direct the proxy request to the web server. Finally, start the HTTP proxy server by clicking on the **Start** button in the lower part of the panel and start surfing to your WildFly.

When you have completed your recording, click on the **Stop** button in the **HTTP Proxy Server** panel. The HTTP request items created in **WorkBench** can eventually be dragged into your test plan.

Standalone and distributed load generation

Your hardware's capabilities will inevitably limit the number of threads you can effectively run with JMeter. If you need to set up a large scale test and you cannot afford to execute the JMeter GUI, you can consider launching JMeter using the command line. The following parameters can be used to run JMeter from the command prompt:

- -n: This specifies that JMeter is to run in the non-GUI mode
- -t: This specifies the name of the JMX file that contains the test plan
- -l: This specifies the name of the JTL file to log the sample results to
- -r: This is used to run all the remote servers specified in the properties of JMeter
- -H: This specifies the proxy server hostname or IP address if it is run using firewall/proxy
- -P: This specifies the proxy server port if it is run using firewall/proxy

An example where JMeter will execute the test plan contained in the test1.jmx file and log the sample results to the logfile.jtl file, would look as follows:

```
jmeter -n -t test1.jmx -l logfile.jtl
```

 It's still possible to use different listeners in the JMeter GUI to analyze the logfile.jtl file after the execution. One way is to use the **WorkBench** area, add the chosen listener, and then use its file-loading box to load the generated result file.

Sooner or later, during extensive load testing, the actual load generator, operating system, and available memory will limit the amount of possible threads. JMeter supports the possibility to run several JMeter slave instances on multiple servers and use a master instance to control the lifecycle and reporting of the tests.

Performing the following schematic steps will allow you to efficiently run JMeter in the distributed mode:

1. Make sure that the load-generator machines have the same version of JMeter, and any data input files used by the test cases as these files will not be propagated from the master node.

2. Start different slave servers (on host1, host2, host3, and so on), $JMETER_HOME/bin/jmeter-server.

3. Start the master node specifying the slave nodes, `$JMETER_HOME/bin/jmeter -R127.0.0.1,host1,host2,host3`, and so on (the node list can also be specified in the `jmeter.properties` config file).

4. Start the distributed test from the master in the following ways (the slaves will follow automatically):

   ○ Using GUI, navigate to **Run | Remote Start All**

   ○ Using command line, use the `jmeter -n -t script.jmx -r` command

 Do not overuse listeners and assertions, as they may slow JMeter down and, therefore, limit the load that a JMeter instance can generate. The most memory-effective combination would be running JMeter in the non-GUI mode with no assertions and just using the listener named **Simple Data Writer**.

Summary

In this chapter, we have discussed the tools and processes based on three key features of performance tuning:

- Profiling
- Monitoring
- Load generation

We have talked about what use these features provide during performance tuning and how they fit into the different layers of an enterprise stack. For each feature, we have discussed at least one well-versed tool that brings a lot of value to the tuning process.

With regards to profiling, we focused on the very versatile JVM tool, VisualVM. We described how to make it and WildFly play well together with `jstatd` and the `http-remoting-jmx`.

Moving onto monitoring, we discussed various OS-specific tools. These are primarily useful for resolving problems in the lower layers of the stack. As such, they often relate to CPU, memory, disks, and network. They also give important clues about the real source of a problem if it has arisen in the upper layers such as poor design, code, or configuration.

We have briefly talked about the tools bundled with WildFly: CLI, Management Console (HAL), and API (DMR).

When discussing load generation, Apache JMeter was our tool of choice. For this, we revealed some of its many possibilities in terms of protocol support, standalone usage, and distributed master-slave behavior.

In this chapter, we mentioned the JVM and things such as the garbage collector which are related to it. In the next chapter, we will dig deeper into the JVM and its various components, their settings, and optimal values.

3
Tuning the Java Virtual Machine

Like every other Java application, the WildFly application server requires an engine to operate. This engine can interpret and handle Java bytecode. As such, it has been named **Java Virtual Machine (JVM)**.

With every release of Java, a lot of changes and improvements to JVM have been introduced. Over time, it has become increasingly faster and more intelligent in determining how it should configure itself in order to give its best for any particular situation and environment. The result is a highly advanced runtime that has become easier to use but still needs some of our love and understanding from time to time.

So, we need to understand how JVM operates, how to interpret what it tells us, and how to tune it to make it work even more efficiently. In order to properly reach these goals, we will learn a lot more about JVM in this chapter by discussing the following topics:

- The basic theory of JVM, focusing on its memory areas, and garbage collector
- Possible (and for some scenarios, optimal) JVM settings
- What a memory leak is and how it can be found
- Reasons for various out-of-memory errors and their resolutions
- JVM settings in WildFly
- How and what to log from JVM in a production environment

JVM

When we talk about JVM, it is important to first put it in its context of **Java Runtime Environment (JRE)**. JRE consist of, among several things, JVM, libraries (with core Java classes), and some components (such as supporting files, Java Web Start, and the Java Plugin). It does not, however, include tools for performing tasks such as compiling and debugging. These are all part of the **Java Development Kit (JDK)** distribution.

JVM is the execution engine for all Java applications. It is responsible for platform security, memory management, and bytecode (compiled code) execution. With bytecode execution, JVM creates a foundation for platform independence.

The JVM specification (`http://docs.oracle.com/javase/specs/jvms/se7/html/index.html`) stipulates what an implementation should adhere to. As we focus on Java SE 7 based on the Oracle JDK 7 distribution in this book, we'll follow that trail by looking at its VM implementation named **Hotspot**.

JVM memory areas

Memory-wise, JVM is made up of two major generic storage types: **stack** and **heap**.

The JVM stack and native stack

A stack is a **last in, first out (LIFO)** type of storage. For each JVM thread of execution, there is a **JVM stack**. In this stack, entries called **frames** are stored. The frames can hold object references, variables values, and partial results. During the execution of a Java application, these frames are added (push) to, or removed (pop) from the JVM stack.

In JVM, there is also the concept of a **native stack**. Normally, there exists one stack per JVM thread, and it is used to support native (written in a platform-native language such as C/C++) functions/methods as the regular JVM stacks can't hold them.

As a concept, a stack is quite easy to control. When a frame is no longer needed, it gets removed (pop), and its memory area is freed by the simple operation of adjusting a pointer to the next frame in the stack.

The heap

The heap is a memory area that, according to the specification, doesn't have to be contiguous but, implementation-wise, it often is. The heap is created during the JVM startup and is shared by all JVM threads. Its size can be static but can also grow to a certain size as per the needs of the executing application. In the heap class, instances and arrays are stored. Hence, this memory area is often denoted as the real data storage of JVM.

This is mainly due to the fact that data structures, with some restrictions, can be allocated at any memory position within the heap. Also, as these data structures are no longer live, the memory they allocated will sooner or later be freed or reclaimed, causing fragmentation of the heap.

Inside the heap, there are several separated memory areas whose sizes depend on the size of the amount of memory available in the heap by default. These areas are denoted as generational memory areas and are named as follows:

* Young generation
* Old (or tenured) generation
* Permanent generation

The Young generation consists of three memory areas:

* Eden
* Survivor space 0 (S0)
* Survivor space 1 (S1)

Data structures are stored in the different memory areas of the young generation and in the tenured generation, depending on how long they have been alive. Here, life is defined in the number of collections made by the **garbage collector (GC)** of JVM. In fact, the main reason for having all these memory areas is to optimize GC performance and, thereby, the memory usage.

In the **permanent generation (PermGen)**, data structures and meta-information of our classes stored. We will discuss all of this in more detail in the upcoming sections:

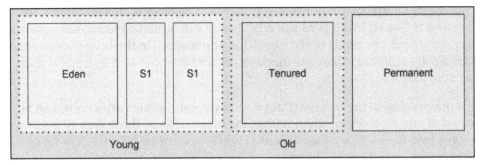

The heap with its submemory areas (sizes are not proportional)

Other JVM memory concepts

It should be noted that, in the Hotspot JVM, there also exist concepts such as the **program counter (pc)** Register, Method Areas, and Runtime Constant Pools. Though they're highly important and interesting, we won't go into further details of these concepts.

GC

Closely related to the memory areas of JVM is GC. Conceptually, GC is an automatic storage-management system. It manages how allocations in memory that no longer live should be freed, thereby making the memory available for new allocations. From this, we reveal that the golden rules of GC are as follows:

- **Collect all garbage**: Due to concerns of, for example, optimizations, this rule can be somewhat floating when interpreted in various GC implementations. It is, therefore, sometimes more correct to rephrase the rule as *collect all garbage, eventually*.

- **Never collect a live object**: This, on the other hand, is an absolutely sacred rule. If it is broken, the GC cannot be trusted or used at all, as faults in the software that executes in JVM will follow.

The Java GC specification does not specify any particular algorithm for how collection is supposed to be done as long as the preceding rules are abided to. It is, therefore, possible to choose an algorithmic strategy, with its related implementation, depending on what needs your specific environment and application have. Hence, you can write you own GC, specific for your own application.

A common fallacy is that Java GC eats a lot of system time and thus degrades the overall system performance. Such claims can be calmed by noting that it is not, since the Java GC does not operate in kernel time, but in user time. This should calm administrators but, as a developer, you still have to have a controlled GC.

Today's JVMs are, however, quite skilled at selecting a good GC. Sometimes, though, there might be a need to change or tweak it a bit. We'll get back to GC strategies later in this chapter.

Before we venture further into configuration of JVM and its components, let's have a look at how memory areas and GC work together in general with object allocations and freeing of memory, respectively.

JVM memory management with the GC

In the following diagrams, we have the heap memory areas, **Eden**, **S0**, **S1**, and **Tenured**, repeated in the rows numbered **1** to **13** (to the right-hand side of each row). Each row represents how the memory areas look at a certain age time.

Objects allocated in the memory areas are depicted with numbers inside them, denoting the generation or age that they belong to. Generation is a measure of how many times an object has moved from one memory area to another. A generation is complete when a memory area is filled up with objects and needs to move all of its live objects to the next memory area.

In step **1** in the following diagram, objects are being created and hence start to allocate memory in **Eden**. New data structures always start their lives in **Eden**, and their generational number is set to **1**.

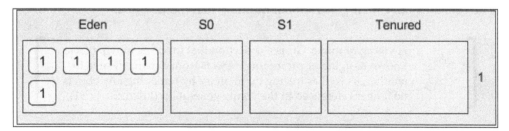

The heap at generational age 1

Step **2** shows us more objects allocating room in Eden and some objects that are no longer in use. These are shown in the following diagram as objects without numbers. The memory that is no longer in use will be collected in upcoming GCs. For now, however, all of these areas are still locked and can't yet be de- or re-allocated.

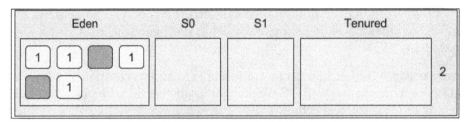

The heap at step 2

As we reach step **3**, **Eden** is full and no more allocations can be made here. Eden is, however, where new allocations are made, as shown in the following diagram:

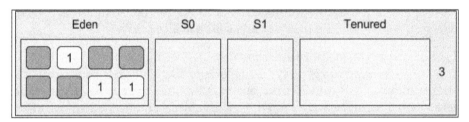

The heap at step 3

Now, between steps **3** and **4**, a minor collection is performed by GC and, after that, as we can see in step **4** in the following diagram, the live objects have been moved into **S0** and the entire **Eden** swept clean in order to receive new allocations. Note how all live objects now have their generational number incremented to **2**.

 A young or minor GC is a collection that involves moving (also known as aging or promoting) objects from a memory area to another, as well as freeing up memory by removing any objects no longer referenced in the young generation (Eden, S0, or S1).

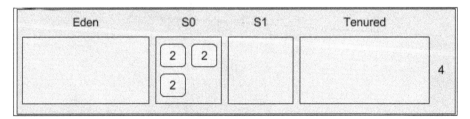

The heap at step 4

In step **5**, as shown in the following diagram, this starts all over again. Now, generation **1** allocations are made in Eden and, in **S0**, one allocation is no longer live.

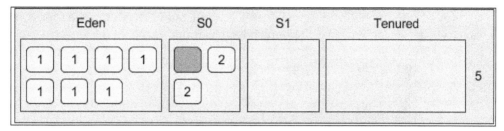

The heap at step 5

Step **6** shows us how Eden once again is full and how many allocations are not live. In S0, another allocation is no longer live, as shown in the following diagram:

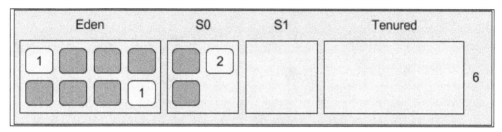

The heap at step 6

Between steps **6** and **7**, another GC executes, moving live objects from S0 to S1, upgrading their generational number from **2** to **3**, and also moving and upgrading any live objects from Eden to S1, thus cleaning both Eden and S0. This is shown in the following diagram:

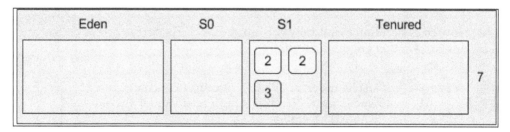

The heap at step 7

This behavior is then repeated in the following steps. As a memory area fills up, GC is commanded to work. Live objects are moved from Eden, a working survival space becomes a free survival space, and their generational age is increased one step each time. This continues until the tenured age limit is hit. When it is, all allocations of this age are moved into the tenured memory area as depicted in step **13** in the following diagram, where we pretend that the tenured age is four.

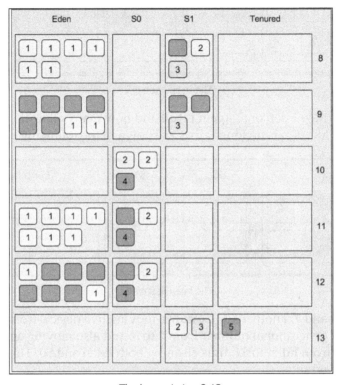

The heap at step 8-13

As the tenured generation eventually fills up, a Full GC is performed to collect any allocations therein that are no longer live.

 An old, major, or Full GC is freeing up memory by removing any objects no longer referenced in the old (tenured) generation.

Performing a Full GC is very costly in comparison to collecting in Eden. From a performance perspective, it is, therefore, desirable to mostly have relatively short-lived objects and objects that are not promoted to tenured space too fast. It is often also desirable to keep long-lived objects (that make it into tenured space) alive as long as possible.

Configuring the JVM

The JVM has lots and lots of configuration possibilities. In this book, we will focus on just a few, but these are the ones that, over the years, have proved most valuable in terms of information and performance-related impact.

Default settings

The Hotspot JVM is nowadays ergonomic. This means that, based upon the platform configuration, it will select the runtime compiler, heap configuration, and GC that, according to its documentation, will produce a *good to excellent performance for most applications*. To get the best possible performance, specific tuning might, however, still be required.

Starting up, JVM is already configured with a set of options. Some are just defaults, while others are dynamically, or ergonomically, set by JVM itself during startup and after the analysis, of, for example, the available hardware that the JVM is executing on. Lastly, a set of options, which by default can be of a static or dynamic nature, can be set as JVM arguments.

To find out about the options that are set for a specific environment in JVM, execute the java command with the VM parameter, -XX:+PrintFlagsFinal, for example:

```
java -XX:+PrintFlagsFinal -version
```

This will show us a long list of the available options in an alphabetical order. The list is over 600 lines long so we won't list them all here. A few typical lines can look as shown in the following code snippet:

```
 bool IncrementalInline     = true {C2 product}
uintx InitialCodeCacheSize = 2555904 {pd product}
uintx InitialHeapSize      := 268435456 {product}
uintx InitialRAMFraction   = 64 {product}
uintx InitialSurvivorRatio = 8 {product}
uintx MaxHeapFreeRatio     = 70 {product}
uintx MaxHeapSize          := 4294967296 {product}
```

As you can see, each line is divided in to five distinct columns of information from left to right; we denote these columns by the following names:

- Type
- Name
- Operator
- Value
- Category

The *type* column tells us the data type that the option value is in. For example, `boolean`, `int`, `double`, `uintx`, and more. Obviously, these are not Java types but native ones. Moving on to the *name* column, this is the option name or key.

The *operator* can be = or :=. The first one tells us that the default value of JVM is used and the last one tells us that the value is changed from the default. It can have been changed after some internal analysis of JVM itself or by a JVM argument given to it.

The *value* column is simply the value of the option. Finally, in the *category* column, we find various information about the option such as whether it is an internal value only, whether it is experimental and not officially supported, or whether it belongs to a specific compiler type.

Client versus Server VM

The Hotspot JVM has two configuration flags that make it use a **Client VM** or a **Server VM**. There is no real visible or functional difference between these VMs, other than the fact that they are configured and optimized differently. The Client VM normally starts faster and the Server VM runs faster over time. As the Client VM starts faster, it is better suited to run client applications as the start up speed is more important than the processing speed. In reality, however, this is very seldom utilized today. Instead, the optimization of the Server VM is the prevailing variant. This has become even more obvious, as the ergonomic choice of the VM that is selected depends on the available hardware. Any relatively modern computer of today (Java SE 6 and 7, that means, having two or more CPUs and at least 2 GB RAM) is considered a server class computer and here the Server VM will automatically be selected.

Should you ever need to override the automatic selection, the Client's VM can be explicitly defined using the configuration flag to the `java` command, as follows:

```
-client
```

Similarly, to explicitly define the Server VM, use the following command when dealing with enterprise applications:

```
-server
```

As you are reading this book, you must have some really strong and new arguments to use anything but the Server VM.

The stack

Using the default, platform-dependent size value for the stack is often a good starting strategy. The stack size can be altered by adding this VM parameter with a new size value: `-Xss<size>`.

For JVMs running out of memory, it can be relevant to lower the stack size. As JVMs with many threads can potentially use a lot of memory, it is a good idea to inspect and correlate the values of the stack size with the memory usage.

Should you encounter the infamous `java.lang.StackOverflowError`, you probably have an application whose stack is exhausted due to recursive calls or a really deep call chain. An overview of how your application is designed and what it actually does in terms of thread life cycle usage is often very relevant at a first encounter. If the validation of the design and implementation turns out to be okay, the stack size will need an increase.

The heap

The heap size can be set to an initial value, a minimum value, and a maximum value. In older JVMs, it was considered good practice to set the minimum and maximum values equal. This made sense as the cost of resizing the heap was very expensive.

Today, the general recommendation is to not set the minimum value at all. The JVM will be perfectly proficient to do that itself by its ergonomic intelligence. The focus should instead be on finding a good maximum size for the heap.

Another way of looking at the heap is shown in the following diagram. Here, the dynamicity of the heap and its subareas is shown by the Allocated (all non-Virtual) and **Virtual** columns. Within each subarea of the heap, the Allocated areas are reserved for holding objects, while the Virtual are unused areas that are available for growth.

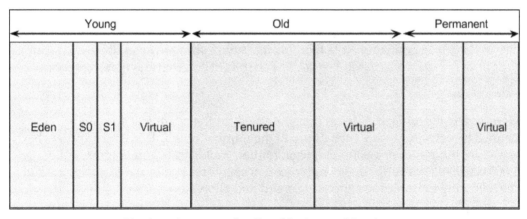

The dynamic memory allocation of the heap and its subareas

In the upcoming subsections, we will go through the various size- and ratio-related VM parameters of the different memory areas. For the size-oriented parameter, the following diagram will act as a visual guide and reference. Red-colored arrows are for the heap excluding the PermGen area. Yellow arrows are for the young generation and blue arrows are for the permanent generation. Note that the sum of both the red-marked Initial arrows equals the initial size value of the heap (set by the Xms parameter).

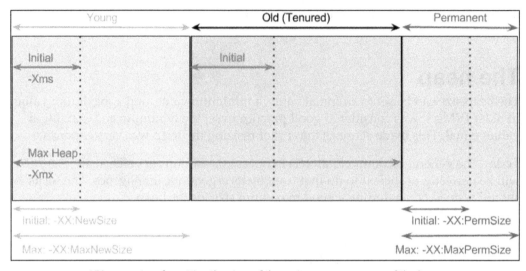

VM parameters for setting the sizes of the various memory areas of the heap

Setting the maximum heap size

Setting the maximum heap size of JVM is done by setting the Xmx flag with a defined size to the `java` command. Note that this maximum size, however, does not include the PermGen space discussed later in this chapter. The generic syntax is as follows:

```
-Xmx<size>
```

Here, size is the number of bytes to be reserved for the heap. The size can be defined by actually stating each figure in the number or with a metric prefix such as k (kilo, thousand, or 1,000), M (mega, million, or 1,000,000), or G (giga, billion, or 1,000,000,000). The suffix is allowed to both upper- and lowercase characters. All of the following examples are, therefore, valid and allowed:

```
-Xmx4294967296
```

```
-Xmx5000k
```

```
-Xmx256M
```

```
-Xmx4G
```

On a server class computer of today (64-bit), JVM normally sets the maximum heap by default to one-fourth of the available memory on the machine. For example, on a machine with 16 GB RAM, the maximum heap size will be 4 GB.

Setting the initial heap size

Should you realize that the initial heap size, for some reason, is wrong for your application, you can set it in the exact same way as the maximum size. The only difference is the name of the flag. The initial or minimum (as it was previously known as) size of the heap is set using the Xms flag. Using a generic syntax, the flag look as follows:

```
-Xms<size>
```

On a server class computer of today (64-bit), JVM normally sets the initial heap by default to 1/64th of the available memory on the machine. So, for example, on a machine with 16 GB RAM, the initial heap size will be 256 MB.

It's also worth noting that, on a 32-bit machine, the limit of available addressable memory is just (2^32=) 4 GB. With this type of computer architecture, the limitations in memory often create quite a lot of problems. The addressable memory in a 64-bit machine is over (2^64=) 18 ExaByte (1.8*10^19). As pretty much all computers of today use 64-bit architectures, being able to physically use enough memory is barely a problem any longer.

Determining what maximum size the heap should be

It is important to award JVM with at least as much memory as estimated (or measured) for peak usage. Giving your application way too much memory isn't good either, as it will lock up more resources than needed and also make your system unnecessarily expensive.

Setting the correct maximum heap size of JVM for an application is one of the most essential—and probably the most common—tuning tasks in relation to the memory handling of the JVM.

Finding the maximum heap size for any application running in a JVM involves monitoring the heap while the system is under load. Monitoring should be done as the load is consistent and also during peak times. The maximum peak value in the heap usage should be noted as in the following image:

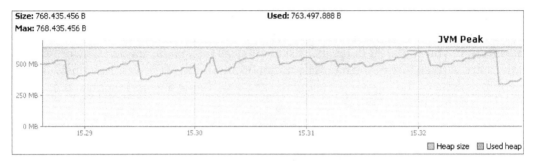

The maximum heap size is determined from the highest peak value used by the heap

The maximum heap size must be somewhat higher than the maximal monitored value. It should also be adjusted so that not more than around 75 percent of the heap is occupied during the normal load. If more of the heap is used, the frequency of GC might interfere with the application performance.

An old rule is that the maximum heap size shouldn't be too large, or the GC will take a long time. This is still true in some scenarios but, as the heap size now is more adaptive and GC strategies have evolved, the importance of this rule has diminished.

Determining what initial size the heap should be

The ergonomic features of Hotspot make it quite unnecessary to choose the initial size of the heap. If we have an application that requires more initial memory than Hotspot can foresee, then there might be some minor but still unnecessary time spent on heap resizing. To improve the time, we could find out, and possibly set, the initial heap size.

Similar to when we determined the maximum heap size, we monitor the heap during the load. As GC is activated, we should start to see the jagged pattern of the utilized heap memory dropping as the collector kicks in and then rising again until the collector once again becomes active. The level that the heap is at the lowest of these points is the value of what the initial heap size should be set to. An example of marking this level is given in the following image:

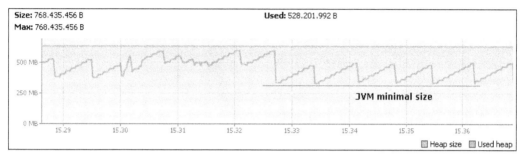

The initial heap size is determined by the minimal value of the heap usage after stabilization

Setting the size of the young and old generations

If the young generation is too small, short-lived objects will be moved too quickly into the old generation, where they are more costly to collect. On the other hand, if the young generation is too large, there will be a lot of unnecessary copying of objects that should end up in the old generation eventually anyway. Should the young generation be more than half the entire heap in size, it negates its ability to perform a copy collection and results in a Full GC. This is also known as the **young generation guarantee**.

The young generation guarantee ensures that the minor collection can complete even if all the objects are live. Enough free memory must be reserved in the tenured generation to accommodate all the live objects arriving from the survivor spaces. When there isn't enough memory available in the tenured generation to accommodate all these objects, a major collection will occur.

Relying on Hotspot's ergonomicity, setting these values is often good enough, especially if your application runs smoothly and no OutOfMemoryErrors occur. Should you, however, need to find a better weight value between the young and old generations; this can only be done by systematic monitoring, measurements, and tuning. Remember to only change one value at a time and retest iteratively.

When designing an application, strive to use mainly short-lived objects as these will die in the young generation where they will be removed with a relatively cheap minor GC. Using some long-lived objects is often necessary and completely valid, but bear in mind that these will require a relatively costly Full GC as they reach the tenured age and memory area.

As for the Heap, the initial and the maximum value of the young generation can be set to absolute values by flags to the `java` command. To set the maximum size of the young generation, use the following flag:

```
-XX:MaxNewSize=<size>
```

For the initial size, use the following flag:

```
-XX:NewSize=<size>
```

When setting the maximum size, great care has to be taken as it also impacts the old generation. The greater the size we award to the young generation, the smaller the old generation will get. Normally, the old generation should be considerably larger than the young generation. It can, therefore, make more sense to set a relative size ratio between the old and young generations. For this, you can use the following flag:

```
-XX:NewRatio=<ratio>
```

Setting this with a `ratio` value of, for example, 3 will mean that the old generation is three times larger than the young generation. So, one-quarter of the space belongs to the young generation and three-quarters to the old. The default when using the server configuration is 2. Commonly, a `ratio` value of 2 or 3 is used for a majority of the applications we've come across.

Now, combining the absolute and relative will give a complete definition of the young-old generations' sizes. Consider the following example:

```
java -XX:NewSize=64m -XX:MaxNewSize=1g -XX:NewRatio=3 MyApp
```

Here, JVM will try to keep the size of the old generation three times larger than the young, but the young will also be kept larger than 64 MB and will never get bigger than 1 GB.

Setting the size ratio of Eden and the survivor spaces

Having a relatively small-sized Eden is generally not good as objects will have to be quickly moved into the survivor spaces and GCs become triggered quite often. Similarly, having survivor spaces that are not good as they will fill up too quickly and, consequently, objects will mature into the old generation too quickly.

Finding the balance of Eden and the survivor spaces is just as important as finding it for all other memory areas. Finding and using the correct settings also follows the same approach.

Leave the ergonomic settings of Hotspot alone if your application works fine. Otherwise, monitor and tune in the controlled way: change one thing, retest, and so on. Learning about the age distribution of objects is particularly useful in this work.

Using the following parameter will list the age distribution of all objects in the survivor spaces on each minor (young) GC. More details of this parameter will be given in the *VM parameters in production* section later on in this chapter:

`-XX:+PrintTenuringDistribution`

Just as with setting the size ratio between the young and old generations, we can set the ratio between Eden and one of the survivor spaces. This is done using the following flag:

`-XX:SurvivorRatio=<ratio>`

Setting this with a `ratio` value of, for example, `10` will mean that Eden is ten times larger than each of the survivor spaces. Consequently, Eden will own 10/12 of the young generation and S0 and S1 will both own one-twelfth each. The default is `8` and, most commonly, a `ratio` value between `8` and `12` is used for a majority of the applications we've come across.

The tenuring threshold is a term that denotes the number of times an object survives a young collection and is aged enough to be promoted to the old (tenured) generation. The initial and maximum tenuring thresholds, respectively, can be set by the following two parameters:

`-XX:InitialTenuringThreshold=<threshold>`

`-XX:MaxTenuringThreshold=<threshold>`

Note that `threshold` here is an integer value. To specify at what percent the "to" survivor space should be utilized before a minor GC kicks in can be set by the following parameter:

```
-XX:TargetSurvivorRatio=<ratio>
```

Here, `ratio` is an integer that denotes a percentage. A `ratio` value of 90 would hence denote that 90 percent of the "to" survivor space should be filled before the collection kicks in. How all these values come in to play is shown by running a VM with the `PrintTenuringDistribution` parameter.

PermGen

The last of the major memory areas we will explore is PermGen. This area is separate from the rest of the areas in the heap as it doesn't handle the storage of objects that are moving around between areas. Instead, PermGen is used to store the object metadata that lasts the JVM lifetime. Reloading and recycling of classes happens here as an application server reloads classes. PermGen has a history of poor optimizations; as a developer using an application server or some other Java tool that loads a lot of classes, you're very likely to have seen the very familiar and pesky `java.lang.OutOfMemoryError: PermGen space` that we will discuss more in detail shortly. Setting the maximum size of the PermGen area is done using the `java` flag as follows:

```
-XX:MaxPermSize=<size>
```

> In **Java SE 8**, PermGen has been removed, which certainly is something that many will feel happy about (at least initially). Instead, we will be introduced to a new memory area called **Metaspace**. This area will handle metadata and is similar to solutions available in the JRockit and IBM VMs. How this will play out remains to be seen, but there are some disturbing signs. As the new memory area is located in the native memory space that is outside of the Java-controlled space, it will certainly introduce new challenges in terms of analysis and monitoring. This is especially obvious as tooling currently is close to nonexistent.

Large objects

When designing and implementing an application, it is worth remembering to avoid allocating very large objects that are kept alive for a long time. The problems with these objects are that they have the potential to severely fragment the heap. Despite good GC strategies and improved defragmentation techniques, consequences can, in the end, be catastrophic for JVM, often in the shape of a `java.lang.OutOfMemoryError` error.

Large objects that have a short lifespan will be collected relatively fast and won't cause many problems. If these large objects are also allocated at the same time, they can be stored as continuous memory space, fragmentation can be kept to a minimum. They are also likely to be collected at the same time.

Another good solution is to chop the large objects up in to smaller ones, as this will make their long lifespan less cumbersome for the memory handling of JVM. Should none of these techniques be an option, the solution of enabling large memory pages might do the trick.

Large memory pages

Modern CPUs have a feature named *large memory pages*. This feature allows applications that require a lot of memory to make 2 to 4 MB-sized allocations instead of the standard 4 KB. Needless to say, this can improve the performance significantly for some applications. It can, however, also cause degraded performance when shortage of memory (that often occurs in systems with long uptime, where memory has become so fragmented that new memory reservations are not allowed) leads to excessive paging.

The large memory pages feature is available in the 64-bit JVM, where the parameter for enabling it is the following one:

```
-XX:+UseLargePages
```

By default, large memory pages is disabled in Java on most major platforms (Linux, OS X, and Windows) but enabled for some (such as Solaris). You will need to adapt your operating system settings accordingly.

The java.lang.OutOfMemoryError error

It is sometimes said that a programmer has not really experienced anything until he or she has come across a `java.lang.OutOfMemoryError` (OOME) error. The Java SE 7 javadoc (`http://docs.oracle.com/javase/7/docs/api/java/lang/OutOfMemoryError.html`) describes the OOME as follows:

> *Thrown when the Java Virtual Machine cannot allocate an object because it is out of memory, and no more memory could be made available by the garbage collector. OutOfMemoryError objects may be constructed by the virtual machine as if suppression was disabled and/or the stack trace was not writable.*

When this error turns up, the OOME hints, in its message, what memory area has been exhausted or what other memory-related problem it pertains to. Most commonly, it points out the heap or PermGen.

The responses among different organizations and individuals vary. Many try to create more or less clever workarounds in order to avoid the nasty OOME that will crash the VM of their valuable system and require it to be restarted. Some often seen, but not recommended, walkarounds include daily restarts, where and somewhat more advanced versions actually check whether the heap level is critical before restarting.

Others will just increase the heap and PermGen until there is no crashing. It is often valid to increase the heap to some level—as we've previously explored. To increase the heap to just avoid or postpone an OOME is not good enough, though. Instead, we must understand what causes the OOME and, if it is a memory leak, how to find and resolve it. We will discuss how to find the source of a memory leak shortly but, first, we need to understand the most common types of OOME.

From the heap

Should the OOME have a message that states that the problem lies within the "Java Heap space", we need to consider a few options. More heap memory might actually be needed by the application. Alternatively, the application holds on to too many object references for too long. In this case, we have what is commonly known as a memory leak.

In either way, an analysis of how the heap utilization looks over time is necessary. A heap with an uneven allocation curve (not the nice, shark-fin shaped one) that grows both its initial (minimum) and maximum limits is a clear suspect for a leak.

From the PermGen

An OOME message that states the "PermGen space" means that the PermGen space is full. This can happen whenever an application needs to load a large number of classes. Resolving this problem could be aided by carefully considering class usage in the application. Unfortunately, this is never realistic during development; for existing applications, it might require a total redesign. Instead, here is the solution to increase the PermGen space with the previously mentioned -XX:MaxPermSize VM parameter.

The PermGen space often gets exhausted after redeploying an application a few times. This is due to the fact that, every time you deploy an application, the application is loaded using its own classloader. Simply put, a classloader is a special class that loads .class files from JAR files. When you undeploy the application, the class loader is discarded and all the classes that it loaded should be collected by the GC sooner or later. The problem is that web containers do not collect the garbage of the classloader itself and the classes it loads. Each time you reload the webapp context, more copies of these classes are loaded; as these are stored in the permanent heap generation, it will eventually run out of memory. Thus, restarting the JVM from time to time is a much better idea than just raising the PermGen size.

Too large an array

When the details of an OOME message state the "requested array size exceeds VM limit", an application will attempt to allocate an array that is larger than the heap size. For example, if an application attempts to allocate an array of 512 MB but the maximum heap size is 256 MB, then an OOME will be thrown with this message. If this object allocation is intentional, then the simple way to solve this issue is by increasing the maximum size of the Java heap. If not, some clever redesign of the application will hopefully be the solution.

Not enough native threads

An OOME message that says "unable to create new native thread" can indicate that the computer user that runs JVM is not being allowed to create enough user processes (these are dependent on the platform but are named user threads in Java). The following command will list how many user processes the current user on a UNIX-system is allowed to execute:

```
ulimit -a
```

Changing the number of processes the user is allowed to execute is done by issuing the following command (preferably in a shell startup script or something similar, so it won't need to be given manually), where 4096 now will be the new number of the allowed user processes:

```
ulimit -u 4096
```

Memory leaks

A very common performance problem in software development is **memory leaks**. The creators and maintainers of the Java language have done a lot to minimize this problem by the garbage collection of released (set to null) and unreferenced object instances for example, but poor code can and will still create problems. When an OOME occurs and the problem is suspected to be due to a memory leak, it is time to start investigating the real cause(s).

The rule of thumb to identify a likely heap leak is as follows:

> *If the heap size usage keeps increasing for a while after each time a Full GC has executed, it implies a likely memory leak*

For the best estimate, the same type and amount of operations should be performed iteratively during each cycle before/after the Full GCs.

By using a tool such as VisualVM, it can, in some obvious cases, be possible to identify a leak directly by simply looking at the graph of the heap space memory. If it keeps growing despite Full GCs being executed, it is time to investigate.

A leak-finding process

A simple but effective process to find memory leaks can be defined in the following three steps:

1. Find suspect-leaked class instances
2. Find where the suspects have been instantiated
3. Find the reason(s) why the leak exists

A step-by-step example using VisualVM

Using the VisualVM tool that was introduced in the previous chapter, we have managed to find and resolve quite a few leaks by following the simple process mentioned previously. Here, the process has been broken down into a number of fine-granular tasks and operations while using the VisualVM Profiler. Perform the following steps:

1. In VisualVM, connect to the JVM that runs your WildFly with a possible memory-leaking application.
2. In the **Profiler** view, enable the **Settings** checkbox and go to the **Memory** settings tab.

3. Here, check the **Record allocations stack traces** checkbox as shown in the following screenshot:

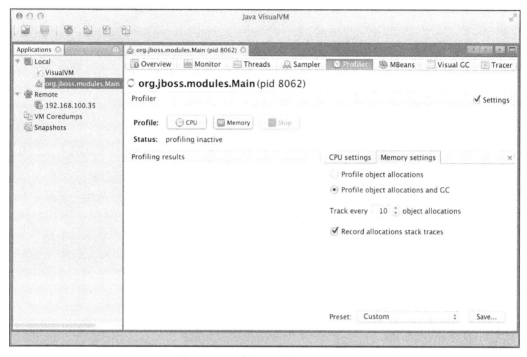

The settings of the Profiler in VisualVM

4. Uncheck the **Settings** checkbox again. The changes are saved.

5. Click on the **Memory** button to start memory profiling. This will take quite some time to start as the bytecode will be instrumented.

6. When the application is in a steady state, perform a GC and then take a snapshot by clicking on the **Snapshot** button. It will show up as a leaf node under the VM instance node in the **Applications** tab to the left.

7. Wait for a while to let the profiled application leak memory. This might happen as the system sits idle but could probably happen as it performs some tasks (preferably as automated and deterministic tests).

8. After the application has run (and leaked memory) for a while, take another snapshot like the one taken previously (including a GC before the snapshot).

9. Select both snapshot nodes under the VM instance in the **Applications** tree.

10. Right-click on the selection of both snapshots and choose **Compare** from the pop-up menu.

11. A new **Snapshots Comparison** view will show up as shown in the following screenshot; in it, the differences between allocated objects will be displayed:

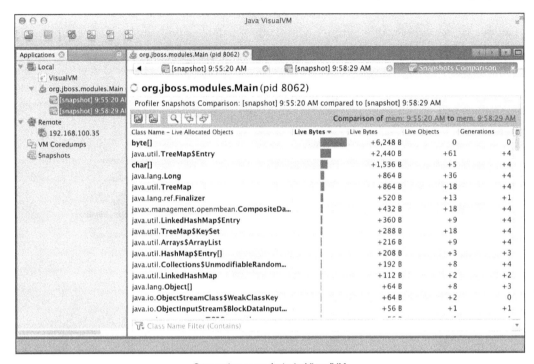

Comparing snapshots in VisualVM

12. The top elements are the ones that have increased in numbers the most, and these are the main suspects as the cause of a memory leak.

13. Go back to the two snapshot views again and select the identified suspect in both.

14. Right-click on the selection and choose **Show Allocation Stack Traces** from the pop-up menu. Alternatively, click on the **Allocation Stack Traces** button in the bottom of the view.

 Note that allocation stack traces can only be taken when profiling. The option does not work when performing the sampling.

15. Identify the methods where there is a large difference in the contribution to the total count.

16. These might be where leaked objects have been instantiated. Many believe that the work is done here, but that's not always quite true. It is important to keep in mind that the leaking object is very likely to *leak* from some place other than where it got created. Therefore, we will need to figure out the object that actually holds the reference to the leaking object. This is the point of leakage.

17. Take a heap dump from the VM instance in the tree by right-clicking on it and selecting **Heap Dump**.

18. The heap dump will show up as a leaf node under the VM instance in the tree to the left.

19. Open the view of the heap dump and look into the **Classes** sub-view. You can see the objects holding references to your suspected leaking object. Sometimes, you can find enough clues about what you're looking for here but, when there are a lot of instances involved and code you can't control (or have the source code for), it might not be enough. If needed, use the filter functionality in your view to be able to focus on relevant data and not be disturbed by an overwhelming amount of data.

20. Double-clicking on the suspect in the **Classes** sub-view will open up the **Instances** sub-view. Here, all instances of the suspect class are shown as follows:

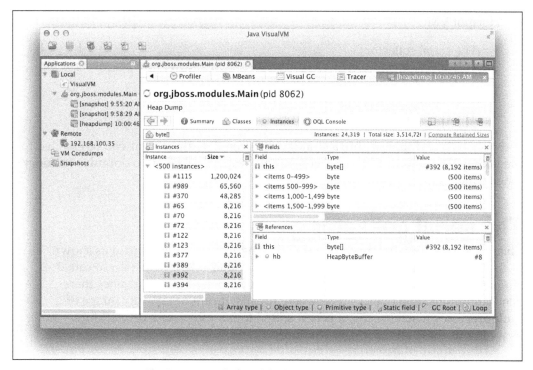

The Instances subview of the heap dump in VisualVM

21. Make sure the **Instances**, **Fields**, and **References** buttons to the top-left section of the sub-views menu bar are all selected.

22. Here, it is gets a bit iterative, and especially so if there are many instances (as there almost always are). Select an instance and look at its references.

23. Here, the references that hold the leaked object are found — and thus the reason for the leak.

24. Many references of the same sort are often a likely indication of where your leaked object could be. Verify for falsification of the leak by giving the related code a thorough inspection.

Following these steps is by no means a guarantee to finding a leak, but they have proved fruitful and should be considered a template that you can adapt for your specific environment and needs.

Types of GC strategies

There are several different collector types of the GC. These types are also known as strategies and they are, in turn, realized by different implementations depending on the JVM manufacturer. Today, many different implementations exist and these are mixtures of the basic strategies. First, let's have a look at most common strategies of the Hotspot VM:

- The serial collector
- The parallel collector
- The concurrent collector
- The **Garbage First (G1)** collector

It should be noted that, within a strategy, different GC algorithms can be enabled for the young generation and the old generation, respectively — all to optimize memory management and performance.

The serial collector

The serial collector performs garbage collection using a single thread as shown in the following diagram. This thread stops all other JVM threads — a so called stop-the-world behavior. While it is a relatively efficient collector, since there is no communication overhead between threads, it cannot take advantage of multiprocessor machines. So, it is best suited for single-processor machines — and as we know, these are no longer common.

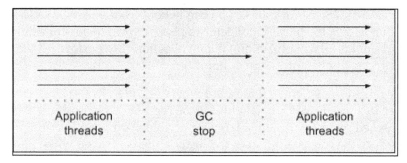

The serial collector at work

The serial collector is selected by default on the hardware and operating system configurations that are not elected as server class machines or can be explicitly enabled with the following VM parameter:

`-XX:+UseSerialGC`

The parallel collector

The parallel collector, also commonly known as the throughput collector, is the default collector on server grade machines for Java SE 7. It can also be explicitly enabled with the following VM parameter:

`-XX:+UseParallelGC`

The parallel collector performs minor collections in parallel, which can significantly improve the performance of applications that have lots of minor collections.

As you can see from the next diagram, the parallel collector still requires a so-called *stop-the-world* activity. However, since the collections are performed in parallel, making good utilization of many CPUs, it decreases the garbage collection overhead and hence increases the application throughput.

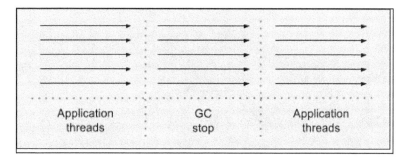

The parallel collector at work

Since the release of J2SE 5.0 update 6, you can benefit from a feature called *parallel compaction* that allows the parallel collector to also perform major collections in parallel. Without parallel compaction, major collections are performed using a single thread, which can significantly limit scalability.

This collector includes a compaction phase where GC identifies the regions that are free and uses its threads to copy data into those regions. This produces a heap that is densely packed on one end with a large empty block on the other end. In practice, this helps reduce the fragmentation of the heap, which is crucial when you are trying to allocate large objects.

Parallel compaction is enabled by default as of the Java SE 7 update 4 release. It can otherwise be explicitly enabled by the `-XX:+UseParallelOldGC` VM parameter and disabled by the `-XX:-UseParallelOldGC` parameter

Many think that the word `Old` in the name of GC refers to it as being old or deprecated. Nothing could be more wrong. `Old` simply refers to the old generation memory area and this GC is often preferred over the regular parallel collector.

The concurrent collector

The concurrent collector is a low-pause collector more commonly known as the **Concurrent Mark Sweep (CMS)** collector. It performs most of its work concurrently with the application still executing. This optimizes performance by keeping GC pauses short.

Basically, this collector consumes processor resources for the purpose of having shorter major collection pause times. This can happen because the concurrent collector uses a single garbage collector thread that runs simultaneously with the application threads. Thus, the purpose of the concurrent collector is to complete the collection of the tenured generation before it becomes full.

The following diagram gives us an idea of how the concurrent collector operates:

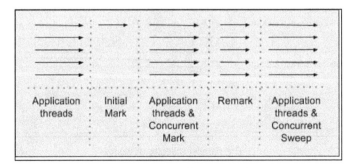

The concurrent collector at work

At first, the collector identifies the live objects, which are directly reachable in an **Initial Mark** phase. Then, in the **Concurrent Mark** phase, the collector marks all the live objects that are reachable while the application is still running. A subsequent **Remark** phase is needed to revisit objects that are modified in the concurrent marking phase. Finally, the **Concurrent Sweep** phase reclaims all objects that have been marked.

The reverse of the coin is that this technique, used to minimize pauses, can actually reduce the overall application performance. Hence, it is designed for applications whose response time is more important than overall throughput.

The concurrent collector is enabled with the `-XX:+UseConcMarkSweepGC` VM parameter.

The G1 collector

The G1 collector is included — and fully supported — in the Oracle JDK 7 update 4 distribution of Java SE 7. G1 and is targeted at server environments with multicore CPUs equipped with large amounts of memory. It is called a regionalized parallel-concurrent collector and is enabled by using the `-XX:+UseG1GC` VM parameter.

When using G1, the heap is divided into equal-sized regions between 1 and 32 MB. JVM sets this size at startup. The goal is to have no more than 2048 regions in a VM. The **Eden (E)**, **Survivor (S)**, and **Tenured (T)** generation are divided into logical non-continuous sets of these regions, as visualized in the following diagram:

S	E		S	E	
	E	T	T		S
T	S	T		T	
E	T	E	T	S	T
			E		

The heap with its sub memory areas; using the G1 collector

G1 is not a real-time collector, but it tries to meet user-defined pause time targets using a pause prediction model by adjusting the amount of regions used by the different memory areas. Heap fragmentations are reduced by the compaction realized by parallel copying of objects between sets of regions — called **Collection Sets (CSet)**.

Object references in the regions are tracked by independent **Remembered Sets** (**RSet**). These enable parallel and independent collection between regions since scanning can be minimized to a region instead of the entire heap.

It is worth noting that, for the G1 collector, the JVM footprint can be a bit larger in comparison to other collectors. This is due to the CSet and RSet data structures and is nothing to worry about.

The goal of G1 is to always stay within any pause time and to reclaim as much memory as possible, starting with areas that contain the most reclaimable space.

All this makes the G1 collector very stable in terms of minimal interrupts for the collection and compaction and effective in terms of memory usage.

The Oracle website states that:

> *Applications that require a large heap, have a big active data set, have bursty or non-uniform workloads or suffer from long garbage collection induced latencies should benefit from switching to G1.*

This can certainly be true for many applications but, in reality, the G1 collector is still seldom used in production. This might be due to the fact that it is relatively new and, as such, so few know about it. Many do not even bother tuning GC at all. For most others, though, the CMS is "good enough" for most applications.

Which collector to use

Which collector is really the best? The answer is that it depends a lot on the machine type and memory area allocations, for example. In the following table, we summarize some of the major benefits of each collector mentioned previously:

Collector	When to use
Serial	Single-processor machines and small heaps
Parallel	Multiprocessor machines and applications that require high throughput
Concurrent	Fast processor machines and applications with strict SLAs that require quick response times
G1	Multiprocessor server machines with applications using large heaps (>6GB) and in need of minimal GC latency

As you can see, the serial collector is not really an option for enterprise solutions of today.

Should your application be deployed on a multiprocessor machine and require to complete the highest possible number of transactions in a time window, the parallel collector is a good choice. This is the case for applications that perform batch processing activities, billing, and payroll applications.

Having fast processors and an application that needs to serve every single request by a strict amount of time is generally a case for the concurrent collector. The concurrent collector is particularly suited to applications that have a relatively large set of long-lived data since it can reclaim older objects without a long pause. This is generally the case in web applications where a consistent amount of memory is stored in the HttpSession.

The new G1 collector is a useful, but not widely used, replacement for the parallel or concurrent collectors when one ore more of the following situations are noticeable for an application:

- More than half the heap is occupied with live data
- There are long GC or compaction pauses (longer than half a second)
- The rate of object allocation or promotion varies a lot

Setting VM parameters in WildFly

Setting JVM parameters to be picked up by the JVM running WildFly can be done in several ways. The most common ways are as follows:

- Setting the parameters to an environment variable directly in the shell that starts the JVM.
- Setting the parameters in the server startup script, for example, in `$WILDFLY_HOME/bin/standalone.sh` or `domain.sh`.
- Setting the parameters in the server configuration file, that is, in `$WILDFLY_HOME/bin/standalone.conf` or `domain.conf`.

The first alternative is in practice not very useful for anything other that testing out new variables.

The second alternative can be used, but previously set parameters might be lost. Also, putting the configuration on the wrong line can easily mess up the rest of the logic in the script.

The last alternative is the recommended one for pretty much all situations as the configuration is persisted and versioned in a way that separates configuration from logic.

It is customary to use the environment variable, JAVA_OPTS, to set JVM parameters. All of the mentioned alternatives make use of this variable as it gets picked up and used by the startup scripts of WildFly.

To not lose any previously set VM parameter, a good practice is to set the environment variable to refer to itself on adding new parameters. This is done by using the following syntax:

```
JAVA_OPTS="$JAVA_OPTS <new-vm-params>"
```

The following command will, as an example, start WildFly with a maximum heap of 2 GB, where any old VM parameters previously set to JAVA_OPTS are ignored (they are removed as the variable is set by the new value):

```
JAVA_OPTS=-Xmx2g
```

Having the relevant information available

If, or rather when, you start to encounter problems in your production environment, it is vital that you have as much relevant information available in order to be able to resolve the problem.

Should the information not be available, chances are often slim that you can figure out what went wrong and how it can be fixed. A bad but common scenario is when a serious problem occurs and no relevant information is available in logs or elsewhere. In these cases, you will most likely need to make adjustments in code and configuration that will allow you to gather interesting information and let the problem occur (at least) one more time. Recreating serious problems in a production environment is naturally something that should be avoided at all costs.

Logging lots of various types of information for different purposes (such as security, business, and even performance) is often required in an application and its application server. As logging can be a source for performance degradation, an opposing requirement is normally to not log (too) much in the production environment. Finding the right level for a specific application or system is a matter of practically weighing the various requirements from the different parts of an organization against each other – business, quality, and operations, to mention a few.

VM parameters in production

The following VM parameters should always be set in your production environment to log relevant information. Even if they come with a small price in terms of performance costs (mostly disk I/O), if they are not set, you have quite a challenge ahead of you to resolve any VM-related problems (memory, GC, and so on) in your applications.

verbose:gc

To retrieve basic memory details after each collection, add the following parameter:

```
-verbose:gc
```

The logged output looks like the following for a minor and major GC, respectively:

```
[GC 85310K->39093K(173056K), 0.0123160 secs]
[Full GC 39093K->25698K(173056K), 0.1902890 secs]
```

First, on each line, `GC` means that a minor GC is executed, whereas `Full GC` naturally means that a full or major GC has executed.

The numbers before and after the arrow (`->`) tell us how much memory in the heap was allocated by objects before and after the GC, respectively.

Then comes a number in parentheses. This number is the total committed amount of heap space.

Finally, at the end of each row, we have the time the GC took to execute.

PrintGCDetails

For more information about the individual memory areas within the heap, the `-XX:+PrintGCDetails` parameter can replace the `verbose:gc` parameter. It actually overrides the previous command and output. This parameter is also often considered to be the minimal level of information that can be useful for tools' support.

The logged output looks like the following for a minor and major GC, respectively:

```
[GC [PSYoungGen: 31715K->6683K(93696K)] 56498K->31474K(161792K),
   0.0071920 secs] [Times: user=0.03 sys=0.01, real=0.01 secs]
[Full GC [PSYoungGen: 6683K->0K(93696K)] [ParOldGen: 24790K-
   >18597K(68096K)] 31474K->18597K(161792K) [PSPermGen: 43415K-
   >42377K(77824K)], 0.1933750 secs] [Times: user=0.78 sys=0.01,
   real=0.19 secs]
```

This output is very similar to the one by `verbose:gc`. First, `GC` or `Full GC` tells if there was a minor or major collection, respectively.

Then, within brackets, for the young generation, we first see what collector is used. Then, still within the same brackets, before and after the `->`, we see how much memory area was allocated before and after the collection, respectively. Finally, within the same brackets, the number within parentheses tells us how much memory in total is committed by the young generation.

While a log of a minor GC shows us the corresponding data for the entire heap, the major GC will show us the data for the old generation (including which collector is being utilized for that memory area), the heap, and then, for PermGen, in serial sequence.

Finally, we have four time values: the time the collection took and then three time values — user, sys and real — that are similar to the output of the time command.

> The ratio of the *user/real* gives us an approximation of the increase in speed you're getting from different collectors.
>
> The system time can be an indicator of the system activity that is slowing down the collection — should, for example, paging occur, sys will be high.

PrintTenuringDistribution

Retrieving information about premature promotion is important as it includes information about the correct size of memory pools. To enable the output of this information, the following flag should be added to the JVM:

`-XX:+PrintTenuringDistribution`

The output looks like the following:

```
[GC Desired survivor size 19922944 bytes, new threshold 7 (max 15)
87601K->39197K(174080K), 0.0133280 secs]
```

Indicating that this is a minor collection, is given by the initial `GC`.

We then see that the size of the "to" survivor space is (here, almost 20 MB) what the current *tenuring threshold* is (in this case 7) and what the maximum tenuring threshold is set to (max 15).

Before and after -> is the size of allocated objects that we are given in the heap before and after the collection, respectively. Then, within parentheses, we get the total committed size of the heap.

Finally, the time that the collection took is given.

loggc

When you suspect or know that a problem that needs analyzing exists, you do not want to parse out the GC log data from the regular logs (console/stdout). Here, the GC log data would be mixed with other data from WildFly or your application since by default all log data ends up in $WILDFLY_HOME/standalone/log/server.log by default. The degree depends somewhat on how you have configured your logging framework(s), but there will be mixed types of information that can be hard to read or parse. To ease this pain, make sure that you always point out a specific file to where the GC-log data should end up by using the following parameter:

```
-Xloggc:<file>
```

By directing the GC log data in this way, a timestamp is also added to each line in the log. This timestamp tells us at what relative point in time the collection occurred, which is counted in seconds (and with three decimals' accuracy) from when JVM started. The same effect can also be realized by using the PrintGCTimeStamps parameter.

Saving the GC log data to a disk can't be recommended highly enough. It is always worth it! A disk is relatively cheap in comparison to the cost of, more or less blindly, chasing problems when no information is available. Also the indirect disturbance to business when chasing around for clues can be significant. Remember that if you won't be able to catch the information about an error right away, you will need for it to occur at least twice before you can start the forensics!

Retrieving GC data can also be done by accessing the javax.management.MXBeans runtime. Using MXBeans can, however, have a negative impact on the running application and they may cause GC problems on their own. Logs, on the other hand, are more useful as they can contain more information and have less relative impact on performance.

Saved log data files can be postprocessed and used by tools for calculations and visualizations that will aid any search for problems.

Using tools

To effectively analyze JVM-related log data, using tools is not only encouraged, it is required in practice. Without proper tool support, analysis is really limited to guessing as it is virtually impossible to get an overview of the vast amount of data that comes from JVM. Tooling can be anything from simple scripts that compare the memory area sized between GCs to advanced graphical visualization tools that can alert you of irregularities and allow you to hone in-focus areas. We won't go into depths about how to use any specific tool here, but you should be aware of the fact that there are several freely available alternatives to licensed products. Some very useful tools are as follows:

- Tools that come with Oracle JDK 7: jstat (JVM Statistics Monitoring), jmap (Memory Map), and jhat (Java Heap Analysis Tool)
- GCViewer
- GarbageCat
- IBM GCMV for Eclipse (search for "GCMV" on the Eclipse Marketplace)
- HPjmeter

VM and GC stability

VMs (in our case Hotspot) and collectors have improved immensely in many performance-related aspects over the years, both in major as well as minor versions. The changes can involve internal behavior that might affect your application in both positive and negative ways. Either way, the changes and their effects are seldom possible to realize by just reading the release notes.

The changes can also quite often be externally visible. The output of various VM parameters, such as the ones for GC logging, has changed many times.

All of these changes are rarely documented in a satisfactory way and changes that can affect your entire application might turn up even in minor releases. To handle this in an orderly fashion involves, as per usual, rigorous and strategic tests.

No VM upgrade, changes in GC strategy, or adaption of VM parameters should be allowed in the production environment without proper tests. As always, change one thing, and one thing only, between each test!

Summary

The JVM is the engine for all Java-based applications. It has evolved tremendously over the years, enabling Java applications to execute faster and to be more memory-efficient. The JVM is good at setting its own default values using ergonomics based on the environment but often needs tuning as, for example, memory runs short or the JVM runs slow.

Memory areas for holding objects are the heap with its subareas, young generation—with Eden and the Survivor spaces S0 and S1—and old (tenured) generation. The size of these areas can be tuned individually and sometimes relative to each other, all to ensure that the best possible configuration for a specific application can be met.

The PermGen memory area is part of the heap but separately holds metadata and isn't involved in object allocation or collection. As with the rest of the memory areas, PermGen can be sized individually.

GC moves aging objects within the heap and removes any unused ones, thus freeing memory. Depending on specific application needs, different GC strategies can be applied in JVM.

As JVM runs out of memory, an `OutOfMemoryError` error will occur. Identifying the cause of this error and resolving it can be a relatively standard but comprehensive process that always requires tool support.

By proactively logging the relevant information, you will be well prepared to handle problems as they occur, instead of being reactive.

Now, we're finally ready to move on to performance-tune WildFly!

4
Tuning WildFly

In this chapter, we will talk about the various subsystems of WildFly as well as their individual tuning possibilities. To get a better understanding of how these subsystems work together, an introduction to the overall history and architecture of WildFly is also given.

An application server is a rather complex piece of software that consists of several enterprise components that must cooperate to fulfill the Java EE specifications. Tuning such a beast can be a daunting task. It's not enough to just understand the Java EE specification and its subspecifications. The real challenge often lies in the understanding of how an application server of choice has been implemented and making practical use of these specifications.

WildFly is, as of 2013, the new name of the historically famous and well renowned **JBoss Application Server (JBoss AS)**. As arguably the most prolific open source application server in the market, JBoss AS made itself famous for being very modular. It embraced other open source products that enabled it to efficiently forge a complete Java EE server. As such, it has made a strong case in personifying the force and strength of open technologies. The successful use of separate modules and third-party open source artifacts continues in WildFly as it achieves full Java EE specification compliance. With lots of separate implementations, it's often not enough to just browse through the core documentation of the application server itself. To really understand the possibilities when fine-tuning an individual component, you must also study how the specific components operate and how they interact with each other.

WildFly's history

The history of WildFly, especially under the previous name JBoss AS, is filled with several market-leading technology innovations and architectural decisions.

It started out as an EJB container called **Enterprise Java Bean Open Source Software** (**EJBOSS**) in 1999. The name was later changed to JBoss as Sun Microsystem, the owner of the EJB trademark, asked the project to stop using "EJB" as part of the application's server name.

The key features that were introduced in earlier versions included support for *Hot Deploy* and the use of *Dynamic Proxies*, removing the need to generate client stubs for remote EJBs. The reputation of being one of the most modular application servers steadily grew as Version 2 and Version 3 were released. These were based on JMX and just about every component in the product was wrapped and exposed as an *MBean*. The JMX infrastructure was a good choice to build a platform of loosely-coupled components. It was extended with add-ons for lifecycle behavior and artifact dependencies to produce a base that was in use up to and including Version 4.

Even though JBoss AS 3 did comply with the J2EE 1.3 specification, it never became a certified J2EE application server. When Version 4 came and received its J2EE 1.4 certification, the market embraced it and it became a real contender also among the biggest commercial alternatives.

The project decided to abandon the JMX kernel for Version 5 and implemented a new *microcontainer* providing POJO injection between services for fine-grained dependencies. However, these new features came at a price. Version 5 and its minor releases demanded a greater amount of resources (basically memory and CPU) than the previous versions. Therefore, it is generally considered a heavyweight release when compared to the 4.x releases.

The microcontainer was used throughout JBoss AS 5 and 6, but for Version 7 a complete new container was introduced, focusing on parallel execution. This new solution is what makes both JBoss AS 7 and WildFly 8 fast and lightweight. Functionality for and around platform management has also been rewritten. The various "infamous" XML files of the previous versions have been combined into a single one. A new *Domain* execution mode was also introduced, making it simpler to manage a large number of server instances.

The following table explains which application server versions correspond to which versions of the J2EE / Java EE specifications:

JBoss/WildFly release	J2EE / Java EE specification (Not all certified)
JBoss AS 3	J2EE 1.3
JBoss AS 4	J2EE 1.4
JBoss AS 5	Java EE 5
JBoss AS 6	Java EE 6
JBoss AS 7	Java EE 6
WildFly 8	Java EE 7

In the following table, you can see the typical startup times for some of the key releases, as measured on a moderate laptop. As you can see, the latest incarnation, WildFly, is blazingly fast. Thanks to internal cacheing, WildFly becomes even faster at subsequent startups. This quick restart cycle is very useful during development and iterative testing.

JBoss/WildFly release	Configuration mode	JVM	Startup time (in seconds)
JBoss AS 4.0.5.GA	Default	1.4	6.5
JBoss AS 5.1.0.GA	Default	5	20
JBoss AS 6.1.0.Final	Default	6	14
JBoss AS 7.2.0.Final	`standalone-full.xml`	6	3
WildFly 8.0.0.Final	`standalone-full.xml`	7	3

WildFly's architecture

JBoss has a long history of being one of the most modular application servers in the market. This remains true for WildFly 8. The different Java EE components in WildFly, for example **Enterprise JavaBeans (EJB)**, **Java Message Service (JMS)**, **Java Persistence Architecture (JPA)**, and the WebContainer, are all packaged into something called **subsystems** or **extensions**.

All the active extensions in a configuration can easily be located in the activated **server configuration file** (that is, in `standalone*.xml` or `domain.xml`) under the `extensions` tag.

If the application being deployed does not need all the functionality provided by WildFly, subsystems can easily be removed from the configuration file, thus disabling modules with functionality.

This saves memory, threads, and sometimes startup time; it also improves overall performance. In addition to this, there are also quite a few extensions that utilize lazy loading. This means that they will not be loaded until requested and therefore the direct impact of removing these is not as obvious as in earlier versions of the application server. In the older versions, all components were loaded and their resources were allocated directly at startup.

The actual removal is done by removing the appropriate extension from the configuration file. For example, to remove the support for CORBA (implemented in WildFly using a project called JacORB), the following line of configuration should be removed:

```
<extension module="org.jboss.as.jacorb"/>
```

This subsystem also has the following configuration section that needs to be removed:

```
<subsystem xmlns="urn:jboss:domain:jacorb:1.3">
  <orb socket-binding="jacorb" ssl-socket-binding="jacorb-ssl">
    <initializers security="identity" transactions="spec"/>
  </orb>
</subsystem>
```

 Note that there might be dependencies between subsystems that can hinder their removal. For example, removing the transaction subsystem is quite futile, as most parts of WildFly need transaction support.

As another example, you can compare the different standalone server configuration files (`standalone*.xml`) under `$WILDFLY_HOME/standalone/configuration`. Here, you can see how the different configurations contain their own list of active subsystems.

The following are some examples of subsystems that may be of interest to remove (unless utilized, of course):

* `org.jboss.as.jacorb`: This is the support for CORBA that not many applications use nowadays
* `org.jboss.as.sar`: These are the legacy JBoss-AS-specific SAR archive packages of JMX beans
* `org.jboss.as.webservices`: This is the support for web services
* `org.jboss.as.messaging`: This is the support for JMS

You may also want to consider the removal of unused default resources that have been configured, such as datasources and drivers—for example, the default datasource `ExampleDS` and its driver for the H2 database, all of which are located in the *datasources* subsystem.

Various subsystem configurations

In a high-performance environment, every costly resource instantiation needs to be minimized. This can be done effectively using pools. The different subsystems in WildFly often use various pools of resources to minimize the cost of creating new ones. These resources are often threads or various connection objects. Another benefit is that the pools work as a gatekeeper, hindering the underlying system from being overloaded. This is performed by preventing client calls from reaching their target if a limit has been reached.

In the upcoming sections of this chapter, we will provide an overview of the different subsystems and their pools.

The thread pool executor subsystem

The thread pool executor subsystem was introduced in JBoss AS 7. Other subsystems can reference thread pools configured in this one. This makes it possible to normalize and manage the thread pools via native WildFly management mechanisms, and it allows you to share thread pools across subsystems.

The following code is an example taken from the WildFly Administration Guide (`https://docs.jboss.org/author/display/WFLY8/Admin+Guide`) that describes how the *Infinispan* subsystem may use the subsystem, setting up four different pools:

```
<subsystem xmlns="urn:jboss:domain:threads:1.0">
  <thread-factory name="infinispan-factory" priority="1"/>
  <bounded-queue-thread-pool name="infinispan-transport">
    <core-threads count="1"/>
    <queue-length count="100000"/>
    <max-threads count="25"/>
    <thread-factory name="infinispan-factory"/>
  </bounded-queue-thread-pool>
  <bounded-queue-thread-pool name="infinispan-listener">
    <core-threads count="1"/>
    <queue-length count="100000"/>
    <max-threads count="1"/>
    <thread-factory name="infinispan-factory"/>
  </bounded-queue-thread-pool>
```

```
<scheduled-thread-pool name="infinispan-eviction">
  <max-threads count="1"/>
  <thread-factory name="infinispan-factory"/>
</scheduled-thread-pool>
<scheduled-thread-pool name="infinispan-repl-queue">
  <max-threads count="1"/>
  <thread-factory name="infinispan-factory"/>
</scheduled-thread-pool>
</subsystem>
...
<cache-container name="web" default-cache="repl"
  listener-executor="infinispan-listener"
  eviction-executor="infinispan-eviction"
  replication-queue-executor="infinispan-repl-queue">
  <transport executor="infinispan-transport"/>
  <replicated-cache name="repl" mode="ASYNC" batching="true">
    <locking isolation="REPEATABLE_READ"/>
    <file-store/>
  </replicated-cache>
</cache-container>
```

The following thread pools are available:

- unbounded-queue-thread-pool
- bounded-queue-thread-pool
- blocking-bounded-queue-thread-pool
- queueless-thread-pool
- blocking-queueless-thread-pool
- scheduled-thread-pool

The details of these thread pools are described in the following sections:

unbounded-queue-thread-pool

The *unbounded-queue-thread-pool* thread pool executor has the maximum size and an unlimited queue. If the number of running threads is less than the maximum size when a task is submitted, a new thread will be created. Otherwise, the task is placed in a queue. This queue is allowed to grow infinitely.

The configuration properties are shown in the following table:

max-threads	Max allowed threads running simultaneously
keepalive-time	This specifies the amount of time that pool threads should be kept running when idle. (If not specified, threads will run until the executor is shut down.)
thread-factory	This specifies the thread factory to use to create worker threads.

bounded-queue-thread-pool

The *bounded-queue-thread-pool* thread pool executor has a core, maximum size, and a specified queue length. If the number of running threads is less than the core size when a task is submitted, a new thread will be created; otherwise, it will be put in the queue. If the queue's maximum size has been reached and the maximum number of threads hasn't been reached, a new thread is also created. If `max-threads` is hit, the call will be sent to the handoff-executor. If no handoff-executor is configured, the call will be discarded.

The configuration properties are shown in the following table:

core-threads	Optional and should be less that max-threads
`queue-length`	This specifies the maximum size of the queue.
`max-threads`	This specifies the maximum number of threads that are allowed to run simultaneously.
`keepalive-time`	This specifies the amount of time that pool threads should be kept running when idle. (If not specified, threads will run until the executor is shut down.)
`handoff-executor`	This specifies an executor to which tasks will be delegated, in the event that a task cannot be accepted.
`allow-core-timeout`	This specifies whether core threads may time-out; if false, only threads above the core size will time-out.
`thread-factory`	This specifies the thread factory to use to create worker threads.

blocking-bounded-queue-thread-pool

The *blocking-bounded-queue-thread-pool* thread pool executor has a core, a maximum size and a specified queue length. If the number of running threads is less than the core size when a task is submitted, a new thread will be created. Otherwise, it will be put in the queue. If the queue's maximum size has been reached, a new thread is created; if not, `max-threads` is exceeded. If so, the call is blocked.

The configuration properties are shown in the following table:

core-threads	Optional and should be less that max-threads
queue-length	This specifies the maximum size of the queue.
max-threads	This specifies the maximum number of simultaneous threads allowed to run.
keepalive-time	This specifies the amount of time that pool threads should be kept running when idle. (If not specified, threads will run until the executor is shut down.)
allow-core-timeout	This specifies whether core threads may time-out; if false, only threads above the core size will time-out.
thread-factory	This specifies the thread factory to use to create worker threads

queueless-thread-pool

The *queueless-thread-pool* thread pool is a thread pool executor without any queue. If the number of running threads is less than max-threads when a task is submitted, a new thread will be created; otherwise, the handoff-executor will be called. If no handoff-executor is configured the call will be discarded.

The configuration properties are shown in the following table:

max-threads	Max allowed threads running simultaneously
keepalive-time	The amount of time that pool threads should be kept running when idle. (If not specified, threads will run until the executor is shut down.)
handoff-executor	Specifies an executor to delegate tasks to in the event that a task cannot be accepted
thread-factory	The thread factory to use to create worker threads

blocking-queueless-thread-pool

The *blocking-queueless-thread-pool* thread pool executor has no queue. If the number of running threads is less than max-threads when a task is submitted, a new thread will be created. Otherwise, the caller will be blocked.

The configuration properties are shown in the following table:

max-threads	Max allowed threads running simultaneously
keepalive-time	This specifies the amount of time that pool threads should be kept running when idle. (If not specified, threads will run until the executor is shut down.)
thread-factory	This specifies the thread factory to use to create worker threads

scheduled-thread-pool

The *scheduled-thread-pool* thread pool is used by tasks that are scheduled to trigger at a certain time.

The configuration properties are shown in the following table:

max-threads	Max allowed threads running simultaneously
keepalive-time	This specifies the amount of time that pool threads should be kept running when idle. (If not specified, threads will run until the executor is shut down.)
thread-factory	This specifies the thread factory to use to create worker threads

Monitoring

All of the pools just mentioned can be administered and monitored using both CLI and JMX (actually, the Admin Console can be used to administer, but not see, any live data). The following example and screenshots show the access to an unbounded-queue-thread-pool called `test`.

Using CLI, run the following command:

```
/subsystem=threads/unbounded-queue-thread-pool=test:read-
resource(include-runtime=true)
```

The response to the preceding command is as follows:

```
{
    "outcome" => "success",
    "result" => {
        "active-count" => 0,
        "completed-task-count" => 0L,
        "current-thread-count" => 0,
        "keepalive-time" => undefined,
```

```
            "largest-thread-count" => 0,
            "max-threads" => 100,
            "name" => "test",
            "queue-size" => 0,
            "rejected-count" => 0,
            "task-count" => 0L,
            "thread-factory" => undefined
        }
    }
}
```

Using JMX (query and result in the JConsole UI), run the following code:

```
jboss.as:subsystem=threads,unbounded-queue-thread-pool=test
```

An example thread pool by JMX is shown in the following screenshot:

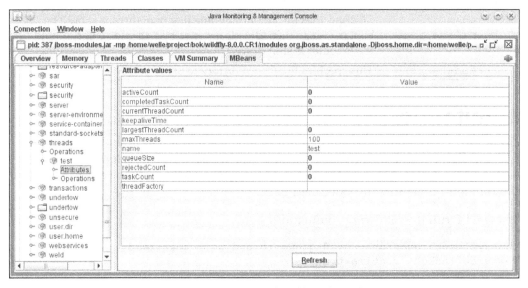

An example thread pool by JMX

The following screenshot shows the corresponding information in the
Admin Console

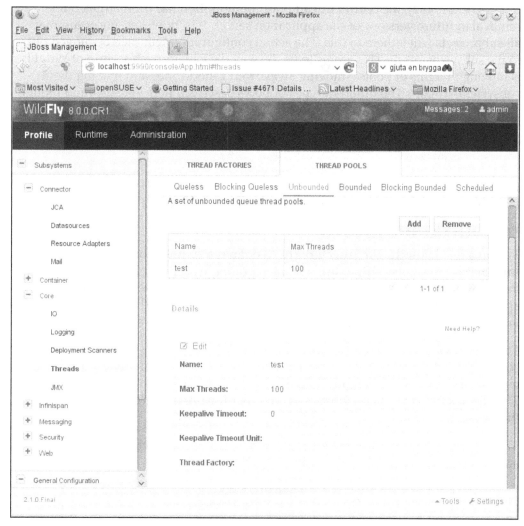

Example thread pool—Admin Console

The future of the thread subsystem

According to the official JIRA case WFLY-462 (`https://issues.jboss.org/browse/WFLY-462`), the central thread pool configuration has been targeted for removal in future versions of the application server. It is, however, uncertain that all subprojects will adhere to this. The actual configuration will then be moved out to the subsystem itself. This seems to be the way the general architecture of WildFly is moving in terms of pools—moving away from generic ones and making them subsystem-specific. The different types of pools described here are still valid though.

Note that, contrary to previous releases, Stateless EJB is no longer pooled by default. More information of this is available in the JIRA case WFLY-1383. It can be found at `https://issues.jboss.org/browse/WFLY-1383`.

Java EE Connector Architecture and resource adapters

The **Java EE Connector Architecture (JCA)** defines a contract for an **Enterprise Information Systems (EIS)** to use when integrating with the application server. EIS includes databases, messaging systems, and other servers/systems external to an application server. The purpose is to provide a standardized API for developers and integration of various application server services such as transaction handling.

The EIS provides a so called **Resource Adaptor (RA)** that is deployed in WildFly and configured in the *resource-adaptor* subsystem. The RA is normally realized as one or more Java classes with configuration files stored in a **Resource Archive (RAR)** file. This file has the same characteristics as a regular **Java Archive (JAR)** file, but with the `rar` suffix.

The following code is a dummy example of how a JCA connection pool setup may appear in a WildFly configuration file:

```
<subsystem xmlns="urn:jboss:domain:resource-adapters:2.0">
  <resource-adapters>
    <resource-adapter>
      <archive>eisExample.rar</archive>
      <!-- Resource adapter level config-property -->
      <config-property name="Server">
        localhost
      </config-property>
      <config-property name="Port">
        6666
      </config-property>
      <transaction-support>
```

```
      LocalTransaction
    </transaction-support>
    <connection-definitions>
      <connection-definition
        class-name="ManagedConnectionFactory"
        jndi-name="java:/eisExample/ConnectionFactory"
        pool-name="EISExampleConnectionPool">
        <pool>
          <min-pool-size>10</min-pool-size>
          <max-pool-size>100</max-pool-size>
          <prefill>true</prefill>
        </pool>
      </connection-definition>
    </connection-definitions>
  </resource-adapter>
 </resource-adapters>
</subsystem>
```

By default in WildFly, these pools will not be populated until used for the first
time. By setting `prefill` to `true`, the pool will be be populated during deployment.
Retrieving and using a connection as a developer is easy. Just perform a JNDI lookup
for the factory at `java:/eisExample/ConnectionFactory` and then get a connection
from that factory. Other usages that will be running for a long time will not benefit
from pooling and will create their connection directly from the RA. An example of
this is a **Message Driven Bean** (**MDB**) that listens on a RA for messages.

The settings for this connection pool can be fetched in runtime by running the
following command in the CLI:

```
/subsystem=resource-adapters/resource-adapter=eisExample.rar/connection-
definitions=EISExampleConnectionPool:read-resource(include-runtime=true)
```

The response to the preceding command is as follows:

```
{
    "outcome" => "success",
    "result" => {
        "allocation-retry" => undefined,
        "allocation-retry-wait-millis" => undefined,
        "background-validation" => false,
        "background-validation-millis" => undefined,
        "blocking-timeout-wait-millis" => undefined,
        "capacity-decrementer-class" => undefined,
        "capacity-decrementer-properties" => undefined,
```

```
            "capacity-incrementer-class" => undefined,
            "capacity-incrementer-properties" => undefined,
            "class-name" => "ManagedConnectionFactory",
            "enabled" => true,
            "enlistment" => true,
            "flush-strategy" => "FailingConnectionOnly",
            "idle-timeout-minutes" => undefined,
            "initial-pool-size" => undefined,
            "interleaving" => false,
            "jndi-name" => "java:/eisExample/ConnectionFactory",
            "max-pool-size" => 100,
            "min-pool-size" => 10,
            "no-recovery" => false,
            "no-tx-separate-pool" => false,
            "pad-xid" => false,
            "pool-prefill" => false,
            "pool-use-strict-min" => false,
            "recovery-password" => undefined,
            "recovery-plugin-class-name" => undefined,
            "recovery-plugin-properties" => undefined,
            "recovery-security-domain" => undefined,
            "recovery-username" => undefined,
            "same-rm-override" => undefined,
            "security-application" => false,
            "security-domain" => undefined,
            "security-domain-and-application" => undefined,
            "sharable" => true,
            "use-ccm" => true,
            "use-fast-fail" => false,
            "use-java-context" => true,
            "use-try-lock" => undefined,
            "wrap-xa-resource" => true,
            "xa-resource-timeout" => undefined,
            "config-properties" => undefined
        }
    }
```

Using JMX (URI and result in the JConsole UI):

```
jboss.as:subsystem=resource-adapters,
  resource-adapter=eisExample.rar,
  connection-definitions=EISExampleConnectionPool
```

An example connection pool for a RA is shown in the following screenshot:

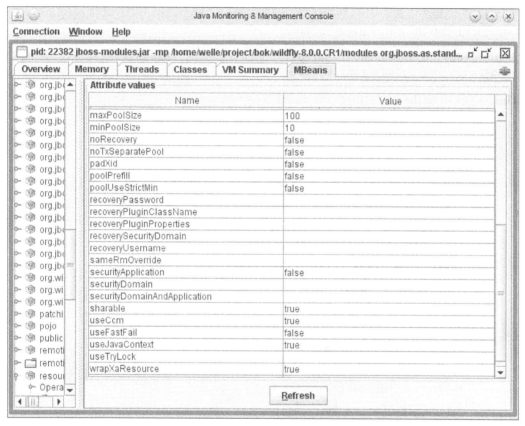

An example connection pool for an RA

Besides the connection pool, the JCA subsystem in WildFly uses two internal thread pools:

- short-running-threads
- long-running-threads

These thread pools are of the type blocking-bounded-queue-thread-pool and the behavior of this type is described earlier in the *Thread pool executor subsystem* section.

The following command is an example of a CLI command to change `queue-length` for the short-running-threads pool:

```
/subsystem=jca/workmanager=default/short-running-threads=default:
write-attribute(name=queue-length, value=100)
```

These pools can all be administered and monitored using both CLI and JMX. The following example and screenshot show the access to the short-running-threads pool:

Using CLI, run the following command:

```
/subsystem=jca/workmanager=default/short-running-threads=default:
read-resource(include-runtime=true)
```

The response to the preceding command is as follows:

```
{
    "outcome" => "success",
    "result" => {
        "allow-core-timeout" => false,
        "core-threads" => 50,
        "current-thread-count" => 0,
        "handoff-executor" => undefined,
        "keepalive-time" => {
            "time" => 10L,
            "unit" => "SECONDS"
        }
        "largest-thread-count" => 0,
        "max-threads" => 50,
        "name" => "default",
        "queue-length" => 50,
        "queue-size" => 0,
        "rejected-count" => 0,
        "thread-factory" => undefined
    }
}
```

Using JMX (URI and result in the JConsole UI):

```
jboss.as:subsystem=jca,workmanager=default,short-running-
threads=default
```

The JCA thread pool can be seen in the following screenshot:

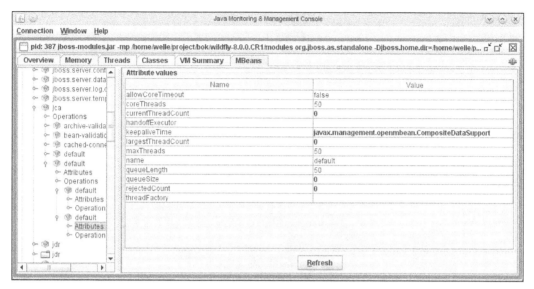

The JCA thread pool

If your application depends heavily on JCA, these pools should be monitored, and perhaps tuned as needed, to provide improved performance.

The Batch API subsystem

The Batch API is new in JEE 7 and is implemented in WildFly by the Batch subsystem. Internally it uses an unbounded-queue-thread-pool (see the description earlier in this chapter). If the application uses the Batch API extensively, the pool settings may need adjustment.

The configuration can be fetched using the CLI or by JMX.

Using CLI, run the following command:

```
/subsystem=batch/thread-pool=batch:read-resource(include-runtime=true)
```

The response to the preceding command is as follows:

```
{
    "outcome" => "success",
    "result" => {
        "keepalive-time" => {
            "time" => 100L,
```

```
            "unit" => "MILLISECONDS"
        },
        "max-threads" => 10,
        "name" => "batch",
        "thread-factory" => undefined
    }
}
```

Using JMX (URI and result in the JConsole UI):

```
jboss.as:subsystem=batch,thread-pool=batch
```

The Batch API thread pool is shown in the following screenshot:

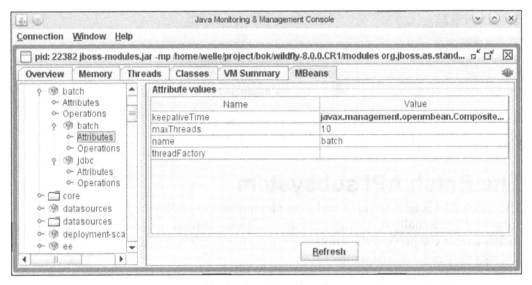

The Batch API thread pool

The Remoting subsystem

The **Remoting** subsystem exposes a connector to allow inbound communications with JNDI, JMX, and the EJB subsystem through multiplexing over the HTTP port (default 8080).

What happens is that the web container (the subsystem *Undertow* in WildFly) uses something called *HTTP Upgrade* to redirect, for example, EJB3 calls to the Remoting subsystem, if applicable. This new feature in WildFly makes life easier for administrators as all the scattered ports from earlier versions are now narrowed down to two: one for the application (8080) and one for management (9990).

All this is based on Java NIO API and utilizes a framework called XNIO (`http://www.jboss.org/xnio`).

The XNIO-based implementation uses a bounded-queue-thread-pool (see the description earlier in this chapter) with the following attributes:

Attribute	Description
task-core-threads	This specifies the number of core threads for the Remoting worker task thread pool
task-max-threads	This specifies the maximum number of threads for the Remoting worker task thread pool
task-keepalive	This specifies the number of milliseconds to keep noncore Remoting worker task threads alive
task-limit	This specifies the maximum number of Remoting worker tasks to allow before rejecting

The settings can be managed using CLI by running the following command:

```
/subsystem=remoting:read-resource(include-runtime=true)
```

The response to the preceding command is as follows:

```
{
    "outcome" => "success",
    "result" => {
        "worker-read-threads" => 1,
        "worker-task-core-threads" => 4,
        "worker-task-keepalive" => 60,
        "worker-task-limit" => 16384,
        "worker-task-max-threads" => 8,
        "worker-write-threads" => 1,
        "connector" => undefined,
        "http-connector" => {"http-remoting-connector" => undefined},
        "local-outbound-connection" => undefined,
        "outbound-connection" => undefined,
        "remote-outbound-connection" => undefined
    }
}
```

The Transactions subsystem

The **Transaction** subsystem has a fail-safe transaction log. It will, by default, store data on disk at `${jboss.server.data.dir}/tx-object-store`. For a standalone server instance, this will point to the `$WILDFLY_HOME/standalone/data/tx-object-store/` directory. The disk you choose to store your transaction log must give high performance and must be reliable. A good choice would be a local RAID, configured to write through cache. Even if remote disk storage is possible, the network overhead can be a performance bottleneck.

One way to point out another path for this object storage is to use the following CLI commands specifying an absolute path:

```
/subsystem=transactions:write-attribute(name=object-store-path,value="/
mount/diskForTx")
reload
```

XA – Two Phase Commit (2PC)

The use of XA is somewhat costly and it shouldn't be used if it isn't necessary with distributed transaction between two or more resources (often databases, but also such things as JMS). If needed, we strongly recommend using XA instead of trying to build something yourself, such as compensating transactions to guarantee consistency between the resources. Such solutions can very quickly become quite advanced and the result will probably not outperform the XA protocol anyway.

Even though WildFly supports **Last Resource Commit Optimization** (**LRCO**), it shouldn't be used for performance optimization. It is only intended as a workaround to provide limited support to use one non-XA resource within an XA transaction.

Logging

Logging information is an indispensable activity both in development and in production. However, you should choose what information is needed for debugging (development phase) and what information is needed for routine maintenance (production phase) carefully. Decide carefully about where to log information and about the formatting of the log messages so that the information can be processed and analyzed in the future by other applications.

Avoid logging unnecessary information. This will make the logging output convoluted and it badly affects the performance of your application.

Make sure that the appropriate log level is used, so you only log necessary information by default. As we will see later on in this chapter, it is possible to adjust the log levels to get clues from a running application server at runtime.

Optimized logging code

If the log level threshold disables a log message, performance is often improved in terms of less data to write to the log. However, as we shall see, this is not always true.

Logging frameworks are normally very quick to check the threshold and can directly reject any log call that has a low log-level. Thus, the only cost, performance-wise, becomes a cheap, in-VM method call.

However, such a call may involve a "hidden" cost in terms of parameter object construction. The following example actually includes concatenate strings, converting both integer and `entry[i]` into a new string object before even calling the logging framework. The code is as follows:

```
LOG.debug("Entry #" + i + " is " + entry[i]);
```

A common pattern that can be used to eliminate this costly parameter object creation is as follows:

```
if (DEBUG) {
    LOG.debug("Entry #" + i + " is " + entry[i]);
}
```

If your logging framework supports parametrized methods (such as `SLFJ`), the following code may also be faster than regular String concatenation:

```
LOG.debug("Entry #{} is {}", i, entry[i]);
```

The following test case uses 30 threads, and calls a servlet that contains 10 DEBUG calls (all are dismissed from ending up in the log file). Each individual DEBUG call consists of 10 string concatenations and a call to a method that sleeps for 1 ms. For non-optimized log calls, the results are as visualized in the following screenshot:

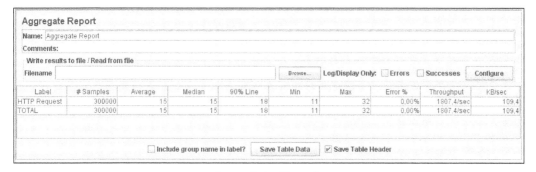

Non-optimized log calls

Optimizing the log calls with the improved parametrized technique will result in an improved throughput of a whooping 450 percent, as shown in the following screenshot (great gains in performance can be made simply by thinking about how to log!):

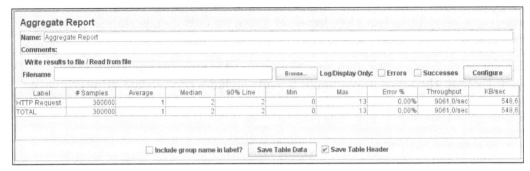

Optimized log calls

Performance tuning logging in WildFly

Logging in WildFly is handled by the *logging* subsystem. By default, logging messages from all deployed applications, together with the output from *stdout* and *stderr*, will be printed to the `server.log` file.

In general, the configuration of the logging subsystem largely consists of defining handlers, loggers, root-logger, and formatters. The following configuration is an example of a default setup:

```
<subsystem xmlns="urn:jboss:domain:logging:2.0">
  <console-handler name="CONSOLE">
    <level name="INFO"/>
    <formatter>
      <named-formatter name="COLOR-PATTERN"/>
    </formatter>
  </console-handler>
  <periodic-rotating-file-handler name="FILE" autoflush="true">
    <formatter>
      <named-formatter name="PATTERN"/>
    </formatter>
    <file relative-to="jboss.server.log.dir"
      path="server.log"/>
    <suffix value=".yyyy-MM-dd"/>
    <append value="true"/>
    </periodic-rotating-file-handler>
    <logger category="com.arjuna">
```

```
          <level name="WARN"/>
        </logger>
        <logger category="org.apache.tomcat.util.modeler">
          <level name="WARN"/>
        </logger>
        <logger category="org.jboss.as.config">
          <level name="DEBUG"/>
        </logger>
        <logger category="sun.rmi">
          <level name="WARN"/>
        </logger>
        <logger category="jacorb">
          <level name="WARN"/>
        </logger>
        <logger category="jacorb.config">
          <level name="ERROR"/>
        </logger>
        <root-logger>
          <level name="INFO"/>
          <handlers>
            <handler name="CONSOLE"/>
            <handler name="FILE"/>
          </handlers>
        </root-logger>
        <formatter name="PATTERN">
          <pattern-formatter pattern="%d{yyyy-MM-dd HH:mm:ss,SSS}
          %-5p [%c] (%t) %s%E%n"/>
        </formatter>
        <formatter name="COLOR-PATTERN">
          <pattern-formatter pattern="%K{level}%d{HH:mm:ss,SSS}
          %-5p [%c] (%t %s%E%n"/>
        </formatter>
    </subsystem>
```

The root-logger header defines which handlers should be active. It may also set the default threshold level (which, in the standard WildFly distribution is set to the INFO level out-of-the-box in WildFly). Individual logger entries control the log level of individual packages. These settings are very important when it comes to performance. You don't want to log more than is necessary as it will use resources. You should, as a general rule, stick to a less-detailed level of logging for your classes, such as WARN, to minimize logging.

Remember that it is always possible to change levels at runtime whenever required. For example, the level can be changed by using the following CLI:

```
/subsystem=logging/logger=com.your.category:write-
attribute(name=level,value=DEBUG)
```

The logging system also supports filtering, which means that it's possible to write rules that either approve a message to be logged or dismiss it. By dismissing a message, you gain performance by not needing to write any data. However, extensive filtering may also consume CPU resources, so this is a trade-off that needs to be investigated case-by-case.

By default, two handlers are defined: one `console-handler` and one `periodic-rotating-file-handler`. The following handlers are available in WildFly:

- `console-handler`: This logs information to the console
- `file-handler`: This logs information to a file
- `periodic-rotating-file-handler`: This logs information to a file that is rotated over time
- `size-rotating-file-handler`: This logs information to a file that is rotated by size settings
- `syslog-handler`: This logs information to the syslog
- `async-handler`: This defines a handler that writes data to the sub-handlers in an asynchronous thread
- `custom-handler`: This defines a custom handler that you write yourself

Logging to the console

It is worth mentioning, from a performance point of view, that `console-handler` should always be removed from a production configuration. Printing text to the console involves a lot of work for the OS during I/O-related operations. Also, on Windows, writing data to the console is a blocking-unbuffered operation. In general, writing lots of data to the console will slow down or block an application.

Let's take the previous test case and change the logging setup in WildFly so that the generated messages of the servlet will be logged and test it on a Linux system. The following screenshot shows a test case where the `console-handler` is enabled and the standard `file-handler` writes to a disk:

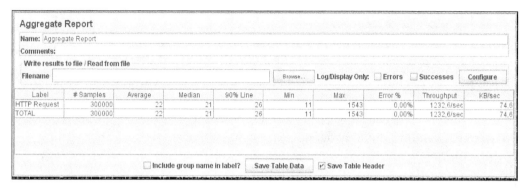

Console logging enabled

In the following screenshot, we have the results of the same test case but with console logging disabled. As we can see, in our case, there is a considerable difference of about 25 percent in throughput.

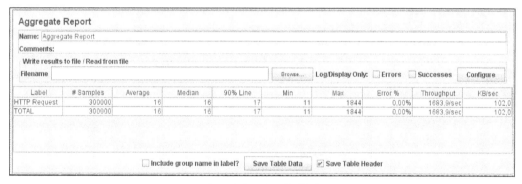

Console logging disabled

Logging to files

There are several different log handlers that write to available disk. All of the handlers benefit in performance by using a dedicated disk for logging. The built-in WildFly default path variable `jboss.server.log.dir` is used (see the usage in the configuration in the *Performance tuning logging in WildFly* section).

Note that this is not a system parameter. If you want to define one yourself and use that instead, the following CLI may be used to change the default `FILE` handler:

```
/path=my.own.wildfly.log.path:add(path=/mount/
diskForLogs)
```

```
/subsystem=logging/periodic-rotating-file-
handler=FILE:change-file(file={relative-to="my.
own.wildfly.log.path", path="server.log"})
```

You can further tune your file based handlers by setting the `autoflush` attribute to `false` in the configuration. By default, a flush operation is executed after writing each event, ensuring that the message is immediately written to the disk. Setting the `autoflush` attribute to `false` can drastically reduce I/O activity, since it will buffer logs in the memory before writing them to the disk. The improvement varies somewhat depending on the host machine, and it can be significantly higher on systems that are heavily I/O loaded.

Using asynchronous logging to improve log throughput

As described earlier, `async-handler` can be used to log events asynchronously. Behind the scenes, this appender uses a bounded queue to store events. Every time a log is emitted, the log call immediately returns after placing events in the bounded queue. An internal thread serves the events accumulated in the bounded queue for the selected handlers to process. The following code is an example of a configuration for an async handler:

```
<async-handler name="async">
    <queue-length value="10"/>
    <overflow-action value="block"/>
    <!-- Which other handlers to call -->
    <subhandlers>
        <handler name="FILE"/>
        <handler name="anotherDefinedHandler"/>
    </subhandlers>
</async-handler>
```

By increasing the `queue-length` option, you can raise the maximum number of logging events that can be buffered in the internal queue.

What happens if the queue reaches its limit and won't accept any more messages? It depends on its configuration attribute called `overflow-action`. The default value is `block`, which means that the caller thread will be blocked until the message can be processed. It is possible to set it to `discard`, but this means of course that messages will be lost and never written to the log target.

Many developers wrongly believe that this async handler is the fastest appender. This is however true only in certain circumstances. The async handler does not automatically improve logging throughput. On the contrary, a non-negligible number of CPU cycles is spent managing the bounded queue and synchronizing the dispatcher thread with various client threads. Thus, logging each event will take a little longer to complete; appending those events will hopefully take place at times where other threads are idle, either waiting for new input to process or blocked on I/O-intensive operations. To summarize, if you are running I/O-bound applications, then you will benefit from asynchronous logging. On the other hand, CPU-bound applications will not.

However, as we said, the async handler does not always increase performance. Do not include it blindly in your setup. Verify by running a benchmark first. If you don't want to experiment too much with your configuration, my advice is to stay with one of the plain file handlers, which is a safe bet.

Logging hierarchy and performance

As you are deciding on a logging strategy, consider that the loggers are organized in a parent-child relationship. For example, a logger for the `org` category is the parent logger of the `org.example` child logger. In the logger hierarchy, the child logger inherits the properties and the logger components from its immediate parent. In short, this means that all the logging events captured by the `org.example` child logger will be processed by the child logger itself and also by its `org` parent logger, in the logger definition, by setting the `use-parent-handlers` attribute of the logger to `false`, as shown in the following code. You can circumvent ancestor loggers, thus improving the performance significantly.

```
<logger category="org.example" use-parent-handlers="false" >
    <level value="INFO" />
    <appender-ref ref="FILE"/>
</logger>
```

Per-deployment logging

Per-deployment logging is a way to configure logging in a deployable artifact, but Per-deployment logging is a way to configure logging in a deployable artifact, but it is completely separate from the logging configuration in WildFly. Per-deployment logging can be realized by adding a logging configuration file to the deployment artifact (EAR, WAR, JAR, RAR, and so on). Such a file should be located in the META-INF (or WEB-INF for web applications) directory of your deployment.

The following configuration files are allowed:

* `logging.properties`
* `jboss-logging.properties`
* `log4j.properties`
* `log4j.xml`
* `jboss-log4j.xml`

Also, the `jboss-deployment-structure.xml` file can be used to disable the loading of the JBoss logging module (`org.jboss.logging`) altogether.

The principles of performance tuning that we have discussed in this chapter are applicable regardless of the underlying framework you use.

Summary

A modern application server such as WildFly is a complex beast to conquer. It comprises multiple subsystems, many of which are projects in their own right, and as such have their own project lifecycle. Many of them you may already recognize as they are well-known open source projects. Keep in mind that, when you try to resolve a performance issue with WildFly, it may not be enough to look at the Wildfly documentation; you many need to dig further and look at the subprojects documentation.

Several of the subsystems that have not been addressed in this chapter are so important that they have been discussed in their own dedicated chapters. They are as follows:

* EJB3
* JPA
* HornetQ (JMS)
* Undertow (the web container)

Starting from the next chapter, we will go through the various performance settings and design tips for EJB3 in WildFly.

5
EJB Tuning in WildFly

In this chapter, we will go through the different types of Enterprise JavaBeans from an optimization perspective. We will talk about the common best practices, look at their configurations within WildFly in more detail, and introduce Enterprise JavaBeans. An **Enterprise JavaBean** (**EJB**) is a component whose purpose is to encapsulate business logic and make various types of interfaces available. The encapsulation is performed by letting the EJBs methods expose what services should be visible for a client. A client can both be *local* (that is, within the same deployed artifact: EAR or WAR) or *remote*.

An EJB is basically a **Plain-Old-Java-Object** (**POJO**) that runs in a server-side environment, providing patterns and best practices for common services such as thread-safe code, transactions, security, and remote access. For EJBs, this environment is called an EJB container, and you can regard an EJB as a portable component that needs this container to be able to execute. The container allows the developer to focus on the business logic without having to worry about complicated issues and the common services just mentioned. The default behavior of the container can be overridden by the following:

- Annotations in the application code
- XML in specific configuration files

Some partial adjustments can also be made in the configuration of the application server and its internal components.

The history of EJBs

In 1999, the EJB specification (JSR 220) was released. It embraced the component model of development in order to increase reuse and simplify business implementations.

After some hype, it started to get a bad reputation for not being able to deliver what it promised. The programming model was much too complex for developers, and the specification allowed for arguably too much freedom among vendors that contributed to poor compatibility between containers.

Alternatives soon emerged. Spring came along with its **Inversion of Control** (**IoC**) container and **Dependency Injection** (**DI**). Instead of the EJB Entity Beans, which had severe performance problems, Hibernate provided a better alternative with its **Object Relational Mapping** (**ORM**) model.

Under pressure, Java EE 5 was delivered with the very much improved and simplified EJB 3.0 and JPA 1.0 specifications. Session beans stayed in the EJB specification, while the Entity Beans were re-engineered into a brand new POJO-based component that could also be used outside a Java EE container. To further simplify development, annotations were introduced along with default configuration values. The use of XML and some interfaces became optional.

This work has continued through the following specifications of JEE6 (with EJB 3.1) and JEE7 (with EJB 3.2), enabling the developers of today to use even simpler and more efficient enterprise frameworks where they can focus on the business functionality instead of the boilerplate code. WildFly 8 is JEE7 certified and thus supports EJB 3.2.

The different types of EJBs

Here, we will give you a brief introduction of the different EJB types.

Stateless Session Beans (SLSB)

Stateless Session Beans (**SLSB**) are business objects that do not have a state associated with them; they are typically used for one-off operations such as fetching a list of elements from a legacy system. Instances of stateless session beans may be pooled. If they are pooled and a client accesses one of them, the EJB container checks whether there are any available instances in the pool. If any available instance is present, the instance is returned to the client.

If no instances are available, the container creates a new instance (unless the pool has reached its max size) that will be returned to the client. In this case, the number of clients that can be served is not unlimited.

As mentioned previously, some implementations don't use a pool. In these cases, instances are normally created and destroyed with each invocation. This might be slower than using a pool as it consumes resources to create new instances.

Stateful Session Beans

Stateful Session Beans (**SFSB**) are business objects that have a state, that is, they keep track of which calling client they are dealing with throughout a session. Thus, access to the bean instance is strictly limited to only one client at a time.

A typical scenario for SFSB is a web store checkout process, which might be handled by a stateful session bean that would use its state to keep track of items the customer is purchasing.

Stateful session beans remain alive in the EJB container until they are explicitly removed, either by the client or the container when they time out. Meanwhile, the EJB container might need to passivate inactive stateful session beans to disk. Passivation requires an overhead and constitutes a performance hit to the application. If the passivated stateful bean is subsequently required by the application, the container activates it by restoring it from the disk.

By explicitly removing SFSB-instances when they are no longer needed, applications will decrease the need for the passivation and minimize container overhead and improve performance. Also, by explicitly removing SFSB-instances, you do not need to rely on timeout values.

Singleton Session Beans

Singleton Session Beans have a global shared state within the JVM and only exist in one single instance. The typical usage of Singleton Session Beans is for caches or configuration data.

 It is common to use a Singleton Session Bean with the @Startup and @PostConstruct annotations as a simple way to kick-start application code that needs to be executed at deployment and undeployment.

Message Driven Beans (MDB)

Another type of EJB is the **Message Driven Bean** (**MDB**). In comparison to Session Beans, MDBs are triggered by incoming messages instead of method calls. They connect to the **Message Oriented Middleware** (**MOM**) infrastructure, usually (but not exclusively) by using the **Java Message Service** (**JMS**) API. Note that MDBs are not tied to the JMS API, though. MDBs subscribe to message queues or message topics, and their execution is triggered as messages.

MDBs are similar to Stateless Session Beans, but a client can't look up MDBs. Hence, direct client access to an MDB is not possible.

Performance tuning EJBs in WildFly

Most of the performance tuning of EJBs in WildFly consists of tuning various pools. The following sections will go more into detail about each of the EJB types and their actual tuning. First though, we will start with some generic information about enabling detailed statistics in WildFly and a few optimizations of local and remote method calls.

Enabling detailed statistics

By default, detailed statistics aren't generated in WildFly. To generate statistics, it must be enabled using the following CLI command:

```
/subsystem=ejb3:write-attribute(name=enable-statistics,value=true)
```

Optimizations of Local and Remote method calls

Session beans have two possible interfaces, `@Local` and `@Remote`. The difference is that when the local interface is used, it makes it possible for the application server to perform a *pass-by-reference* instead of a *pass-by-value* call. When using references, the method-call parameters are sent as memory references (like any other standard Java call within the same VM), but when using the remote interface, all parameters need to be serialized.

The pass-by-value approach is easy to understand when using remote clients as memory references doesn't work, but the fact is that if the remote interface is used within the application server, it will still have to go through the serialization process, as this is required by the EJB3 specification. So, the recommendation is that you always use the local interface when possible. The following diagram illustrates the difference between the two approaches:

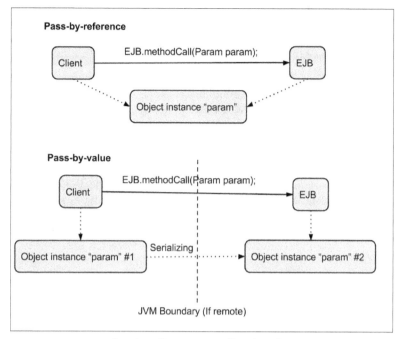

Pass-by-reference versus Pass-by-value

In the top *pass-by-reference* case, the **Client** makes a local method call. No serialization is needed. Only the reference of (or address to) the object instance for the parameter is actually passed to the EJB. The EJB will then look at the same object instance located as the position in memory as the **Client** used and has referenced.

Using the bottom *pass-by-value* case, the object instance parameter is serialized and copied from the **Client** to the **EJB**, where it is deserialized and used, as the **Client** performs the method call to the **EJB**. Here, there is more than one object instance of the parameter in memory.

So when is it not possible? As mentioned previously, remote clients need to use the remote interface, but actually, all clients that are located outside the EAR file are prohibited to use the local interface, even if they are running within the same application server.

From a technological point of view, it is possible for an application server to optimize remote interface calls within the same VM and use pass-by-reference instead of pass-by-value; this breaks the EJB specification contract though. As such, it should only be utilized after thorough consideration of architecture and future platform plans (as updated versions of the application server might not include this functionality).

To enable optimization in WildFly, you can execute the following CLI command:

```
/subsystem=ejb3:write-attribute(name=in-vm-remote-interface-invocation-
pass-by-value, value=false)
```

> Note that pass-by-reference will only be used if the
> client and EJB have access to the same class definitions
> (meaning identical classes loaded from the same
> classloader). WildFly will perform a shallow check to
> verify whether the optimization is enabled and will
> return to non-optimized calling if needed. A shallow
> check, in contrast to a deep check, only checks the
> top-level object and will not continue checking any
> references within it to others. This means that you may
> get `ClassCastException`, so only use it if you are sure
> that the client is using the same classloader as EJB.

If remote interfaces are used, it is a good idea to minimize the number of network calls done by using the *coarse grained approach*.

Looking at the following diagram, we see an example of a client making many calls to an EJB, setting one attribute at time:

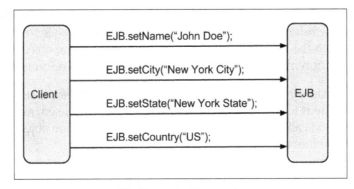

The fine grained approach

The preceding diagram is an example of what is considered to be a *fine grained approach*. This works relatively fine if local interfaces (and pass-by-reference) are used as there will be local in-VM method calls. However, should the client access an EJB through remote interfaces (and using pass-by-value), the calls will go over the network, resulting in relatively high performance-related costs.

The coarse grained approach illustrated in the following diagram uses a data object (person) that is populated with information on the client side (using all deployment-local and in-VM calls) and is then sent to the EJB in only one remote call (`EJB.setData(person)`). This minimizes the necessary network-related calls and improves performance and overall efficiency.

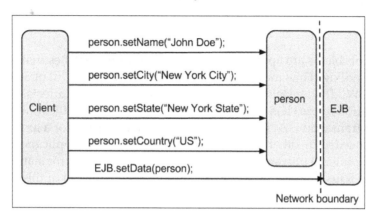

The coarse grained approach

Session beans and transactions

If you are using **Container Managed Transaction (CMT)**, which is the default transaction strategy, the container will automatically start a transaction for you because the default transaction attribute is REQUIRED. This guarantees that the work performed by the method is within a global transaction context.

However, transaction management is an expensive affair and you need to verify whether your EJB methods really need a transaction. For example, a method that simply returns a list of objects to the client usually does not need to be enlisted in a transaction.

For this reason, it's considered a best practice in tuning to remove unneeded transactions from your EJB. Unfortunately, this is often underestimated by developers who find it easier to define a generic transaction policy for all methods in the deployment descriptor. For example, in the following example configuration, all methods of TestEJB will use the Required transaction attribute:

```
<container-transaction>
  <method>
    <ejb-name>TestEJB</ejb-name>
    <method-name>*</method-name>
  </method>
  <trans-attribute>Required</trans-attribute>
</container-transaction>
```

Using EJB3 annotations, you have no excuse for your negligence; you can explicitly disable transactions by setting the transaction type to NOT_SUPPORTED with a simple annotation, as shown in the following code:

```
@TransactionAttribute(TransactionAttributeType.NOT_SUPPORTED)
public List<PayRoll> findAll() {
    ...
}
```

The common problems are applications with long-running batches that include transaction handling. They may hit the default transaction timeout of 300 seconds (5 minutes) in WildFly. Instead of just increasing this setup that affects all transactions on the application server, it is better to override the timeout for the individual EJB that starts the transaction. A "hanging" call may lock resources for a long time, which are resources needed by other callers, thus slowing down the application due by queueing. Keeping the transaction timeout at a reasonable level for standard calls and increasing it just for specific ones; this minimizes the impact of this happening. Instead the locked resources will be released at an early time-out.

The default timeout can be managed by issuing the following CLI command:

```
/subsystem=transactions:read-attribute(name=default-timeout)
{
    "outcome" => "success",
    "result" => 300
}
```

Setting the timeout to a specific value can be done by the following CLI command (we're setting it to 600 seconds here):

```
/subsystem=transactions:write-attribute(name=default-timeout, value=600)
```

A specific timeout value can also be configured in code with the following annotation:

```
@TransactionTimeout(value = 600, unit = TimeUnit.SECONDS)
```

Or, it can be configured in the jboss-ejb3.xml configuration file by using the following code:

```
<container-transaction>
  <method>
    <ejb-name>MyBean</ejb-name>
    <method-name>*</method-name>
  </method>
  <tx:trans-timeout>
```

```
        <tx:timeout>600</tx:timeout>
        <tx:unit>Seconds</tx:unit>
      </tx:trans-timeout>
   </container-transaction>
    . . .
```

 Note that it is only valid when using the transaction attributes REQUIRED (if the current bean is the actual creator of the transaction) or REQUIRES_NEW (if a new transaction should be created for every call to the bean).

In WildFly, it is possible to activate statistics for the transactions. It is disabled by default for performance reasons but can be enabled using the following CLI command and then restarting the application server:

```
/subsystem=transactions:write-attribute(name=enable-statistics,
value=true)
```

Execute the following CLI command to list the available transaction statistics' attributes:

```
/subsystem=transactions:read-resource-description
```

The attributes that may be of interest for monitoring are as follows:

- number-of-transactions
- default-timeout
- number-of-application-rollbacks
- number-of-aborted-transactions
- number-of-inflight-transactions
- number-of-timed-out-transactions
- number-of-committed-transactions
- number-of-resource-rollbacks

A JMX MBean with the ObjectName `jboss.as:subsystem=transactions` is also available for monitoring. An example using JConsole for listing it and its attributes is shown in the following screenshot:

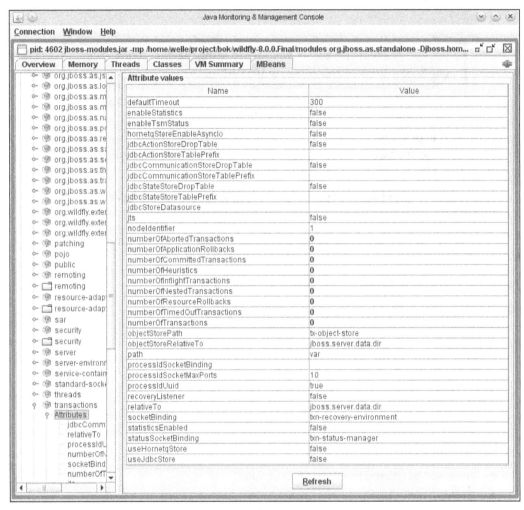

Transaction information MBean

In the following screenshot, the **Transaction Metrics** view in **Management Console** provides an overall view of the transactions:

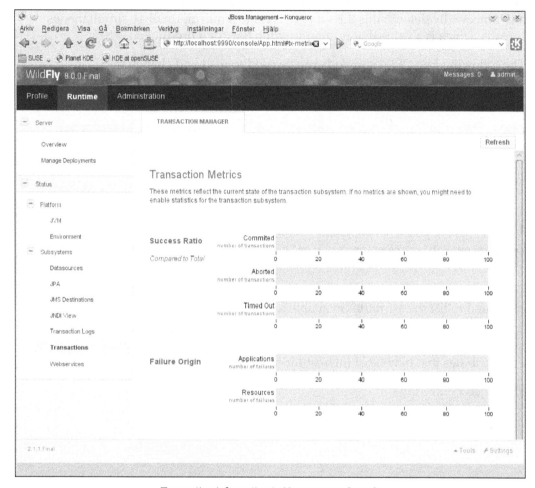

Transaction information in Management Console

Remote EJB calls

For the examples in this chapter, we are using JMeter with a special EJB Sampler (both test-cases and the sampler are available at https://bitbucket.org/wptbook2014/ wildfly-performance-tuning-ch5). As this sampler is being executed in the JMeter JVM and not within WildFly, it is regarded as a remote EJB client.

In WildFly, there is a special thread pool used for all remote access that we need to tune. This pool consists of a `max-threads` size and a queue (of tasks) with no upper bound. If no threads are available for a task, this task will be put in the queue without any timeout. By default, this thread pool is set to a maximum of `10` simultaneous threads, which is a value that is often way too low for a production setup.

The following two CLI commands can be used to read and change the `max-threads` configuration:

```
# Get max threads
/subsystem=ejb3/thread-pool=default:read-attribute(name=max-treads)
{
    "outcome" => "success",
    "result" => 10
}
# Set max threads
/subsystem=ejb3/thread-pool=default:write-attribute(name=max-threads,
  value=100)
```

This thread pool can also be monitored using CLI. Execute the following CLI command to list the attributes available for monitoring:

```
/subsystem=ejb3/thread-pool=default:read-resource-description
```

The attributes that may be of interest for monitoring are as follows:

- `max-threads`
- `largest-thread-count`
- `current-thread-count`
- `activeCount`
- `task-count`
- `completed-task-count`
- `rejected-count`
- `queue-size`

A JMX MBean with the ObjectName `jboss.as:subsystem=ejb3,thread-pool=default` is also available for monitoring. The following screenshot shows you how it uses JConsole:

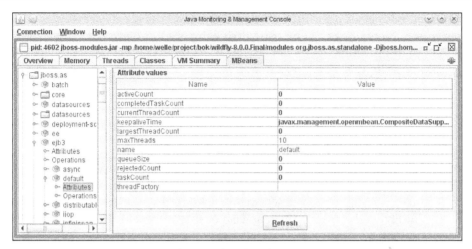

The EJB3 thread pool MBean

The following screenshot shows you **Management Console**, which only provides a configuration view on this pool and not any runtime information:

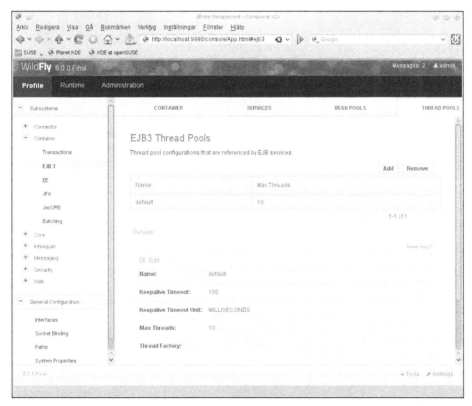

The EJB3 thread pool in the Management Console

As this thread pool is used for EJB3 asynchronous and timer calls as well as for remote access, you may need to investigate it even if you do not have any remote clients in your application.

For the remainder of this chapter, test results depend on the `max-threads` parameter in the EJB3 thread pool setting being set to `100`. If it's not set to `100`, none of the tests will be able to execute more than 10 simultaneous calls.

Optimizing Stateless Session Beans

If SLSB isn't costly to instantiate (no heavy `@PostConstruct`), pooling may be slower than just creating new instances when needed. This behavior is actually default in WildFly, and it means that each caller thread creates its own instance of the needed SLSB.

The downsides are that it can be counterproductive when SLSB takes a long time to be created or in a scenario where you have resources that are starving. For example, you might need to have exact control of your SLSB if they are strictly dependent on an external resource such as a JMS queue.

Enabling instance pooling for SLSB can be done by the following CLI command which activates an already shipped and configured pool:

```
/subsystem=ejb3:write-attribute(name=default-slsb-instance-
  pool,value=slsb-strict-max-pool)
```

The approach to be used depends on a lot of criteria and the best decision is based (as usual) on real tests. As there is not much to optimize if the default behavior is used, besides minimizing lifecycle callbacks, we focus the rest of the discussion on a scenario when SLSB pooling is enabled.

When enabling SLSB pooling, the default maximum pool size in WildFly is set to `20`.

The following two CLI commands retrieve and set the maximum size of the pool:

```
# Get the max pool size
/subsystem=ejb3/strict-max-bean-instance-pool=slsb-strict-max-
  pool:read-attribute(name=max-pool-size)
# Set the max pool size
/subsystem=ejb3/strict-max-bean-instance-pool=slsb-strict-max-
  pool:write-attribute(name=max-pool-size, value=30)
```

If there is no instance available in the pool, the caller will be put on hold for a maximum of 5 minutes (default). This can be changed by executing the following CLI commands:

```
# Get the unit for the timeout value
/subsystem=ejb3/strict-max-bean-instance-pool=slsb-strict-max-
  pool:read-attribute(name=timeout-unit)
# Get the timeout value
/subsystem=ejb3/strict-max-bean-instance-pool=slsb-strict-max-
  pool:read-attribute(name=timeout)
# Set the timeout value
/subsystem=ejb3/strict-max-bean-instance-pool=slsb-strict-max-
  pool:write-attribute(name=timeout, value=10L)
```

In the following examples, we will show you how an SLSB pool can be monitored. SLSB is named `StatelessSessionTestBean` and is located in the `MyEJB.jar` example rtifact, which in turn, is deployed within EAR, `MyEAR.ear`.

Use the following CLI command to explore the available attributes of the SLSB pool for any given bean deployed:

```
/deployment=MyEAR.ear/subdeployment=MyEJB.jar/subsystem=ejb3/
stateless-  session-bean=StatelessSessionTestBean:
read-resource-description
```

The attributes that may be of interest for monitoring are as follows:

- `pool-max-size`
- `pool-current-size`
- `pool-available-count`
- `peak-concurrent-invocations`
- `invocations`
- `pool-create-count`
- `pool-remove-count`

To find the peak load value of an already deployed SLSB, have a look at the `peak-concurrent-invocations` attribute.

As usual, there is also an MBean available to provide the same information. In this case the JMX MBean has the ObjectName `jboss.as:deployment=MyEAR.ear,subdeployment=MyEJB.jar,subsystem=ejb3,stateless-session-bean=StatelessSessionTestBean`, and it's output can be seen using JConsole as shown in the following screenshot:

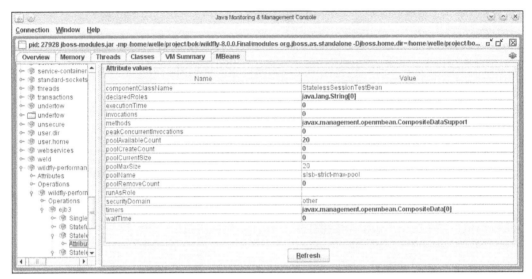

Statistic MBean for a SLSB

Unfortunately, the **Management Console** only provides a configuration view on this pool and not any runtime information. The setup possibilities can be seen in the following screenshot:

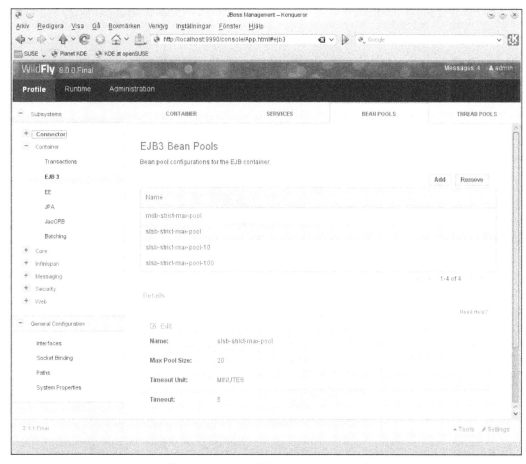

Management Console's view of a SLSB pool

Tuning the SLSB pool

Let's run a test case with 100 simultaneous threads calling a SLSB that just sleep for 1 second, where each thread executes 10 iterations without any pause in between. The following screenshot shows you the JMeter report of this test:

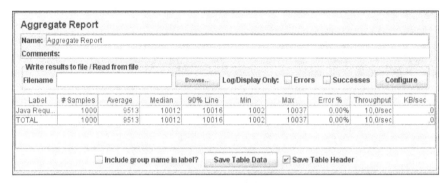

The JMeter result SLSB

For the remaining examples in this chapter, we will focus on the **Throughput** column. In real life, you probably want to investigate the other measurements as well. For example, whether the call time values (**Average**, **Median**, **90% Line**, **Min**, and **Max**) can be checked in order to find any extreme values that may point to some resource starvation, synchronization problems, and so on.

So let's turn to the **Throughput** column. Shouldn't the throughput be around 20 invocations/sec as the pool size is 20? Let's look at the pool usage for the SLSB using the JMX MBean during the test using JConsole, as shown in the following screenshot:

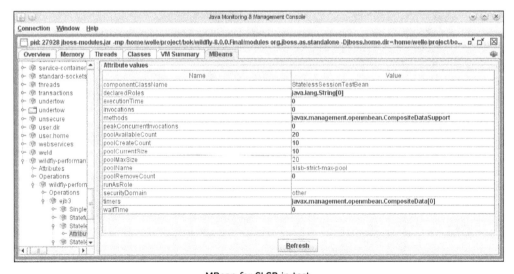

MBean for SLSB in test

WildFly has only created 10 instances in the pool, but shouldn't it be 20?

The answer is that we actually hit the limit of the EJB remote thread pool mentioned in the beginning of this chapter. Let's change it to `100` using the CLI command:

```
/subsystem=ejb3/thread-pool=default:write-attribute(name=max-threads,
   value=100)
```

After the change and re-testing, the following screenshot displays the result from JMeter:

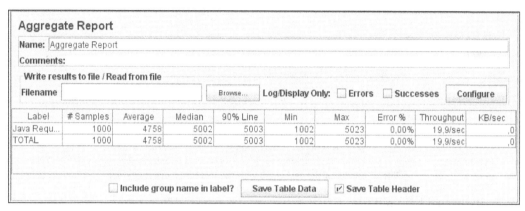

The JMeter result of the test SLSB with the increased EJB3 pool

Now, we have reached the expected throughput of around 20 invocations/sec, and watching the JMX MBean for the SLSB confirms that 20 instances have been created and used.

So what if the default size of 20 is not enough for the application. One solution would be to increase the default setting. This would, however, affect all SLSB in the container. It is also possible to create a new pool and let the individual SLSB use that pool instead. First, we create a new pool named `slsb-strict-max-pool-100`, using the following CLI command:

```
/subsystem=ejb3/strict-max-bean-instance-pool=slsb-strict-max-pool-
   100:add(max-pool-size=100, timeout-unit=MINUTES, timeout=5L)
```

Then, we can use it in our bean with the WildFly/JBoss specific annotation, as shown in the following code:

```
@org.jboss.ejb3.annotation.PPool(value="slsb-strict-max-pool-100")
```

Or, we can use the `jboss-ejb3.xml` configuration file as shown in the following code:

```
<p:pool>
   <ejb-name>MyBean</ejb-name>
```

```
    <p:bean-instance-pool-ref>slsb-strict-max-pool-100</p:bean-instance-
    pool-ref>
    </p:pool>
    . . .
```

Now we really are getting this bean to fly. A new test run shows us the results from JMeter in the following screenshot:

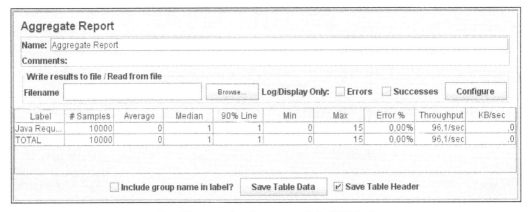

Aggregate Report

Name: Aggregate Report

Comments:

Write results to file / Read from file

Filename [ ] Browse... Log/Display Only: ☐ Errors ☐ Successes Configure

Label	# Samples	Average	Median	90% Line	Min	Max	Error %	Throughput	KB/sec
Java Requ...	10000	1001	1001	1002	1000	1079	0,00%	98,9/sec	,0
TOTAL	10000	1001	1001	1002	1000	1079	0,00%	98,9/sec	,0

☐ Include group name in label?   Save Table Data   ☑ Save Table Header

The JMeter results of the test SLSB with the increased instance pool

With all this said, do not forget that these test cases are a bit unrealistic. Clients very seldom call the same SLSB over and over again with no pause. So, there is normally no need to blindly correlate the pool's size with the expected number of callers.

Let's run a test case with 100 simultaneous threads, which calls SLSB with an instance pool set to `10`. Each caller thread sleeps for one second between calls and the SLSB return the execution immediately without any sleep. The result from JMeter is shown in the following screenshot:

Aggregate Report

Name: Aggregate Report

Comments:

Write results to file / Read from file

Filename [ ] Browse... Log/Display Only: ☐ Errors ☐ Successes Configure

Label	# Samples	Average	Median	90% Line	Min	Max	Error %	Throughput	KB/sec
Java Requ...	10000	0	1	1	0	15	0,00%	96,1/sec	,0
TOTAL	10000	0	1	1	0	15	0,00%	96,1/sec	,0

☐ Include group name in label?   Save Table Data   ☑ Save Table Header

The JMeter results of a more realistic SLSB test

The **Throughput** column shows you that a pool of 10 is probably enough for this scenario as we match the load that should generate 100 calls/sec.

Optimizing Stateful Session Beans

As we discussed earlier, with SFSB the passivation process requires overhead and constitutes a performance hit to the application. If the passivated SFSB is subsequently required by the application, the container activates it by restoring it from the disk.

By explicitly removing SFSB when finished, applications will decrease the need for passivation, minimize container overhead, and improve their performance. Also, by explicitly removing SFSB, you do not need to rely on timeout values for the removal of stale beans.

The default setup of passivation in WildFly uses a cache called `simple`. This is a cache that doesn't passivate anything. This means that all SFSB are kept in memory without any timeouts. Unless removed by the application or their timeout setting, these can cause an out-of-memory exception in extreme cases. The following CLI command shows you the default setup:

```
/subsystem=ejb3:read-attribute(name=default-sfsb-cache)
{
    "outcome" => "success",
    "result" => "simple"
}
```

It is highly recommended that you change the setup to enable disk passivation in WildFly. This can be done using the following CLI command:

```
/subsystem=ejb3:write-attribute(name=default-sfsb-cache,
  value=passivating)
```

The threshold that specifies the maximum number of SFSB in memory before passivation will start (the default is `100000`) and can be retrieved and configured with the following two CLI commands:

```
/subsystem=ejb3/passivation-store=infinispan:read-attribute(name=max-
size)
{
    "outcome" => "success",
    "result" => 100000
}
/subsystem=ejb3/passivation-store=infinispan:write-attribute(name=max-
size, value=50000)
```

A default timeout for the removal of old unused SFSB isn't available in WildFly, so it's good practice to use the @StatefulTimeout annotation in the SFSB to instruct the container to remove the bean. Otherwise, it will be kept forever (or at least to the next restart). The following example sets it to 30 minutes:

```
@StatefulTimeout(value=30)
```

The same attribute and value set in XML using the deployment descriptor is shown in the following code:

```
<stateful-timeout>
  <timeout>30</timeout>
  <unit>Minutes</unit>
</stateful-timeout>
```

Disabling passivation for individual SFSB

As WildFly supports EJB 3.2, it also provides the possibility to disable passivation for an individual SFSB. This can be done in code using annotations, as shown in the following code:

```
@Stateful(passivationCapable=false)
```

The same attribute and value set in XML using the deployment descriptor is shown in the following code:

```
...
<session>
  <ejb-name>MyBean</ejb-name>
  <ejb-class>org.myapp.MyStatefulBean</ejb-class>
  <session-type>Stateful</session-type>
  <passivation-capable>false</passivation-capable>
</session>
...
```

The overuse of passivation disabling may lead to the application running out of memory, as all instances must be kept in memory.

Individual SFSB can be monitored using the CLI. Execute the following CLI command to list the available attributes:

```
/deployment=MyEAR.ear/subdeployment=MyEJB.jar/subsystem=ejb3/stateful-
session-bean=StatefulSessionTestBean:read-resource-description
```

The attributes that may be of interest for monitoring are as follows:

- `total-size`
- `invocations`
- `cache-size`
- `peak-concurrent-invocations`
- `passivated-count`

A JMX MBean with the ObjectName `jboss.as:deployment=MyEAR.ear,` `subdeployment=MyEJB.jar,subsystem=ejb3,stateful-session-` `bean=StatefulSessionTestBean` is also available for monitoring and is presented using JConsole, as shown in the following screenshot:

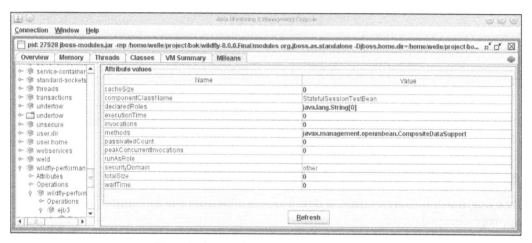

JConsole showing the statistic MBean for a SFSB

Optimizing Singleton Session Beans

Part of the basic idea of Session Beans is that the container is responsible for disallowing concurrent calls to the same instance. This helps in the construction of robust systems as the programmer doesn't have to produce thread-safe code.

A disadvantage of this is that the robustness can often lead to performance problems. This is especially common when using Singleton Session Beans; as there's only one instance, it can easily become a performance bottleneck if it is left with its default behavior.

This is demonstrated in the following test case. Here are 10 client threads running simultaneously performing 10 calls to a Singleton Session Bean method that takes 1 second to process before returning. The result is a throughput of only 1/second (60/min) as seen in the following screenshot of the JMeter report:

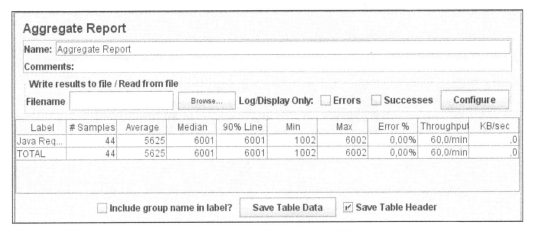

The JMeter result for a Singleton EJB

If you study WildFly's system log you are likely to see a few timeouts as well, as it took the client more than the default 5 seconds to obtain an instance.

Adjust lock mechanisms and time-outs

By using the @Lock annotation, a developer can instruct the EJB container to apply appropriate read or write locks more effectively, as shown in the following code:

```
@Singleton
@AccessTimeout(value=60, timeUnit=SECONDS)
@Lock(READ)
public class ExampleSingletonBean {
  private String info;

  public String getInfo() {
    return info;
  }

  @Lock(WRITE)
  public void setInfo(String info) {
    this.info = info;
  }
}
```

This bean will now use a read lock for all methods with the exception of the `setInfo` method, which will have a write lock. The timeout for getting access is set to 60 seconds.

Running the same test case against a Singleton Session Bean with read lock enabled gives us a throughput of almost 10 per second (**9.1**/sec), as shown in the following screenshot:

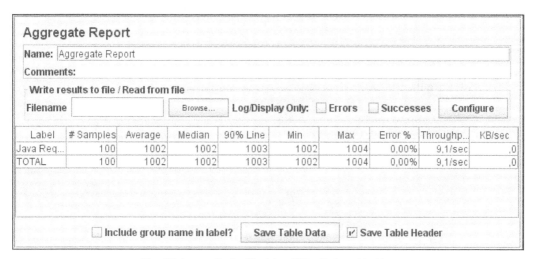

The JMeter result of a Singleton EJB with tuned locking

Container Managed Concurrency versus Bean Managed Concurrency

When the EJB container is responsible for handling concurrency (with the optional help of the `@Lock` annotation), it is called **Container Managed Concurrency** (**CMC**). It is also possible for a programmer to take full control by changing the bean to use **Bean Managed Concurrency** (**BMC**) by using the following annotations:

```
@ConcurrencyManagement(BEAN)
@Singleton
public class ExampleSingletonBean {
  // Threadsafe code
}
```

 Note that any code in this bean now really must be thread-safe! No assistance is given by the container.

Monitoring

Each Singleton Session Bean can be monitored using CLI. Execute the following command to list the available attributes:

```
/deployment=MyEAR.ear/subdeployment=MyEJB.jar/subsystem=ejb3/singleton-be
an=SingletonSessionTestBean:read-resource-description
```

The attributes that may be of interest for monitoring are as follows:

- `peak-concurrent-invocations`
- `invocations`

A JMX MBean with the ObjectName `jboss.as:deployment=MyEAR.ear,subdeployment=MyEJB.jar,subsystem=ejb3,singleton-bean=SingletonSessionTestBean` is also available and can be seen in the following JConsole screenshot:

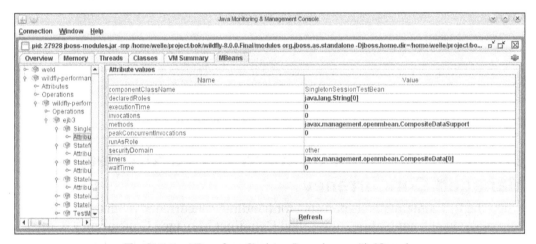

The Statistics MBean for a Singleton Bean shown with JConsole

Optimizing Message Driven Beans

MDB is a Java EE component that asynchronously processes messages, often from an incoming **Resource Adaptor (RA)**. The default adaptor is the built-in JMS provider in WildFly.

 As JMS is often used together with MDBs, proper tuning of the JMS provider and the connected destinations is also very important for the overall performance. More about tuning the WildFly JMS provider, its messages, and destinations will be addressed in an upcoming chapter.

As messages can be processed simultaneously, MDB instances need to be pooled in the same way as, for example, a SLSB. The default pool size for MDBs in WildFly is 20. This can be verified and modified using the following CLI commands:

```
# Get the max pool size
/subsystem=ejb3/strict-max-bean-instance-pool=mdb-strict-max-pool:read-attribute(name=max-pool-size)
# Set the max pool size
/subsystem=ejb3/strict-max-bean-instance-pool=mdb-strict-max-pool:write-attribute(name=max-pool-size, value=30)
```

It is easy to draw the conclusion that this number corresponds to the number of RA listeners on a JMS destination as well. This means that an MDB that listens to messages from a JMS queue would make the application server set up 20 listeners to that queue. This is actually not the case. These listeners are configured separately with RA-specific parameters.

In WildFly, the default adaptor is HornetQ (which is the JMS provider), and it uses the `maxSession` property (the default value is `15`), which can be set in the `@ActivationConfigProperty` annotation in MDB, as shown in the following code:

```
@MessageDriven(activationConfig = {
    @ActivationConfigProperty(propertyName = "destinationType",
        propertyValue = "javax.jms.Queue"),
    @ActivationConfigProperty(propertyName = "destination",
        propertyValue = "queue/testQueue"),
        @ActivationConfigProperty(propertyName = "maxSession",
        propertyValue = "20"),
    @ActivationConfigProperty(propertyName = "acknowledgeMode",
        propertyValue = "Auto-acknowledge") })
public class TestMDB implements MessageListener {
    public void onMessage(Message message) {
...
    }
}
```

Each MDB can be monitored using CLI. Execute the following command to list the available attributes:

```
/deployment=MyEAR.ear/subdeployment=MyEJB.jar/subsystem=ejb3/message-driven-bean=TestMDB:read-resource-descriptiondescriptiondescriptiondescription
```

The attributes that may be of interest for monitoring are as follows:

- `invocations`
- `peak-concurrent-invocations`
- `pool-available-count`
- `pool-current-size`
- `pool-create-count`
- `pool-remove-count`

Just like the other bean types, there is a JMX MBean with the ObjectName `jboss.as:deployment=MyEAR.ear,subdeployment=MyEJB.jar,subsystem=ejb3,message-driven-bean=TestMDB`.

The following screenshot visualizes the result using JConsole:

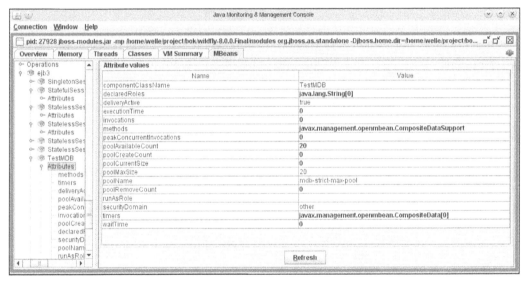

Statistics MBean for MDB shown with JConsole

A common scenario is that the application needs to process the messages not only asynchronously, but also in a strict serial order. The solution is often to configure the `maxSession` parameter to `1`, thus making a "singleton MDB". This is of course, bad for performance and it would be much better to redesign the application to allow the messages to be processed in parallel.

As MDBs are often used for long-running tasks, remember what we talked about in the section about transactions. Make the transaction runtime as short as possible, perhaps by splitting up a long task into several smaller ones.

 If the loss of messages is acceptable in case of failures, an alternative to using MDBs could be asynchronous EJBs to improve performance.

Summary

In this chapter, we studied the different performance issues and configurations of the various types of EJBs. In WildFly, the default setup of SLSB isn't using a pool, and this may be adequate for some applications but certainly not for all. The use of SFSB needs to be analyzed to keep the passivation to a minimum, and the default passivation configuration is unlikely to fit a production scenario. For Singleton Session Beans, the default locking strategy should be scrutinized before entering a production environment.

Next, we will turn our focus on how to tune persistent content handling in a Java EE application stack.

6
Tuning the Persistence Layer

Data persistence is a key ingredient of any enterprise application, and it has been a part of JDK since its very first release. Most readers certainly agree that data persistence is the most common cause of bottlenecks in applications. Unfortunately, isolating the root of the problem is not a straightforward affair and requires investigating areas from the SQL code to the interfaces used to issue SQL statements. Other potential areas that may affect your data persistence are the database configuration and the underlying network and database hardware.

For this reason, we have divided this chapter into the following three main sections in order to cover all the major factors that can drag down the performance of your data persistence:

- The first section introduces some principles of good database design. If your database design doesn't conform to some commonly agreed rules, chances are high that you will find it hard to achieve the performance needed for a successful application.

- The next section illustrates how to improve the performance of the **Java Database Connectivity (JDBC)** API, which allows connecting to a legacy database by means of drivers released by database vendors.

- The last section covers the core concepts of the **Java Persistence API (JPA)** and the Hibernate framework, which is used by WildFly as the persistence engine.

The majority of persistent storage solutions in the enterprise world are and have been relational databases for the last decades. There is a good reason for this as they proved very reliable and flexible. Other solutions include document databases, Big Data systems, and data grids. These techniques will not be covered in this book, but it is interesting to see how several of these solutions try to implement the JPA standard as they get more mature.

Designing a good database

Even if modern development tools and processes tend to make it easier to push the database design phase towards the end of the development cycle, it is crucial to not do so. Once the application has been implemented, it's simply too late to fix an inaccurate database design, leaving no other choice but to buy a larger amount of fast, expensive hardware to cope with the problem — if possible.

Designing a database structure is usually the task of a database administrator. However, it's not rare in today's tight-budget world that the software architect takes care to design the database schemas as well. That's why you should be aware of basic concepts such as database normalization, database partitioning, and good indexing.

Continuous database design, sanity checks, and early performance tests in parallel with the development process will minimize future headaches.

Database normalization and denormalization

One fundamental cornerstone of database design is normalization. Its purpose is to eliminate redundant data and support data integrity. An example of a denormalized database and its normalized counterpart is visualized in the following diagram (note how the normalized version allows adding more cities to a company without any alteration to the database design):

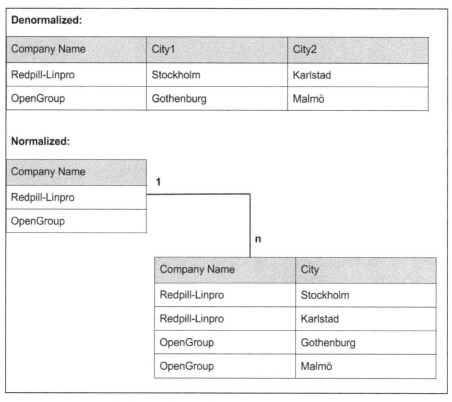

The denormalized and a normalized database tables

To measure and check how normalized a database design is, several so-called **Normal Forms** (**NF**) have evolved over the years. These NFs can be seen as collections of criteria to measure the normalization. Edgar F. Codd, who invented the database relational model, also defined the first three NFs (NF1, NF2, and NF3) in the early 70s. Over the years, several other NFs have emerged, but a database that complies with NF3 is commonly regarded as a normalized database. A detailed walkthrough of the different NFs is not in the scope of this book, but we encourage you to investigate these on your own.

Databases intended for **Online Transaction Processing** (OLTP) are typically more normalized than databases intended for **Online Analytical Processing** (OLAP). The reason for this, from a performance view, is that normalization generally favors updates and inserts while denormalization favors reads.

Your first goal in the design process should be to normalize your data. Next, you can test your design with realistic data and transactions. At this point, if you see that denormalization helps, then you can apply it by all means. However, don't assume that you need to denormalize data until you can prove (through testing) that it's the right thing to do.

> With JPA object-relational mapping, you can use the @Embedded annotation for denormalized columns to specify a persistent field whose @Embeddable type can be stored as an intrinsic part of the owning entity and can share the identity of the entity.

Database partitioning

If you are designing a database that can potentially be very large, holding millions or even billions of rows, you should consider the option of partitioning your database tables. Different database vendors have different supports and add-ons to help with this, but we will stick to the overall principles in this book. You can partition your database either horizontally or vertically.

Horizontal partitioning

Horizontal partitioning involves splitting a large table into smaller tables. The following diagram shows an example of how it can be done:

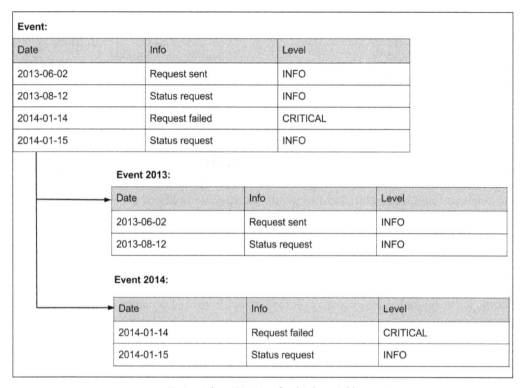

Horizontal partitioning of a database table

The main advantage of this is that it is generally much faster to query a single small table than a single large table. The performance of some queries can improve dramatically if the heavily accessed rows are located in one of the smaller tables, as both the table and its indexes may fit in memory.

Vertical partitioning

By using the vertical partitioning scheme, we split a table with many columns into multiple tables with fewer columns. Now, only certain columns are included in a particular dataset, with each partition including all rows.

For example, a table that contains a number of very wide text or **BLOB** columns that aren't referenced can often be split into two tables with the most-referenced columns in one table and the seldom-referenced text or **BLOB** columns in another. The following diagram shows an example of vertical partitioning:

Product	Info		Product	Picture
Screwdriver	Size 14		Screwdriver	<BLOB>
Wrench	Metric		Wrench	<BLOB>

Vertical partitioning of a database table

Using JPA/Hibernate mapping, you can easily map the preceding case with a lazy one-to-many relationship between the tables. The second table contains a less frequently accessed **BLOB** data type that can be lazily loaded. Hence, it is queried and retrieved just when the client requests the specific fields of the relationship.

Using indexes

The database *index* functionality is one of the best ways to improve the read performance of a database schema. Just like the reader searching for a word in a book, an index helps when you look for a specific record or set of records with a WHERE clause.

Since index entries are stored in a sorted order, indexes also help when processing GROUP BY and ORDER BY clauses. Without an index, the database has to load the records and sort them during execution.

Though indexes are indispensable for fast queries, they can have some drawbacks, as well, when the time comes to modify records in particular. As a matter of fact, any time a query modifies the data in a table, the indexes on the data must change too. Try to use a maximum of four or five indexes on one table, not more. If you have a read-only table, then the number of indexes may be safely increased.

There are a number of guidelines to build the most effective indexes for your application that are valid for every database, in particular the following:

- **Index on appropriate columns**: In order to achieve the maximum benefit from an index, you should choose to index the most common column, that is, in your WHERE, ORDER BY, or GROUP BY clauses for queries against this table.

- **Keep indexes small**: Short indexes are faster to process in terms of I/O and are faster to compare. An index on an integer field provides optimal results.

- **Choose distinct keys**: If the fields bearing the index have small or no duplicate values, this is highly selective and provides the best performance results.

- **Structure a composite (multicolumn) index correctly**: If you create a composite index, the order of the columns is very important. Put the most unique data element, the element that has the biggest variety of values, first in the index. The index will then find the correct page faster.

> To help you investigate whether indexes are used effectively for a particular query, most database vendors provide the possibility to get feedback from the query analyzer within the database server. As an example, you can use the EXPLAIN command in PostgreSQL for this, as shown in the following line of code:
>
> ```
> EXPLAIN SELECT * FROM product WHERE family=13;
> ```
>
> Few JPA/Hibernate users seem to know that it is possible to define indexes in the table configuration with Hibernate. For example, if you need to define an index named index1 on the columns column1 and column2, you can use the following simple annotation:
>
> ```
> @Table(appliesTo="tableName", indexes = {
>     @Index(name="index1",
>         columnNames={"column1","column2"})})
> ```

Tuning the Java Database Connectivity API

Java Database Connectivity (JDBC) is the Java standard that defines how a client accesses a (in most cases, relational) database. The different database vendors provide an implementation of this API, often called a JDBC driver.

Even if the basic purpose of JDBC is to provide a standardized way of executing native SQL statements and handling the result sets, it's often used as a foundation for other frameworks, for example, JPA or Hibernate.

Performance-tuning JDBC consists of the following processes:

- Introducing a database connection pool that reuses your connections

- Making use of proper JDBC features, such as fetch size and batch size

- Using prepared statements in your application and configuring a prepared statement cache at application server level

Connection pooling

The first basic rule you need to follow when programming JDBC is to use a connection pool when accessing a database. Establishing database connections, depending upon the platform, can take from a few milliseconds up to one second. This can be a meaningful amount of time for many applications, if done frequently.

A connection pool allows the reuse of physical connections and minimizes expensive operations in the creation and closure of sessions. Also, maintaining many idle connections is expensive for a database management system, and the pool can optimize the usage of idle connections (or disconnect, if there are no requests).

A common misconception among many Java developers is that acquiring and returning connections continuously from the pool stresses your application server excessively. Thus, it's not rare to see implementations with a database manager, which holds static connection fields to be shared across the application.

However, this is not an issue as the overhead for the application server is actually quite small. Of course, this doesn't mean you need to abuse the connection pool when it's not necessary. For example, it's always good to reuse the same connection and statements if you are performing a set of database operations within the same business method.

Sharing your connection instance across several business methods is not a good idea as it can easily confuse whoever is using these classes, and it can easily end up with connection leaks. So, keep your code simple and tidy, and don't be afraid to open and close your connections in every business method.

Performance tuning a connection pool in WildFly

A connection pool in WildFly is also called a **DataSource**, and it is managed by the subsystem *DataSources*. The pool may be defined whenever the underlying JDBC driver is deployed, using the CLI, the Admin Console, or a special deployable XML file. The following CLI command is a minimal example of a connection pool (bundled with WildFly for the H2 database) with all the default values and just the minimum required parameters defined:

```
/subsystem=datasources/data-source=TestDS:add(connection-
    url=jdbc:h2:mem:testDB,jndi-name=java:jboss/TestDS, driver-name=h2)
```

The following table contains selected parameters that may be of interest performance-wise. Fields marked with **depends** in the Performance recommendation column mean that a recommendation depends too much on application, environment, and other factors to be stated:

Value	Description	Default value	Performance recommendation
min-pool-size	This specifies the minimum number of connections for a pool.	0	Normal production usage +10-20 percent; in more extreme cases, set it to the value of max-pool-size
max-pool-size	This specifies the maximum number of connections for a pool. Note that there will probably be a maximum limit for the number of connections allowed by the database to match.	20	Maximum usage observed (in production or relevant tests) +10-20 percent
pool-prefill	This specifies whether the pool should be prefilled.	false	true
initial-pool-size	This is the initial number of connections in a pool.		min-pool-size
pool-use-strict-min	This specifies whether the min-pool-size should be considered strictly.	false	true
blocking-timeout-wait-millis	This is the maximum time to block while waiting for a connection. Note that this timeout is only to apply the lock itself. It will not trigger if creating a new connection takes a long time.		
allocation-retry-wait-millis	This is the time to wait between retrying to allocate a connection.		
idle-timeout-minutes	This is the maximum time a connection may be idle before being closed. The actual maximum time also depends on the scan time of the *IdleRemover* thread, which is half of the smallest idle-timeout-minutes value of any pool.		

Value	Description	Default value	Performance recommendation
allocation-retry	This is the number of allocation tries that should be tried before throwing an exception.		
flush-strategy	This is the flush strategy in case of the following errors: • FailingConnectionOnly • IdleConnections • EntirePool	Failing Connect ionOnly	
check-valid-connection-sql	This is the SQL statement to check validity of a pool connection when it's fetched from the pool.		If not needed, do not use it
valid-connection-checker-class-name	This is a org.jboss. jca.adapters.jdbc. ValidConnectionChecker class that is used for validating a connection.		Used instead of check-valid-connection-sql when there is such a database vendor implementation available, as it is probably more efficient
valid-connection-checker-properties	This is the valid connection checker properties.		
use-fast-fail	This specifies whether a connection allocation should fail directly if the first connection fetched is invalid or keep trying until all connections in the pool are tried.	false	
background-validation	This specifies whether connections should be validated in the background instead of when they are fetched from the pool.	false	true If connection validation is needed, doing it in the background is better than each time a connection is fetched
background-validation-millis	This specifies the time between background validations.		

Value	Description	Default value	Performance recommendation
prepared-statements-cache-size	This is the number of prepared statements per connection in an LRU cache.		
share-prepared-statements	This specifies whether to share prepared statements, that is, whether asking for the same statement twice without closing uses the same underlying prepared statement.	false	
query-timeout	This helps set the query timeout.		
set-tx-query-timeout	This automatically sets the query timeout to the time remaining until the transactions will timeout (if no transaction is active, the value of query-timeout will be used).	false	
spy	This enables logging of SQL statements.	false	false Useful if set to true for obtaining and investigating the executed SQL statements. Enable logging for "org.jboss.jdbc" as well
transaction-isolation	This sets the transaction isolation level: • TRANSACTION_NONE • TRANSACTION_READ_UNCOMMITTED • TRANSACTION_READ_COMMITTED • TRANSACTION_REPEATABLE_READ • TRANSACTION_SERIALIZABLE		See information later in this chapter

Value	Description	Default value	Performance recommendation
`track-statements`	This specifies whether WildFly should check statements and result set closure when a connection is returned. The possible values are: • `false` (Do not track) • `true` (Track and warn when not closed) • `nowarn` (Track but do not warn)	NOWARN	`false` Note that this means you must be sure that the application doesn't leak. To use `true` in all test environments is recommended
`connection-properties`	This specifies the properties that will be fed to the JDBC driver.		Can be used to set JDBC driver-specific optimizations

In order to calculate the optimal pool size, it's important to know how many connections an application requires. Monitoring the pool can be done with the CLI, the JMX, and the Admin Console. By finding the runtime statistics, it is possible to get an inside view of how the pool works during performance tests and in production.

The available statistics about the pool can be investigated by using the CLI. A CLI command for a non-XA DataSource pool (ExampleDS) is as follows:

```
/subsystem=datasources/data-source=ExampleDS/statistics=pool:
read-resource-description
```

A CLI command for an XA DataSource pool (ExampleXADS) is as follows:

```
/subsystem=datasources/xa-data-source=ExampleXADS/statistics=pool:
read-resource-description
```

The same information is available by JMX, as shown in the following screenshot, with the JConsole and the URI:

```
jboss.as:subsystem=datasources,data-source=ExampleDS,statistics=pool
```

For XA, use the URI:

```
jboss.as:subsystem=datasources,xa-data-
source=ExampleDS,statistics=pool.
```

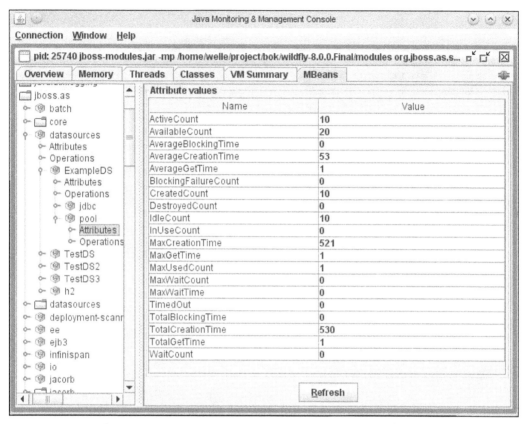

The JConsole displaying statistical information of the ExampleDS DataSource

In comparison to the MBean shown in the JConsole, the WildFly Admin Console in the following screenshot shows limited information:

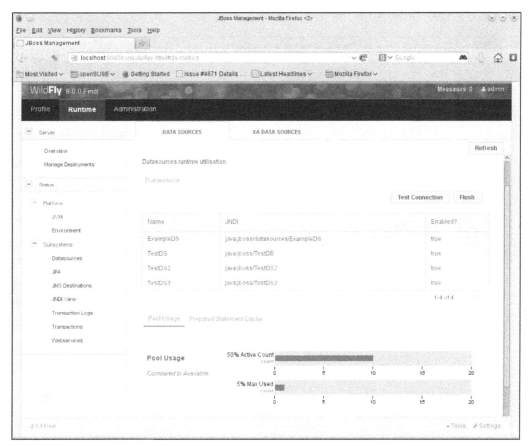

The WildFly Admin Console displaying statistical information of the ExampleDS DataSource

From the programmer's point of view, what WildFly provides you with is a `Connection` object, wrapped by the `org.jboss.jca.adapters.jdbc.jdk7.WrappedConnectionJDK7` class.

For example, if you are interested in retrieving the underlying implementation of an `OracleConnection` from the connection pool in WildFly, you can perform the following operations:

```
Connection conn = myWildFlyDatasource.getConnection();
WrappedConnectionJDK7 wrappedConn = (WrappedConnectionJDK7)conn;
Connection underlyingConn = wrappedConn.getUnderlyingConnection();
OracleConnection oracleConn = (OracleConnection)underlyingConn;
```

You may be wondering what the advantage of retrieving the underlying `Connection` implementation is. One good reason is the need to access some custom properties that are not available through the base `Connection` interface.

For example, if you are using an Oracle thin driver and you need to debug your Prepared Statement Cache Size, you can use the `getStatementCacheSize()` method of the `OracleConnection` object, as shown in the following code:

```
System.out.println("Cache size: " + oracleConn.
getStatementCacheSize());
```

Setting the proper fetch size

The fetch size is the number of rows retrieved from the database at one time, by the JDBC driver, as you scroll through a `ResultSet` using the `next()` method. If you set the query fetch size to `100`, the JDBC driver retrieves the first 100 rows at once when you retrieve the first row (or all of them if fewer than 100 rows satisfy the query). When you retrieve the second row, the JDBC driver merely returns the row from the local memory. It doesn't have to retrieve that row from the database. This feature improves performance by reducing the number of calls (frequently network transmissions) to the database.

To set the query fetch size, use the `setFetchSize()` method on the `Statement` (or `PreparedStatement` or `CallableStatement`) before execution. The optimal fetch size is not always obvious. Usually, the fetch size of one half or one quarter of the total expected result size is optimal. As a general rule, setting the query fetch size is mostly effective for a large result set. If you set the fetch size as much larger than the number of rows retrieved, it's likely that you'll get a performance decrease, not an increase. The default value differs for different database vendors.

 If you plan to increase the default row prefetch for all your statements, then you may be able to do so using a driver-specific connection parameter (for example, Oracle uses `defaultRowPrefetch` and DB2 uses `block size`).

Using batch updates for bulk insert/updates

In situations where you want to issue several inserts or updates in the same unit of work, update batching lets you group the statements together and transmit them to the database as one set of instructions. As with setting the query fetch size, update batching works by reducing the number of network transmissions between the application and the database.

For example, consider a website for online sales. When customers create orders, they often order multiple items. Usually, when the order is recorded, the items on the order are recorded at the same time. Update batching allows the multiple inserts for the order to be transmitted to the database at once.

Update batching is supported for SQL issued via the `Statement`, `PreparedStatement`, and `CallableStatement` classes. As with manipulating the query fetch size, the amount of performance improvement with batching statements varies between database vendors. Also, the network speed plays an important role in determining the real benefit of bulk updates.

Prepared statements

When a database receives a statement, the database engine first parses the SQL string and looks for syntax errors. Once the statement is parsed, the database needs to figure out the most efficient plan to execute the statement. This can be quite expensive computationally. Once the query plan is created, the database engine can execute it.

Ideally, if we send the same statement to the database twice, then we'd like the database to reuse the access plan for the first statement. This uses less of the CPU than if it regenerated the plan a second time. In Java, as well as in other languages, you can obtain a good performance boost by using prepared statements instead of concatenating the parameters as a string, using markers, as shown in the following code:

```
PreparedStatement ps =
    conn.prepareStatement("SELECT a,b FROM t WHERE c = ?");
```

Prepared statements allow the database to reuse the access plans for the statement, and it makes the program execute more efficiently inside the database. This basically lets your application run faster or makes more of the CPU available to users of the database.

Prepared statements can be cached by the application server itself when it's necessary to issue the same statements across different requests. Enabling the prepared statements cache is quite simple; all you have to do is set the `prepared-statement-cache-size` attribute in your connection pool configuration.

In practice, WildFly keeps a list of prepared statements for each database connection in the pool. When an application prepares a new statement on a connection, the application server checks if that statement has already been used. If it has been used, the `PreparedStatement` object instance is recovered from the cache and returned to the application. If not, the call is passed to the JDBC driver and the query or the `PreparedStatement` object is added into that connection's cache. The cache used by prepared statements is a **Least Recently Used (LRU)** cache.

The performance benefit provided by the prepared statement cache is application-specific and can be observed using, for example, the CLI.

The CLI command for a non-XA DataSource (TestDS) is as follows:

```
/subsystem=datasources/data-source=TestDS/statistics=jdbc:read-resource-description
```

The CLI command for an XA DataSource (TestXADS) is as follows:

```
/subsystem=datasources/xa-data-source=TestXADS/statistics=jdbc:read-resource-description
```

As usual, MBean is also available. For a regular DataSource named `ExampleDS`, it can be found at `jboss.as:subsystem=datasources,data-source=ExampleDS,statistics=jdbc`, and for the XA DataSource named `ExampleXADS`, it can be found at `jboss.as:subsystem=datasources,xa-data-source=ExampleXADS,statistics=jdbc`.

The attributes and values of ExampleDS are shown in the following screenshot using JConsole:

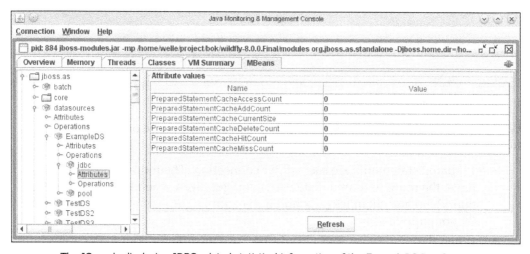

The JConsole displaying JDBC-related statistical information of the ExampleDS DataSource

The WildFly Admin Console presents a somewhat less detailed view, as shown in the following screenshot:

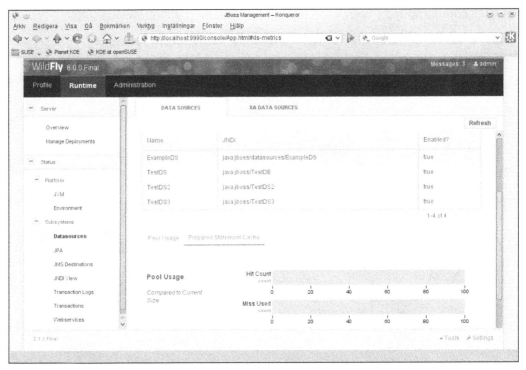

The WildFly Admin Console displaying JDBC-related statistical information of the ExampleDS DataSource

When working with prepared statements, one should be aware of the following two things:

- Prepared statements are cached per connection. The more connections you have, the more prepared statements you get (even when they are the same query). So, use them frugally and don't simply guess how many are needed by your application.

- When the connection pool shrinks because the idle timeout for a connection expires, statements are removed from the pool of cached prepared statements. This can cause an overhead that outweighs the benefits of caching statements.

> One good compromise that has been tried on a few projects is to create two pools for an application: a larger one (let's say with up to 30 connections) with no prepared statement cache, and a smaller one with a prepared statement cache activated and min-pool-size equal to max-pool-size, in order to avoid any shrinking of the pool.

Isolation levels

The levels of transaction isolation are defined by the SQL standard, using the following scenarios:

- **Dirty read**: It occurs when a transaction reads data that has been modified by a concurrent uncommitted transaction

- **Non-repeatable read**: It occurs if a transaction re-reads the same data and the values differ between reads (due to data being committed by another concurrent transaction)

- **Phantom read**: A transaction re-executes a query returning a set of rows that satisfy a search condition, and it finds that the set of rows satisfying the condition has changed due to another recently-committed transaction

The following table explains how these scenario relate to the isolation levels:

Isolation level	Dirty read	Non-repeatable read	Phantom read
TRANSACTION_READ_UNCOMMITED	Possible	Possible	Possible
TRANSACTION_READ_COMMITED	Not possible	Possible	Possible
TRANSACTION_REPEATABLE_READ	Not possible	Not possible	Possible
TRANSACTION_SERIALIZABLE	Not possible	Not possible	Not possible

Selecting the appropriate isolation level depends on the application's requirements. For an application for which there is no risk of concurrent writes when data is read, TRANSACTION_READ_UNCOMMITED may very well be okay. On the other hand, if your application handles really critical data, such as a bank account, you may very well need the safest choice, delivered by TRANSACTION_SERIALIZABLE.

Choosing the correct level is a tradeoff between safety and performance. If the application doesn't need to deal with concurrent transactions at all, the most performance-friendly choice would be TRANSACTION_NONE, which lacks isolation.

Be aware that the selected database may not support all isolation levels. It is actually allowed to "upgrade" to the next level if the selected one isn't supported. PostgreSQL, for example, supports TRANSACTION_READ_COMMITTED (default) and TRANSACTION_SERIALIZABLE.

Tuning JDBC networking

A JDBC connection is, behind the scenes, a socket connection to legacy systems. So, you can apply the same low-level network tuning, which is generally used for socket-data transmission.

For example, it is useful to set the TCP send and receive buffer to a higher value than the default (32 KB) if your system allows it. This can be done in most databases using the following connection properties:

- `tcpSndBuf = 65534`
- `tcpRcvBuf = 65534`
- `tcpNoDelay = true`

> Note that not all JDBC drivers honor the same connection properties; only some of them may provide additional properties that are particularly suited to the underlying database. Therefore, use these properties with caution, and only if you really need to fix or tune network issues with your relational database.

Tuning JPA and Hibernate

Programming with the JDBC API is quite simple as it is merely a thin layer over the database programming interfaces. There are, however, some considerations that you need to take into account:

- First, using the native SQL language in your code exposes your application to a tight coupling with the database where your code had initially been developed. Even if the SQL dialects are similar, each database performs differently depending on the structure of the query, necessitating vendor-specific tuning in most cases.

- Second, when you are using plain JDBC, you need to bridge the gap between the relational model and the object model by creating a layer of intermediate objects or collections that host the data fetched from the database. This is an unnecessary effort because **Object-Relational Mapping (ORM)** tools, such as Hibernate, can do it for you out-of-the-box.

- Finally, by using an intermediate layer that sits between your code and the database, it's possible to add additional services such as caching, which, if properly used, can greatly improve the performance of your applications.

As of Java EE 5, the **Java Persistence API (JPA)** provides a POJO-based persistence model to map between the world of objects (in Java) and relations (database). This allows you to design your persistence layer with the support of a standard specification using Java classes with relations.

Although developed by the EJB 3.0 expert group, JPA is not limited to usage in EJBs. It can be used in application clients, web applications, and standard Java SE applications. As JPA is a specification, it needs an implementation. In WildFly, the implementation provider is the globally renowned ORM project, Hibernate.

WildFly 8.0.0.Final makes use of the JPA 2.1 specification and the bundled module since the provider is Hibernate in Version 4.3.1.

JPA and Hibernate are ORM technologies that are *strategically similar* from one point of view since they are both fit to bridge the gap between the object world of Java and the legacy relational systems. They are, however, *semantically different* because JPA is a standard Java EE specification while Hibernate is a de facto framework that can be used both as a JPA implementation provider and as a standalone technology. Although we focus on Java EE, and thus JPA, in this book, suggesting which strategy delivers the best application design is outside the scope of discussion. We will primarily focus the walkthrough and examples on JPA, but will also give references to Hibernate as we go on.

Optimizing object retrieval

Efficient data loading is the most important factor when we aim at improving the performance of Hibernate and JPA. Since every SQL statement issued to a database bears a cost (from network latency, statement compiling, data handling, and so on), the goal is to minimize the number of statements and know how to tune them so that querying can be as efficient as possible. In the following sections, we will walk you through various optimization techniques and describe how different alternatives may affect performance.

Transactional integrity and performance

Concurrent updates of the same data from different transactions can be very hazardous. Think about ordering flights from a system that won't allow you to be sure that you get any tickets until after the final step of the payment process. An even worse scenario from the health sector, with unthinkable consequences, could be doctors updating the same patient records simultaneously and thus overwriting vital information.

With transactional locking strategies, competing operations in different transactions can be stopped. Using **pessimistic locking** only allows changes to data within the owning transaction. It locks an entire database table row from all changes external to the owning transaction. This is a very secure solution for upholding transactional integrity, but it can also cause deadlocks. It is not very useful or a sound strategy in terms of performance for the often interaction-heavy systems of today because it scales poorly.

Instead, **optimistic locking** is normally recommended. Here, a transaction can perform operations against the same data row that is already "owned" by another transaction. As long as no conflict actually occurs, everything is fine. Should there be a conflict, a `javax.persistence.OptimisticLockException` is thrown when using JPA.

Optimistic locking with row-based versioning is supported in JPA by the use of the `@Version` annotation on an entity's attribute, as shown in the following code:

```
@Version
private Long version;
```

Any update to the entity will cause the `version` attribute to increase by one, making concurrent updates detectable and protecting the transactional integrity.

Limiting retrieved data by pagination

Retrieving more data than is needed from a database is normally a poor design choice that influences performance negatively. Imagine a web-based sales application where you want to show a table list of items; the total amount of items in the database is too large to show in one page of the table, so you should use *pagination*, where a small and manageable set of the total amount of items is shown on each page.

Naturally, you can read all the items from the database with a query, here given in Java using **Java Persistence Query Language** (JPQL), which looks something like the following code:

```
EntityManager em;
Query query = em.createQuery("SELECT i FROM Item i");
```

The JPQL will then translate into the SQL statement:

```
SELECT * FROM Item;
```

This will load all available items from the database into the memory. Depending on your application, you can keep them in the memory and handle sorting and pagination here. Doing so will, however, sooner or later, result in a stale dataset, and any update to the database will not be reflected in your retrieved set of data.

To minimize problems with stale data, you will need to retrieve the dataset each time you flip through the pages of items in the application. Using the same query as mentioned, this will retrieve a lot more data than is needed for a single page. Your application may display 20 lines per page, with an item on each line, while the database may contain thousands of items in total. The overhead of unused data will be overwhelming, and the users will likely suffer from the poor performance of the system.

Instead, you should limit your query to only retrieve the items that will actually be shown (or used) on each page. This is often denoted as *true pagination*. Using JPA, you can use the `setFirstResult(int)` and `setMaxResult(int)` methods of the `javax.persistence.Query` class to set the range of rows that are needed to be retrieved from the database in every situation. Our previous example has now evolved to the following, retrieving 20 items for each page:

```
Query query = em.createQuery("SELECT i FROM Item i");
query.setFirstResult(page * 20);
query.setMaxResults(20);
List<Item> items = query.getResultList();
```

Fetching parent and child objects

All normalized data models pretty much have relations between objects/tables. For the upcoming sections, we will use the object data model given in the following diagram. A `Customer` object can have many orders, and each `Order` instance can contain several `Item` objects:

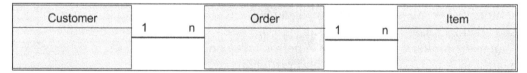

A sample object data model.

In this case, the `Order` object is said to have a *one-to-many* relation to the `Item` object. In JPA, this will be realized by the `@OneToMany` annotation. The following is the (simplified) definition of the items list attribute of the `Order` class:

```
@OneToMany
private List<Item> items;
```

When we retrieve an `Order` object from the database, the related `Item` objects will not be retrieved until they are used (presuming that the `Order` object is attached to the persistence context). This is due to the fact that we use the `LAZY` fetch-type, which is the default for one-to-many relations.

 Using a LAZY strategy is a useful performance strategy when you do not (or rarely) need related objects.

If we want the `Item` objects to be retrieved with the `Order` object right away, we can simply set the fetch-type to `EAGER`. This can be done by defining the `fetch` attribute in the relation annotation as follows:

```
@OneToMany(fetch = FetchType.EAGER)
private List<Item> items;
```

Other relation definitions (and annotations) are one-to-one (`@OneToOne`), many-to-one (`@ManyToOne`), and many-to-many (`@ManyToMany`). The different relation types have different default fetch-behaviors that we encourage all readers to explore as they will affect implementations.

Whether we use the `LAZY` or the `EAGER` fetch-type, the queries to retrieve data can be the same. For example, when one specific `Order` (here `id=10`) is retrieved, the JPQL query will look like the following code:

```
SELECT o FROM Order o WHERE o.id = 10;
```

Then, as we venture into the list of items related to each `Order` object, the `Item` objects will be retrieved by an additional JPQL query, as shown in the following code:

```
SELECT i FROM Item i WHERE i.order.id = 10;
```

As the number of parent objects (here `Order`) increases, these multiple questions can turn out to be a real bottleneck. This is often denoted as **n+1 problem**, and a common solution is to use a single query, using an SQL `JOIN` to retrieve both the parent object and all of its related children objects (`Item`). This is normally much more effective than using multiple queries, but the performance enhancement needs to be weighed against factors of code simplicity and readability.

In our case, the `JOIN` fetch can be implemented in JPQL as follows:

```
FROM Order o LEFT OUTER JOIN FETCH o.items BY o.id
```

Combining pagination and JOIN fetches

Paging features are not implemented internally by JPA, Hibernate, or JDBC but by using the database's native functions that limit the number of records fetched by the query. For this reason, every database will use its *own proprietary syntax*.

This leads to an important aspect to consider: if we query using a JOIN fetch, the logical table created by the database does not necessarily correspond to the collections of objects we deal with. As a matter of fact, the outcome of the join may duplicate orders in the logical tables, but the database doesn't care about that since it's working with tables and not with objects. In order to deal with this problem, Hibernate does not issue a statement with a native SQL instruction (such as LIMIT or ROWNUM). Instead, it fetches all of the records and performs the paging in memory.

 Results from using pagination with firstResult() and maxResults() methods, specified with a collection join fetch, apply in memory in Hibernate.

Using a combination of JOIN fetch and paging often shows fewer throughputs than either of the techniques used separately. So, as a rule of thumb, it is wise to use either JOIN fetches or paging to reduce the time spent in retrieving data. They should, however, not be used together as the result may be a reduction in performance.

Naturally, and as always, you should test and see how the techniques behave in the specific queries in your application and environment.

Improving the speed of collection queries using batches

Imagine a use case with a customer object loading orders lazily. If a Hibernate session or JPA entity manager has 5,000 customers attached to it, then by default, for each first access to one of the customers' order collection, Hibernate will issue an SQL statement to fill that collection. At the end, 5,000 statements will be executed to fetch the order collections.

Batch fetching is an optimization technique of the LAZY select fetching strategy, which can be used to define the identical associations to populate in a single database query. You can apply batch fetching using the Hibernate @BatchSize annotation at class level, as shown in the following code:

```
@Entity @BatchSize(size = 50)
public class Item implements Serializable { ...
```

Alternatively, a default value can be set by the `default_batch_fetch_size` property variable for all classes of a persistence unit, in a `persistence.xml` file, as shown in the following code:

```
<property name="hibernate.default_batch_fetch_size" value="50" />
```

It can also be set per class in an ORM (`orm.xml`) file, as shown in the following code:

```
<class name="Item" batch-size="50">...</class>
```

With these settings, when Hibernate loads its 5,000 customers, it will load the items for the first 50, then for the next 50, and so on.

While referenced collections are seldom loaded, batch fetching is a very effective optimization technique for data retrieval.

Minimizing query compilation with JPA-named queries

Until now, we have used queries defined in the single EJB methods to request data. Instead of spreading queries across methods, JPA provides the possibility to declare them in a standardized way at a class level and to recall them whenever needed. This technique is called **named queries** and is implemented with annotations on (preferably related) the `Entity` classes, as shown in the following example code snippet:

```
@Entity
@NamedQueries({
  @NamedQuery(name = "listAllCustomersWithName",
    query = "FROM Customer c WHERE c.name = :name")
})
public class Customer implements Serializable { ...
```

The advantage, in terms of performance, is that the persistence provider will *precompile* HQL- or JPQL-named queries to SQL as part of the deployment or initialization phase of an application. This avoids the overhead of continuously parsing HQL/JPQL and generating related SQL statements.

Even with a cache for converted queries, dynamic query definition will always be less efficient than using named queries.

Named queries enforce the best practice of using query parameters. Query parameters help to keep the number of distinct SQL strings parsed by the database to a minimum. As databases typically keep a cache of SQL statements on hand for frequently accessed queries, this is an essential part of ensuring peak database performance.

Improving the performance of bulk SQL statements

Many updates to multiple rows and columns in a database can be performed with a single SQL statement. For entity-based inserts and updates, grouping multiple statements into a single SQL statement is considerably more advanced (if even possible) and often not desirable from design and business-flow perspectives.

Instead, looping over similar inserts/updates of an entity is a more common behavior. To avoid the burden of synchronizing the entity classes with the database for every operation, you should set a fetch size as before, and then manually perform a flush as the bulk of operations reaches the desired flush-size level.

The larger the bulk of statements, the better the performance achieved, but the more memory used. It's just one more tradeoff between memory and performance.

Entity caching

A major justification for using object/relational persistence layers against direct JDBC is their potential for caching. Caching structurally implies a temporary store to keep data for quicker access later on. Although nothing beats a good database design and good fetching strategies, there is no doubt that caching can have a serious impact on performance for some kinds of applications.

We will introduce the JPA caching system with its implementation in its provider, Hibernate, and show how to enable and use the first and second level cache. This information and these rules can be applied to caching in general, and they are valid for more than just Hibernate applications.

A cache is a representation of the current database state either in memory or on the disk of the application server machine. In JPA/Hibernate, there are different types of caches, used for different purposes. Let us first take a look at the following cache types:

- **The first-level cache (L1C or 1LC)**: This is related to the JPA persistence context and entity manager, which will translate to the session in Hibernate. This cache caches managed entities within the current persistence context. This is also a mandatory cache that depends on the life-length of the persistence context scope—transaction or extended.

- **The second-level cache (L2C or 2LC)**: This cache works at the JPA EntityManagerFactory (SessionFactory in Hibernate) level and is responsible for caching objects across persistence contexts. This is an optional cache.

- **The query cache**: This is responsible for caching queries and their results. The following diagram shows where Hibernate caches are located in the path of a JDBC connection:

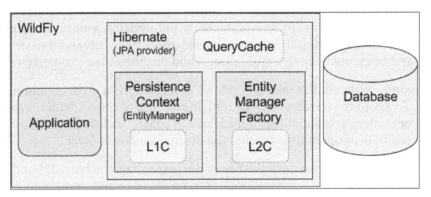

JPA components and caches

The first-level cache

Nothing is needed to enable or use the L1C. It's, by default, on and it cannot be disabled. Using the entity manager operations guarantees that there will be one and only one object instance within a single persistence context for any particular database row. The same entity can, however, be managed in another user's transaction. The optimistic or the pessimistic locking strategy should be used for controlling transactions and the level of integrity.

The second-level cache

The L2C is responsible for caching entities across persistence contexts on the EntityManagerFactory level. This is often known as the *Entity cache*, and caching with L2C is normally transparent to an application.

In JPA 1.0, the specification did not define the concept of a shared cache. As of JPA 2.0, it is defined but optional, so providers do not have to implement it. However, Hibernate and most other major providers do implement it.

 As the L2C existence is still optional for JPA providers, portable applications should not completely rely on its support for SLA compliance.

This cache is beneficial because it avoids database access for already loaded entities and is faster for reading entities that are unmodified and frequently accessed.

On the negative side, L2C can be very memory-consuming for large amounts of objects. Data can be stale for updated objects. Performance can suffer significantly depending on what locking mechanism is used (optimistic/pessimistic). For frequent or concurrently updated entities, L2C scales poorly.

Using L2C in the wrong context may actually degrade performance.

 Use L2C for entities that are read often, modified infrequently, and not critical if stale.

Hibernate also provides a pluggable architecture where different cache implementations can be plugged in and used as L2C. In WildFly, *Infinispan* is utilized as an L2C cache provider for Hibernate.

The L2C is not enabled or configured by default in WildFly or Hibernate. To enable L2C in WildFly with Hibernate, first add the following configuration to the properties block in your application's `persistence.xml` file:

```
<property name="hibernate.cache.use_second_level_cache" value="true"/>
```

A *cache mode* is also set in the configuration file using the `share-cache-mode` tag (as shown in the following code) as the equivalent can naturally be set on EntityManagerFactory in code as well:

```
<shared-cache-mode>ENABLE_SELECTIVE</shared-cache-mode>
```

Depending on what this mode is set to, individual entities may need to be configured in order to be enabled for L2C. The different cache modes are described in the JEE7 documentation as follows:

Cache mode setting	Description
ALL	All entity data is stored in the L2C for this persistence unit.
NONE	No data is cached in the persistence unit. The persistence provider must not cache any data.
ENABLE_SELECTIVE	Enable caching for entities that have been explicitly set with the `@Cacheable` annotation.
DISABLE_SELECTIVE	Enable caching for all entities, except those that have been explicitly set with the `@Cacheable(false)` annotation.
UNSPECIFIED	The caching behavior for the persistence unit is undefined. The persistence provider's default caching behavior will be used.

If the mode is ENABLE_SELECTIVE, we will need to configure each entity that we'd like to enable for L2C with the @Cacheable annotation (Hibernate uses the @Cache annotation) on class level. This can also be configured using XML.

Using annotations, this will look like the following code:

```
@Entity @Cacheable
public class Customer implements Serializable { ...
```

How data is stored in the L2C can be configured using a retrieval-mode property named javax.persistence.retrieveMode. This property can have the values USE (default), BYPASS, and REFRESH of the javax.persistence.CacheStoreMode, and it is set in code for an entity manager as follows:

```
EntityManager em = ...;
em.setProperty("javax.persistence.cache.storeMode", "BYPASS");
```

Alternatively, it is possible to set the retrieval mode per query using a *hint*. Hints are explored in more detail in the next section.

The different property values affect the L2C as follows:

- USE: When data is read from or committed to the database, the cache data is created or updated. If data already exists in the cache, no refresh will be forced when data is read from the database. The cache has moderate speed, but it may contain stale objects.

- BYPASS: The cache is unchanged (bypassed and not updated) when data is read from or committed to the database. This makes the cache fast but very volatile as it sooner or later is likely to contain stale objects.

- REFRESH: When data is read from or committed to the database, the cache data is created or updated on database reads, and a refresh is forced on data in the cache. This is a safer but slower option.

If you want to inspect your objects existing in the cache, it can be retrieved as follows:

```
EntityManager em = ...;
Cache cache = em.getEntityManagerFactory().getCache();
Long pk = ...;
boolean existInCache = cache.contains(Customer.class, pk);
```

Similarly, clearing the cache of one specific object instance (with a given primary key), all objects of one entity type, or all objects, is easily done with the following three method calls, respectively:

```
cache.evict(Customer.class, pk);
cache.evict(Customer.class);
cache.evictAll();
```

The query cache

The entity cache requires that you access your database rows by means of its primary key. Sometimes, this strategy cannot be applied, and you need a more flexible way to collect your data, such as caching the result of a specific query, like in the following code:

```
List<Customer> customers =
    em.createQuery("from Customer c where c.name = :name);
```

Using the query cache, the statement that comprised the query can be cached as well, including any parameter values along with the primary keys of all entities that comprise the result set.

Hibernate does not cache the state of the actual entities in the cache. Only identifier values and results of value types are cached. The query cache should, therefore, always be used along with the L2C for entities that are expected to be part of the result set.

To enable the query cache in Hibernate, first add the following property to the property block in the `persistence.xml` file of an application, as shown in the following code:

```
<property name="hibernate.cache.use_query_cache" value="true"/>
```

Then, the queries that will be stored in the cache need to be defined. This is done by a **query hint** in the annotations on a named query as in the following code:

```
@NamedQueries({
  NamedQuery(name = "findCustomersByName",
    query = "FROM Customer c WHERE c.name = :name",
    hints = { @QueryHint(
    name = "org.hibernate.cacheable",
    value = "true") } )
} )
```

Alternatively, this step can be performed on a specific query by using the following code:

```
Query query = ...
query.setHint("org.hibernate.cacheable", new Boolean(true));
```

Query caching, as with all caching, has a cost. If a query is run only a very few times or seldom, using caching is likely to be more expensive than running a query without it.

You may wonder how your Hibernate caching provider understands whether the data stored in the query cache is synchronized with the content of the database. The answer is in the timestamp cache, which is actually used to decide if a cached query result set is stale. Hibernate looks in the timestamp cache for the timestamp of the most recent insertion, update, or deletion made to the queried table. If it's later than the timestamp of the cached query results, then the cached results are discarded and a new query is issued.

The Hibernate query cache should not be confused with the query cache available for many databases, such as the **Postgres Query Cache** (**PQC**) for PostgreSQL.

Query hints

Using query hints is a powerful feature of the JPA that allows dynamic and even adaptive tuning of queries. Query hints are often performance-related and implementation-specific per provider. For JPA and Hibernate, the following EJB3 hints are available:

Hint	Description
`javax.persistence.cache.retrieveMode`	`CacheRetrieveMode.[BYPASS|USE]`
`javax.persistence.cache.storeMode`	`CacheStoreMode.[BYPASS|REFRESH|USE]`
`org.hibernate.timeout`	Query timeout in seconds (`new Integer(10)`)
`org.hibernate.fetchSize`	Number of rows fetched by the JDBC driver per roundtrip (`new Integer(50)`)
`org.hibernate.comment`	Add a comment to the SQL query, useful for the DBA (`new String("fetch all orders in 1 statement")`)
`org.hibernate.cacheable`	Whether or not a query is cacheable (`new Boolean(true)`); defaults to false
`org.hibernate.cacheMode`	Override the cache mode for this query (`CacheMode.REFRESH`)
`org.hibernate.cacheRegion`	Cache region of this query (`new String("regionName")`)
`org.hibernate.readOnly`	Entities retrieved by this query will be loaded in a read-only mode, where Hibernate will never dirty-check them or make changes persistent (`new Boolean(true)`); default to false
`org.hibernate.flushMode`	Flush mode used for this query (useful to pass Hibernate-specific flush modes, in particular `MANUAL`).
`org.hibernate.cacheMode`	Cache mode used for this query

The hint scopes (global definitions are valid for all lower scopes, but lower-positioned definitions override the global) can be defined as follows:

- For an entire persistence unit: Using properties in the `persistence.xml` file
- For EntityManagerFactory: Using the `createEntityManagerFacotory()` method
- For EntityManager: Using the `createEntityManager()` or `setProperty()` method
- For a named query definition: Using the `@QueryHints` annotation
- For a specific query execution: Using the `setHint()` method

Entity versus query cache

Entity caching takes advantage of the fact that a database row (that reflects an entity's state) can be locked, with cache updates applied with that lock in place. This is extremely useful to ensure cache consistency across the cluster.

There is no clear database analog to a query result set that can be efficiently locked to ensure consistency in the cache. As a result, the fail-fast semantics used with the PUT operation of entity caching are not available; instead, query caching has semantics akin to an entity insertion, including costly synchronous cluster updates.

To make things worse, Hibernate must aggressively invalidate query results from the cache any time any instance of one of the entity classes involved in the query's WHERE clause changes. As stated before, this is done by means of the timestamp cache, which checks the latest timestamp for every operation executed on a query.

As a consequence of these semantics, you need to use query cache with caution and mainly for data that is read-only or seldom updated. Always monitor your application performance with the cache disabled first and then with the cache enabled. If you don't see any substantial benefit from caching your queries, then you should stay away from query cache, which will otherwise consume system resources.

Optimizing data synchronization

For most JPA providers, including Hibernate, the default strategy for flushing data to a database is to set it to `FlushMode.AUTO`. This means that uncommitted changes are flushed before queries and on commit and flush operations. This ensures that the changes are visible for the upcoming query.

The `FlushMode.COMMIT` decouples transaction demarcation from the synchronization. It only flushes changes on explicit commit and flush operations.

By using manual flushing, execution of insertions and updates, that are sent in bulk, can be delayed.

Summary

Performance-tuning the persistent layer means starting at the bottom with a good database design with correct indexes, well tuned queries, and a thought-through choice of isolation level. If JDBC is used directly, make sure that connection pooling is used, and investigate what the application may gain by using fetch size, batch updates, and prepared statements.

With Hibernate and the JPA specifications, the gap between the relational database layer and the Java objects is bridged. In the Java layer, tuning can be performed using the following techniques and strategies:

- Retrieving data with Hibernate and JPA requires applying the correct fetch strategy. Lazily loaded data avoids the cost of early loading relationships. This, however, carries the problem of additional queries executed to fetch the parent-child relationship, also known as *n+1 problem*.

- Pagination can be used by means of the `setFirstResult()` or `setMaxResults()` method of the `Query` class. This allows loading a smaller page of data with consistent time saving.

- Using the `JOIN` fetches, you can combine data extraction of the parent-child relationship with a single SQL statement. In most cases, this optimization is the logical solution to the n+1 problem.

- Batch fetching is an optimization of the `LAZY` select fetching strategy, which can be used to define how many identical associations to populate in a single database query.

The easy appliance and portability of caching is one of the main benefits of Hibernate/JPA over JDBC programming. There are basically three types of caching:

- The first-level cache allows caching objects within the current persistence context (entity manager)

- The second-level cache is responsible for caching objects across the persistence contexts of an `EntityManagerFactory`

- The query cache stores queries, including variables and result sets

You should cache data which is read-only or seldom modified.

Before applying any caching strategy, monitor your system performance without a cache. Then, you can progressively try to introduce caches, verifying whether the performance has increased.

Expect the most consistent performance gains with entity caching. Use query caching with caution as frequent updates may reduce (or negate completely) the benefit of this cache.

After digging around in the persistence layer, we will next discuss how to tune the web container in WildFly. Jump on!

7
Tuning the Web Container in WildFly

In this chapter, we will introduce **Undertow**, which is the brand new web container in WildFly. We will have a quick look at its internals and then continue our performance focus and look at the available tuning configuration options in the container. Finally, we look at the benefits of a web server such as Apache HTTPD with mod_cluster, acting as a frontend to our application server.

Enter Undertow

A vital part of an application server is its web container. In the previous incarnations of WildFly (when it was named JBoss AS), the old container, **JBoss Web Server** (**JWS** — https://www.jboss.org/jbossweb/), that was based on a fork of **Apache Tomcat** (http://tomcat.apache.org/), acted as an embedded Java EE web container.

As of WildFly 8, JWS has been replaced by technologies from the Java-based web server, Undertow (http://undertow.io/). Similar to JWS/Tomcat, Undertow can act both as a web server and a Java EE web container. It can also run in embedded mode, just as it does in WildFly, as well as in standalone mode.

Undertow was initially designed for speed. It is lightweight and adaptable, allowing it to handle new features and advanced technologies such as the **WebSockets** API and **HTTP Upgrades**, which we will discuss further on. The Undertow project is relatively new but has already come far when it comes to its initial goals. As it matures further in areas such as documentation and configuration possibilities, its future looks very bright.

By making use of XNIO (`http://www.jboss.org/xnio/`), which is a framework based on the Java **New Input Output** (**NIO** or **New I/O**) API, Undertow receives vital support for the speed of both blocking and non-blocking I/O. These technologies and techniques are utilized by, for example, WebSockets and asynchronous servlets.

> Although there is support for non-blocking I/O through the core I/O APIs (NIO/XNIO) that Undertow is built upon, most of the things that Java EE applications use are backed by the servlet container and Java servlets are defined to utilize blocking I/O. So, by having servlet-based applications, you never use the non-blocking I/O mode to serve requests unless you're using WebSockets (a new asynchronous technology) or implementing the `io.undertow.servlet.ServletExtension` proprietary interface.

Undertow internals

Internally, Undertow is assembled by listeners and a chain of building blocks, named handlers.

A listener is a component that handles protocol-specific incoming calls that, in turn, are forwarded to a handler chain. At the time of writing this book, the following three listeners are supported out of the box:

- HTTP
- HTTPS
- **Apache JServ Protocol (AJP)**: This has no support for HTTP Upgrades

These listeners are, at their core, XNIO listeners that in turn are a higher level of an NIO channel.

A handler is basically a Java class that can add almost any functionality, for example, security, error page handling, metrics or virtual host support. The handlers in Undertow are chained together and allow the construction of a highly dynamic platform. A platform that can be anything from a simple HTTP processor within your code to a full-fledged Java EE servlet container or more. The handlers are also very dynamic and adaptive as they can select the next handler in the chain based on the current request and its content. This paves the way for HTTP Upgrades. The listeners and a sample chain of handlers are visualized in the following diagram:

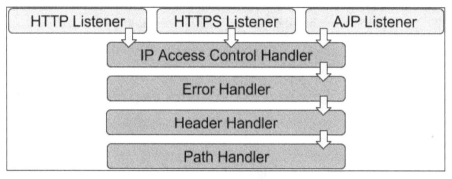

Undertow listeners with a simple chain of handlers

Creating a custom handler can be quite useful. It could, for example, collect performance measurements or metrics, be used as a tool in tuning, and for detailed SLA compliance. At the time of writing this book, it is not possible to simply configure the Undertows handler chain in WildFly. Therefore, we will, only briefly describe how to implement a custom handler by implementing the io.undertow.server.HttpHandler interface as shown in the following code snippet of MyHandler:

```
Import io.undertow.server.HttpHandler;

public class MyHandler implements HttpHandler {
  private final HttpHandler next;

  public MyHandler(HttpHandler next) {
    this.next = next;
  }
  @Override
    public void handleRequest(HttpServerExchange exchange)
    throws Exception {
      // *** your fabulous code here ***
      next.handleRequest(exchange);
  }}
```

HTTP Upgrades

A core feature of Undertow is its support for HTTP Upgrade.

Generically, this involves starting communication with the server by one protocol (often the basic plain-text HTTP 1.1), which is then "upgraded" to another version or, as is more common in WildFly, changed into another protocol entirely. This mechanism is very useful to multiplex between various remote protocols over the standard web container port (which, by default, is set to 8080 in WildFly/Undertow) for HTTP. This is very useful in environments where default port access is normally disabled for everything except for, for example, SSH (22), HTTP (80), and HTTPS (443).

In WildFly, HTTP Upgrade is used for most protocols, including RMI and JNDI.

The default caching of static resources

By default, Undertow is configured to cache static resources. Unfortunately, it seems that no information related to monitoring or configuration is available in the current version of WildFly. To disable the cache, the `default-buffer-cache` attribute needs to be removed by using the following configuration:

```
<servlet-container default-buffer-cache="default"/>
```

Server and container topologies

It is possible to run several web servers or web containers in a single WildFly instance. The practical use for these, however, seems quite limited for the time being. Although Undertow benefits from port reduction and performance improvements, resulting in an overall smaller memory footprint, it is still advisable to not use several web containers in the same WildFly instance.

More than one web container/server would involve a more complex configuration (in the `standalone.xml` or `domain.xml` file). Also, as the console does not (yet) have support for it, administration is limited to CLI.

Starting a new WildFly application server instance is also administratively easy and not a very expensive operation resource-wise. With all this taken into account, there are not much incentive for starting a web container on its own, unless in very extreme cases of performance.

Using XNIO

Undertow has been designed to make full use of the *ultra-high-performance* XNIO framework.

XNIO, in turn, builds on the Java NIO API. XNIO provides full NIO support and enhances it by providing an enriched and simplified API with a partially higher abstraction layer. XNIO also offers other related functionalities, such as callbacks, multicast, and socket support (both blocking and non-blocking).

NIO basics

The Java NIO API itself was introduced with J2SE 1.4, enhancing the overall standard I/O performance and including support for native memory.

The following are the main components of NIO:

- Channel
- Buffer
- Selectors

A NIO *channel* is a component that a client can use to write data to or read data from. The standard channels currently support both file and network (both UDP and TCP) access. They can be asynchronous and they write incoming data to or read outgoing data from NIO buffers.

The NIO *buffers* are used to store data and are based on the datatype of what they can store. The `java.nio.ByteByffer` is probably the most common datatype, but all primitive types are supported. You put data into a buffer, "flip" it (change its read-write mode), and then take data out of it.

A NIO *selector* is a sort of inspector that can handle several channels. This is useful as it optimizes thread usage by letting one thread handle several channels.

XNIO Workers

In XNIO, the buffers are used for fast data storage just as in NIO. New and important is however is the concept of *Workers*. A worker has the role of a coordinator that creates listener channels and manages thread pools. These pools are either for *worker threads*, that are responsible for various user-defined actions, or for *I/O threads* that handle things such as cancellation events and callbacks for reading or writing events.

More of how the WildFly listeners, workers, and buffer pools relate and how they can be configured will be explained more in detail in the following section.

Tuning Undertow

As mentioned earlier, WildFly handles traffic on different protocols through listeners. The only one that is enabled out of the box is the HTTP listener. If support is needed for AJP and HTTPS, the corresponding listeners will need to be configured and enabled. In earlier versions of the application server, there were quite a few settings that had to do with performance tuning on these protocol configurations (mainly thread pools settings). This is not the case in Undertow as thread handling is handled earlier in the stack by the I/O subsystem and using XNIO.

Two key components are configured by the Undertow subsystem. First, there is a XNIO worker pointed out by the worker attribute and named default by default. Secondly, there is a buffer pool pointed out by the buffer pool attribute. Even though clear by context, this is — like so many other things in in the default configuration of WildFly — also named default. We will now have a more detailed look into these components.

Worker

Our first component is the worker. The actual name value of the default worker for a specific listener (in this example, the: http-listener) can be retrieved by the following CLI command:

```
/subsystem=undertow/server=default-server/http-listener=default:read-attribute(name=worker)
{
  "outcome" => "success",
  "result" => "default"
}
```

 Many workers can be defined in WildFly, and each worker can serve one or more listeners.

The same information can also be explored in the Admin Console, as shown in the following screenshot:

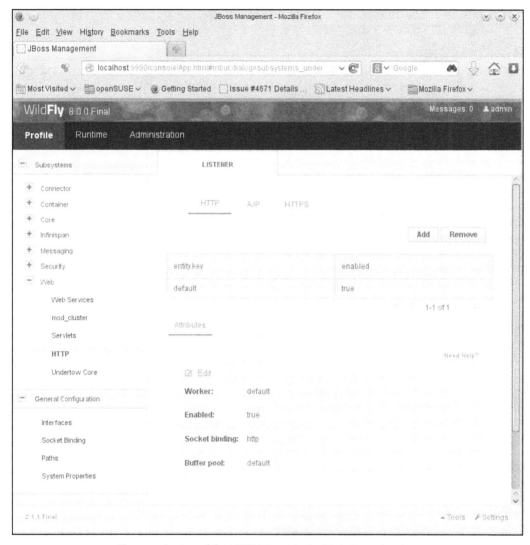

The console view of the HTTP listener in the Undertow subsystem

The name points to a worker configuration in the I/O subsystem called **default**. The available attributes of the worker can be listed using the following CLI command:

```
/subsystem=io/worker=default:read-resource-description
```

The same attributes are also available in the Admin Console, as shown in the following screenshot:

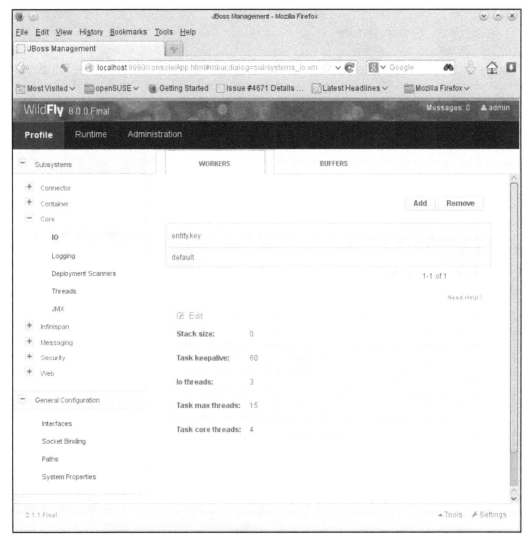

The console view of the default worker in the I/O subsystem

The following table explains the attributes and their impact on performance:

Parameter	Description	Default value	Performance hint
`stack-size`	The stack size of a created thread	0 (uses the default setting of JVM)	The normal thread stack size logic applies. A value that is too large uses an unnecessary amount of memory and a value that is too low may result in OOMEs
`task-keepalive`	The number of seconds to keep a connection from a client alive	60	Very dependent on the use case. If unsure, start with the default value and test, test, test
`io-threads`	The number of IO threads created for non-blocking tasks	3	The Undertow documentation says 1 per CPU core is reasonable, but tests have shown that # *CPU core* * 2 to be even better
`task-max-threads`	The maximum number of threads	15	# *CPU core* * 16
`task-core-threads`	The number of threads created for blocking tasks (such as servlet calls)	4	Depends on the application, but the general advice would be at least 10 per CPU core

The buffer pool

The other component pointed out by Undertow is a buffer pool. Just as with the worker setup, the default name of the pool for a specific listener (in this case, `http listener`) is pointed out by the configuration and can be retrieved by using the following CLI command:

```
/subsystem=undertow/server=default-server/http-listener=default:read-attribute(name=buffer-pool)
{
    "outcome" => "success"
    "result" => "default"
}
```

This points once again to a setup in the I/O subsystem:

```
/subsystem=io/buffer-pool=default:read-resource-description
```

The same attributes are also available in the Admin Console, as shown in the following screenshot:

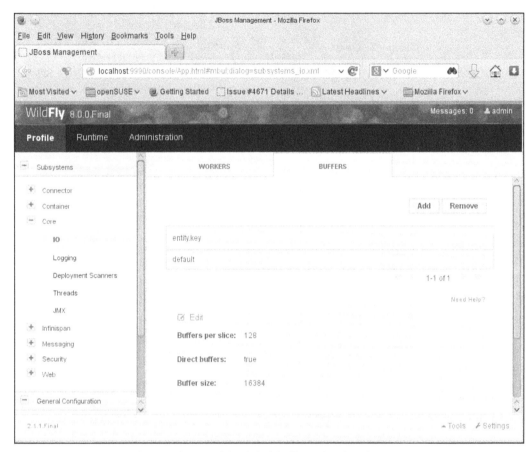

The console view of the default buffer in the I/O subsystem

The following table explains the attributes and their impact on performance:

Parameter	Description	Default value	Performance hint
direct-buffers	Should the buffer pool use direct buffers, this instructs the JVM to use native (if possible) I/O operations on the buffers.	true	true
buffer-size	The size of the buffer	16384	A general suggestion is to match the socket buffer size in the underlying OS (16 kb is the default for Linux)

Tuning the servlet container and JSP compilation

A feature in the servlet container in Undertow that relates to performance is the option to ignore flushes on a servlet output stream. Ignoring flushes can provide better performance in most cases. The current setting can be investigated using the following CLI command:

```
/subsystem=undertow/servlet-container=default:read-attribute
(name=ignore-flush)
```

The default value of the `ignore-flush` attribute is `false` and can be easily changed to `true` using the following command in the CLI:

```
/subsystem=undertow/servlet-container=default:write-
attribute(name=ignore-flush, value=true)
```

An MBean named `jboss.as:subsystem=undertow,servlet-container=default` is also available. The following screenshot shows you the JConsole view of the attributes of the default servlet container:

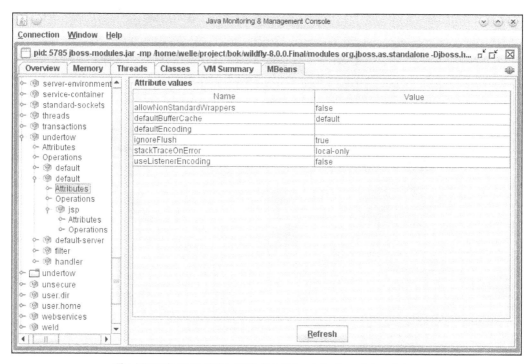

The JConsole view of the attributes of the default servlet container

The setup is also available through the Admin Console, as shown in the following screenshot:

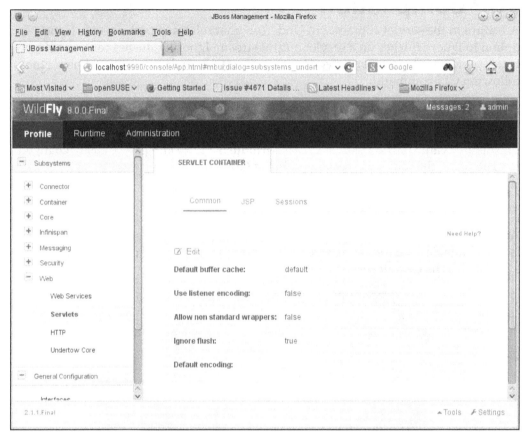

The Admin Console view of the attributes of the default servlet container

Tuning hints for Jastow

The JSP engine in Undertow is called **Jastow** and is a fork of the **Apache Jasper** project. In the following table, we list a subset of the available configuration attributes that are related to performance improvement and that may be of interest in production(-like) environments:

Parameter	Description	Default value	Performance hint
development	Recompiles JSP without the application redeployment	false	false
trim-spaces	Removes unneeded spaces to minimize the response size	false	It may be of interest to set this to true if network is a limitation
tag-pooling	Pools and reuses tag handler instances	true	true
check-interval	These are the number of seconds between checks if a JSP needs to be recompiled (only valid if the flag development is set to true)	0 (=disabled)	Disable it by setting the flag development to false
modification-test-interval	This is the maximum age in seconds before JSP is recompiled (only valid if the flag development is set to true)	4	Disable it by setting the flag development to false
recompile-on-fail	This decides whether failed JSP compilations should trigger recompile for each request	false	false
generate-strings-as-char-arrays	Converts strings into character arrays	false	May improve performance if set to true in some cases

All these values (and others) regarding the JSP compilation can be retrieved using the CLI. The following CLI command lists the available JSP settings together with short descriptions:

```
/subsystem=undertow/servlet-container=default/setting=jsp:read-resource-description
```

It is also possible to get the values through JMX using the Mbean `jboss.
as:subsystem=undertow,servlet-container=default,setting=jsp`. The
following screenshot shows you the JConsole view of the JSP attributes of the
default servlet container:

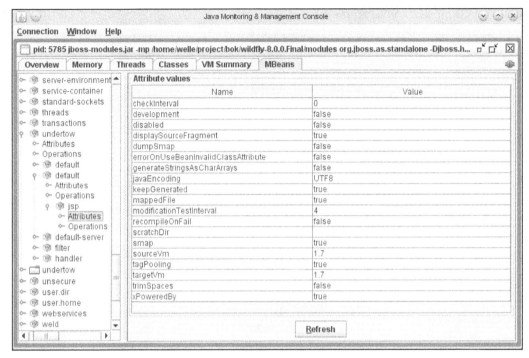

The JConsole view of JSP attributes of the default servlet container

The same information is also available through the Admin Console, as shown in the
following screenshot:

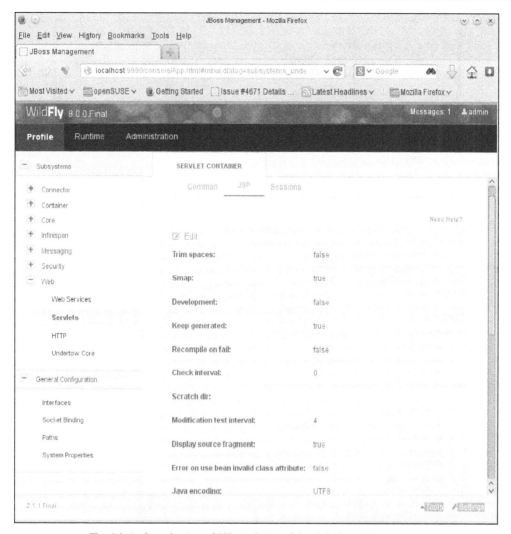

The Admin Console view of JSP attributes of the default servlet container

Using Apache as a frontend

A quite common setup for Java EE application servers, where clients are use HTTP, is to have a native web server, such as Apache HTTPD, acting as a *frontend server*. This setup has the following potential benefits:

- **HTTPS termination**: Handling the computations of HTTPS encryption and decryption takes a lot of CPU usage. A native stack (as in Apache HTTPD) or even designated hardware, is normally more optimized and faster than handling these computations in Java.

> In this book, we use Apache HTTPD as an example, as it is very versatile and is the most common web server in the world. Several options, such as *nginx* and *lighttpd*, are however available and should be evaluated before deciding on which to use.

In most scenarios, it is allowed to terminate HTTPS in the frontend (that can execute on it's own hardware that is separate from the application server) and use unencrypted traffic within the infrastructure of the application server. Your IT security policies and business requirements related to performance should give direction to what is allowed and needed for your environment.

Using a web server such as Apache HTTPD for HTTPS termination relieves the computational burden of encryption/decryption on the application server and its hardware

- **Static content**: Even though the new Java EE web containers have improved in serving static content (using internal caches and so on), an application with much static content may very well benefit from locating that material in a native web server. Thus, it lets the Java EE / servlet web container focus on more dynamic and executing content.

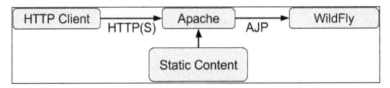

Static content placed in the web server, Apache HTTPD, enables the application server, WildFly, to focus on more runtime tasks and dynamic content

> For applications that are required to handle very large loads, there exist some interesting options in terms of web accelerators. Among these specialized caching solutions, it is worth exploring, for example, Apache mod_cache (http://httpd.apache.org/docs/current/mod/mod_cache.html) and Varnish Cache (https://www.varnish-cache.org/).

- **Demilitarized Zone (DMZ)**: Some infrastructure and security-related scenarios mandate the use of a DMZ in front of all applications that interact with internal systems. In these cases, a web server put in the DMZ can act as a frontend for the WildFly servers that are running in an internal network zone.

The Apache HTTPD web server can act as a gateway in DMZ, handling, for example, traffic traceability and security access to a secured internal zone where application servers such as WildFly run

- **Load balancing**: A web server such as Apache HTTPD can, with some extra modules such as mod_cluster, act as a software load balancer in front of a collection of WildFly instances. The web server (load balancer) then provides functionality for both load balancing and failover. This will be discussed more in detail in the last chapter of the book as we dissect WildFly clusters.

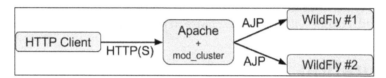

The Apache HTTPD and mod_cluster act as a load balancer, directing traffic, by some balancing algorithm, to the underlying WildFly application servers

HTTP and AJP

The HTTP protocol was not originally designed with focus on performance. Instead, its main focus was simplicity and ease of understanding. Its simplicity actually makes it humanly readable and very easy to work with.

Interpreting the HTTP protocol into a more binary representation requires quite an amount of CPU overhead in terms of both encoding and decoding. An example of this is having a web server frontend where incoming HTTP calls first need to be decoded (after any HTTPS termination is performed) and then encoded to HTTP again before sending the call on to an application server, where a final HTTP decoding must be performed. Outgoing calls must go through the same but reversed operations.

To aid this constant and costly high-level encoding-decoding, **Apache JServ Protocol (AJP)**, http://tomcat.apache.org/connectors-doc/ajp/ajpv13a.html), was invented. It is a binary protocol that can carry everything that HTTP can, but it is less CPU intensive to encode and decode. For performance reasons, it is highly recommended that you use AJP instead of HTTP between the Apache HTTPD web server and WildFly.

The functionality of handling a request dispatch to a backend server is made possible in Apache HTTPD through some module plugins. The most common plugins are listed as follows:

- **mod_proxy**: http://httpd.apache.org/docs/2.4/mod/mod_proxy.html
- **mod_jk**: http://tomcat.apache.org/connectors-doc/
- **mod_cluster**: https://www.jboss.org/mod_cluster

While mod_jk has traditionally been the most commonly used out of these, mod_cluster is more modern, easier to configure, and is also well integrated with WildFly. Therefore, this is also the plugin that we use for all examples in the book. As we use just one WildFly instance in this scenario, the remaining load balancing and failover features of mod_cluster will be covered more in detail in a later chapter.

Configuration

We will set up a scenario where we want to configure an Apache HTTPD web server in front of a single non-clustered WildFly. The mod_cluster subsystem in WildFly is not enabled for non-clustered setups by default, so we need to add it to our setup.

 No matter which Apache plugin you choose, there is a really nice application available at http://lbconfig.appspot.com/, which helps you generate a good setup depending on your topology. Note that the generated JBoss setup is not correct for WildFly but should still provide good information.

The configuration consists of two major parts: one in Apache HTTPD and one in WildFly.

The Apache HTTPD configuration

The easiest way to get an Apache HTTPD with mod_cluster up and running is to download a ready-to-use Apache, bundled with mod_cluster, from: `https://www.jboss.org/mod_cluster/downloads`.

Otherwise, you have to download the required modules from the same website, install them into your existing HTTPD, and add some minimal configuration. Note the IP address (`192.168.1.200`) and port (`6666`), both of which will be used in the WildFly configuration as well. The following lines need to be added in `httpd.conf` (or referenced files):

```
LoadModule proxy_module mod_proxy.so
LoadModule proxy_ajp_module mod_proxy_ajp.so
LoadModule slotmem_module mod_slotmem.so
LoadModule manager_module mod_manager.so
LoadModule proxy_cluster_module mod_proxy_cluster.so
LoadModule advertise_module mod_advertise.so
...
<IfModule manager_module>
  Listen 192.168.1.200:6666
  <VirtualHost 192.168.1.200:6666>
    <Directory />
      Order deny,allow
      Deny from all
      Allow from 192.168.1
    </Directory>

    ServerAdvertise On:192.168.1.200:6666
    EnableMCPMReceive

    <Location /mod_cluster-manager>
      SetHandler mod_cluster-manager
      Order deny,allow
      Deny from all
      Allow from 192.168.1
    </Location>
  </VirtualHost>
</IfModule>
```

The last part that defines `mod_cluster-manager` is optional and provides a status page available at `http://192.168.1.200:6666/mod_cluster-manager`, showing you various kinds of information about the connected WildFly server (or servers, as in most cases).

The WildFly configuration

Enabling the mod_cluster subsystem for a non-clustered WildFly is done by adding the mod_cluster subsystem with minimal configuration and an AJP listener (as WildFly isn't configured with one enabled out of the box) by performing the following steps:

1. Start with adding the mod_cluster extension by using the following CLI command:

    ```
    /extension=org.jboss.as.modcluster:add
    ```

2. Then, add an AJP listener by using the following command:

    ```
    /subsystem=undertow/server=default-server/ajp-
    listener=ajp:add(socket-binding=ajp, scheme="http")
    ```

3. Finally, add a (here minimal) mod_cluster configuration by using the following commands:

    ```
    /subsystem=modcluster:add
    ```

    ```
    /subsystem=modcluster/mod-cluster-config=configuration:add
    (proxy-list="192.168.1.200:6666", connector="ajp")
    ```

    This tells WildFly to send information to `192.168.1.200` on port `6666`, which fits well with the earlier configured Apache's dedicated virtual host for mod_cluster.

After installing mod_cluster and configuring WildFly, as shown in the preceding steps, your web applications deployed on WildFly should be automatically available through the Apache HTTPD frontend server. This allows Apache HTTPD to handle static content and HTTPS termination. An HTTPS setup will need a more detailed configuration, but that is outside the scope of this book. By viewing the mod_cluster status page at `http://192.168.1.200:6666/mod_cluster-manager`, it can be verified that the setup is correct. The following screenshot shows you the content of the mod_cluster status page:

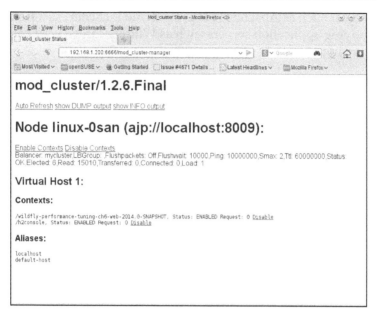

The mod_cluster admin page

The screenshot shows us that there are two web applications deployed on the WildFly server (`wildfly-performance-tuning-ch6-web-2014.0-SNAPSHOT` and `h2console`) and that these will be accessible by clients that go through Apache HTTPD.

Summary

In this chapter, we learned that the old web container — JBoss Web Server — of JBoss AS has been replaced by Undertow. This new web server/container is blazing fast and highly adaptive to handle new technologies.

Support for HTTP, HTTPS, and AJP is available through listeners that connect to a chain of handlers that, in turn, provide dynamic functionality.

Undertow is based on the XNIO framework that, supports and enhances Java NIO.

There are relatively few tuning points in Undertow, but heed should be taken for the available worker pools, buffer pools, and JSP compilation attributes. As always, the needs of your specific use case and environment can only be satisfied by tests.

Using a web server such as Apache HTTPD (with mod_cluster) as a frontend to one or many underlying application servers such as WildFly can be very beneficiary and allows the following:

- HTTPS termination
- Static content handling
- DMZ
- Load balancing

After setting the stage with the foundation of a web container, we now move into the tuning of the actual Java EE web applications that are to be executed in the container.

8
Tuning Web Applications and Services

In this chapter, you will learn about how to write fast and efficient Java EE based web applications and services by the use of some common design and tuning techniques.

From a bird's eye view, all web applications can arguably and roughly be divided into the following two broad areas:

- **Business-to-Consumer (B2C) applications**: In these applications, the user interacts through a **User Interface** (**UI**), usually in a browser, with server-side business logic and data that often resides in one or more legacy systems. The typical archetype of a B2C application based on Java EE is engineered using dynamic web pages (JSP/servlets) and/or frameworks based on a component-driven UI design model (JSF). WebSockets is a new and exciting player in this field.

- **Business-to-Business (B2B) applications**: These typically involve the exchange of information between businesses with legacy systems and makes use of **Service Oriented Architecture** (**SOA**). They are also common paradigms of the integration of heterogeneous systems, which are often used in and by an **Enterprise Service Bus** (**ESB**) platform. In Java EE, a B2B application that uses SOA is most often realized using web services and/or RESTful services.

Although these areas sometimes float together and overlap, especially as SOA becomes increasingly utilized within application stacks, this chapter has been split into two main sections that dissect each respective area. In the first section, we will discuss the performance tuning of web applications with a focus on different Java EE frameworks and related technologies and consequently, in the second section, we will talk about the performance tuning of Java EE based services.

Web applications

Web applications of today are almost always built with some kind of web framework. These frameworks exist in vast numbers that seem to rise by the day. No matter which language you favor, there is likely to be a framework out there for you. Determining what or which frameworks are actually suitable for your organization and use cases is, however, not always an easy task.

Choosing a web framework

When it comes to adopting new technologies, many of the decision points are mainly organizational and related to the business. When an organization intends to adopt an application-development framework, it is typically looking to cover the following requirements:

- Adaptivity and business-related integration possibilities with existing products of interest for the organization (internal and external)

- The ability to cover current and foreseeable business requirements

- Address complexities and maximize the developer productivity, which can often be done by having simple but feature-rich frameworks that minimize or reduce the amount of code (and sometimes even configuration, although this often seems to go in the opposite direction) that developers have to write and maintain

- Allow developers to focus on the business logic and minimize the required amount of boilerplate code and configuration

Following our path with a focus on Java EE, we will mainly address tuning related to the frameworks of the specification. Before going into the gory details of tuning though, we will start with a bit of historic background on dynamic web frameworks with an eye on how to improve overall performance.

The evolution of web frameworks

Initially, dynamic web applications were based on the **Common Gateway Interface (CGI)**, portrayed in the next diagram. These applications were commonly realized by a script that parsed the URI of the incoming HTTP request method call (normally, GET or PUT), performed some business logic, and then returned a response as a generated HTML page. A basic web server with a supporting CGI library would spawn a new OS process for each incoming call. Naturally, this was very ineffective and had its limitations (such as the number of processes and network ports) that quickly became obvious in environments under heavy load.

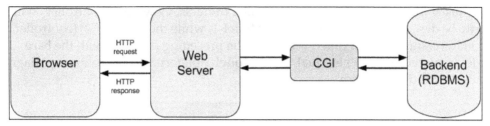

A logical model of Common Gateway Interface

With the introduction of the **Java Servlet API**, a platform called a *web container* for executing Java-based logic came into play. In this container, an incoming call results in a thread being retrieved from a pool of threads and designated to execute the logic of the servlet. Using pooled threads allowed for a much improved performance in comparison to the process of continuously spawning new threads. Earlier, servlet containers actually didn't have a pool of threads but simply spawned a new thread for each incoming call. It was an improvement over spawning processes, but pooling took it up another notch. Although a lot of productivity improvements had also been made to parse incoming calls (including request attributes and values), the bare half-duplex servlets still need to create their HTML output and stream it to an awaiting browser client. The concept of the bare servlet is depicted in the following diagram:

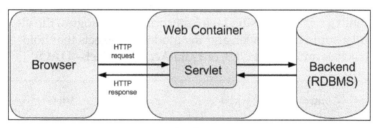

Servlet

As an attempt to make responses more dynamic and increase developer productivity, **JavaServer Pages (JSP)** was introduced. A JSP is really a template page mixed with a markup language notation, which almost always is (X)HTML, and special JSP elements with Java code. When a JSP is called, it is initially compiled (on the first call or precompiled) into a Java servlet. The JSP can be used instead of a regular servlet that contains both logic and view, but the two have come to complement each other. The servlet would initially accept a call and handle any business logic before controlling what JSP it could and would pass on the execution to. The receiving JSP would act as a dynamic template with logic that is relevant only for the view.

Using just a JSP without a separate controller (models, views, and controllers will shortly be described) is a pattern called **Model-1**, while the servlet-JSP (controller and view) combination is called **Model-2**. The preceding diagram with the bare servlet (replaced by a JSP) is equal to the **Model-1** pattern and the following diagram equals the **Model-2** pattern:

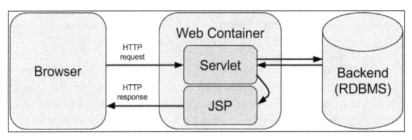

The Java servlet and JSP in a Model-2 pattern setup

At the core of almost any modern application is the data of the organizational business model. This includes how it can be effectively used, controlled, and manipulated by end users through a **Graphical User Interface (GUI)** view. The **Model-View-Controller (MVC)** pattern, as seen in the following diagram, confirms this by separating the business domain object into a *model*, the visualization and rendering of the business data into a *view* suitable for interaction, and the request processing and business logic into a *controller*. Using Java Enterprise technologies, the view could be a JSP, the controller could be a servlet, and the model are objects that holds and possibly persists data (such as an Entity, POJO, or **Data Access Object – DAO**).

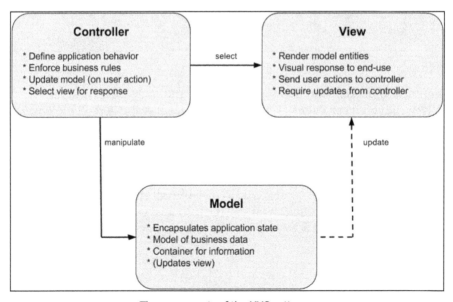

The components of the MVC pattern

One of the initial and strong arguments for the MVC pattern was its *separation of concerns*. Each of the three cornerstones of the pattern would handle its own area of specialization free from the other. This was great and lots of frameworks were, and are, based on the pattern. In reality, though, tight couplings between several of the cornerstones was the result.

As requirements for rich and highly responsive UIs in web applications became increasingly strong, solutions based on just Java servlets and JSPs became more and more inadequate.

JavaServer Faces (JSF) is a server-side component framework, which together with related component libraries, was intended as the next step of evolution in the Java enterprise specifications.

In JSF, a number of life cycle phases were introduced as depicted in the following diagram:

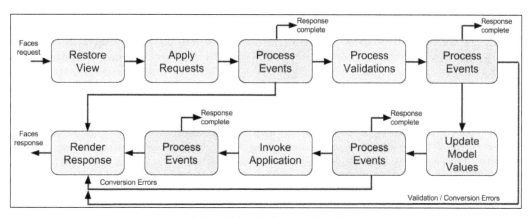

The JSF life cycle phases and paths

From a developer's point of view, these phases are completely isolated from each other in order to secure the separation of concerns. Thus, each phase can also be separately and independently overridden to handle the various tasks the framework enables. To make things even better, should the framework or user (developer) need, the life cycle can be short-circuited to only execute the necessary phases. Should for example, the validation fail (here, in the **Process Validations** phase), the JSF framework will notice it and jump directly to the last (**Render Response**) phase, skipping all intermediate phases, and enable the quick display of the relevant error-related information.

Despite its best intentions, JSF is often criticized for the following points:

1. Being complex and hard to understand
2. Being too "silent" and hard to debug
3. Having poor performance

In comparison to many earlier frameworks, JSF is definitely more complex, as in, it has more steps and paths of execution. As with all things, we must, however, take a step back and think about the entire problem domain and what we are trying to solve for each particular case. The reason that JSF is more complex is that it also solves more problems than its predecessors. A rich enterprise application is for example often required to support (Bean) validation, transactional states, and partial updates of the **Domain Object Model (DOM)** component tree in the GUI. Putting these in perspective, JSF is actually a simple, dynamic, and feature-rich standardized framework that aids productivity and application management. JSF is often misunderstood in terms of complexity, but it is true that it can be hard to interpret where in the life cycle, and why, a problem occurs. A simple aid for this is to enable a simple phase listener such as the `PhaseTracker` class in the following code (note that, in this example, the phase listener is triggered before and after each phase (`PhaseId.ANY_PHASE`) in the JSF life cycle):

```
public class PhaseTracker implements PhaseListener {
  @Override
  public void afterPhase(PhaseEvent phaseEvent) {
    System.out.println("PhaseTracker.afterPhase: " +
      phaseEvent.getPhaseId() + ":" +
      phaseEvent.toString());
  }
  @Override
    public void beforePhase(PhaseEvent phaseEvent) {
      System.out.println("PhaseTracker.beforePhase: " +
        phaseEvent.getPhaseId() + ":" +
        phaseEvent.toString());
  }
  @Override
    public PhaseId getPhaseId() {
    return PhaseId.ANY_PHASE;
  }
}
```

The configuration in `faces-config.xml` can be seen in the following configuration:

```
<lifecycle>
    <phase-listener>util.jsf.PhaseTracker</phase-listener>
</lifecycle>
```

A phase listener can also easily be instrumented to measure the execution time between phases and other performance-related metrics that might be useful for tuning your application.

JSF's reputation of poor performance is both justified and not justified. In the end, it is really all about what you need support for. If you do not need support for what JSF brings to the table, then it just isn't for you. If you, for example, need extremely fast server responsiveness and can ignore features such as validation, transactions, and rich component libraries, looking for another framework is recommended. If you, on the other hand, do need these and other enterprise features as well as a standardized way to develop web applications, JSF should at least be on your short-list of frameworks to evaluate.

Should you opt for putting together a set of frameworks on your own (such as Hibernate for bean validation and persistence and JBoss/Arjuna for transaction support), keep in your mind that you will soon have created an "enterprise"-like web framework stack on your own. This might be completely relevant for your particular situation, but it very seldom is, as it almost always comes with unjustified costs in terms integration complexity, version management, and maintenance.

The JSF render response phase is often identified as the most costly of all phases in terms of both CPU usage intensity and execution time. The good thing, however, is that the JSF architecture supports partial updates of the user interface DOM. By using the **Asynchronous Java and XML (AJAX)** set of technologies (Javascript, HTML, CSS, and so on), request calls from a client can be made to a server-side application that only returns and updates a partial part of the complete DOM tree. This technique enables more responsive UIs and can improve overall performance. AJAX is, therefore, available and increasingly used in the various JSF component frameworks, such as PrimeFaces (`http://www.primefaces.org/`), Richfaces (`http://www.jboss.org/richfaces/`), or IceFaces (`http://www.icesoft.org/`), to mention a few.

Tuning a web component – the data table

When we are talking about web-based GUI components, a button or a text input field are quite likely to be among the most common. The performance tuning possibilities of these are however, quite limited. A larger but still very common and very tunable component is the data table.

To make things interesting, we have looked at the performance of a simple data table that only displays the entity data using the following three technologies:

- Servlet/JSP with the core **JavaServer Pages Template Library (JSTL)**
- Pure JSF (2.2)
- JSF with PrimeFaces (4.x)

Each test used the same data set and displayed the same number of entities (rows) with attributes (columns) in a data table. As each use case and environment will factor in, the actual number of measurements will be quite irrelevant. Hence, we will not list the actual results here but, instead, focus on the relative results.

The data table in the servlet/JSP implementation was implemented as follows in the JSP page:

```
<c:forEach items="${beanList}" var="bean">
  ${bean.attribute1}
  ${bean.attribute2}
  ${bean.attribute3}
</c:forEach>
```

In the pure JSF solution, the head of the data table definition looked similar to the following code in the JSF page:

```
<h:dataTable value="#{tableBean.beanList}" var="bean">
```

Finally, and similar to JSF-PrimeFaces, the head of the data table definition can be seen in the following code:

```
<p:dataTable value"#{tableBean.beanList}" var="bean">
```

The result showed that, in terms of the throughput, the servlet/JSP solution was about twice as good as the pure JSF solution, and the pure JSF solution was slightly better than the one that used JSF-PrimeFaces.

From this, we can simply believe that servlet/JSP solutions are "better" than any of the JSF variants. Now, if you only want to show data without any user interaction, this might just be true. The feature requirements of rich user interfaces, however, imply otherwise. In a modern application, the user interface with a data table is quite likely to support at least some, if not all, of the following features:

- True pagination
- Filtering
- Sorting
- Selecting and view/editing of an element (row or cell), which, on performing an update, might require validation in turn

Implementing these features in a servlet/JSP solution will be quite cumbersome and will require a lot of custom code. Likewise, implementing the pure JSF solution will require quite a lot of code. The JSF-PrimeFaces solution, on the other hand, is extremely simple and productive. Each of the individual features can be enabled by adding an attribute to the data table definition (for example: `paginator="true"`, `sorting="true"` and `selection="#{customersAction.selectedCustomer}"`), plus a relatively simple and straightforward data model class (extending, for example, the `org.primefaces.model.LazyDataModel` class) that retrieves the correct data set to be shown for a given action — a new page, filtering, and so on.

> The different JSF component libraries have evolved separately and continue to do so. Thus, their set of features differ quite a bit and can change radically even between versions. The choice of which JSF component library to be used is very important, as it will impact the developer's productivity, product stability, and user experience heavily. So, before just selecting a library, make sure that you have a well-thought-out set of requirements (including both business and technological) that it should be able to live up to.

Tuning servlet/JSP applications

In this section, we will talk about some common tuning activities related primarily with servlets and JSP pages. Some of these activities are also relevant when using other technologies.

Choose the scope wisely

Storing data objects in the correct scope depending on when and how they are needed is an important design aspect that can and will affect the performance of an application.

For servlets and JSPs, the following are the scopes that exist:

- Servlet/Application
- Session
- Request
- Page (JSPs only where it is default)

From top to bottom of the bullets, the objects put in a certain context will in general live longer and will be accessible from a lower positioned context. So, changing an object in the application scope will for example make the change visible in (and affect) all sessions.

Storing a lot of data including large objects or objects graphs in, for example, the `HttpSession` should be avoided as it will consume memory that won't be released until the session dies and it can carry a heavy computation overhead due to serialization.

Should you need to, you can store an object in the session as follows:

```
HttpSession session = request.getSession();
session.setAttribute("user", objectToStoreInSession);
```

In a JSP page, a JavaBean object can be stored in a given scope as follows (selecting one of the four listed scopes):

```
<jsp:useBean id="myName"
  scope="page|request|session|application"
  class="MyClass">
</jsp:useBean>
```

As data objects stored in one scope and no longer need to be there, they should be removed. Removing an object associated with a specific attribute from the session is done using the following line of code:

```
session.removeAttribute("user");
```

Should you need to clear (invalidate) the entire session, this can be done by using the following line of code:

```
session.invalidate()
```

Session timeouts

Setting a session timeout that is adequate for your specific use case is very important. Setting the timeout to a high number will in effect limit the number of sessions that can exist in memory over time on a server. Setting a number that is too small will annoy your customers (as they might get prematurely logged out due to "short" periods of inactivity) and have negative effects on the business.

Defining the session timeout for all sessions in a web application can be done in the `web.xml` file of the application. Its configuration is as follows (note that it should be an integer and that it defines the timeout in *minutes*):

```
<web-app ...>
  <session-config>
    <session-timeout>20</session-timeout>
  </session-config>
</web-app>
```

Setting the timeout can also be done programmatically per session, as follows (note that here, the timeout is defined in *seconds*):

```
HttpSession session = request.getSession();
session.setMaxInactiveInterval(20*60);
```

JSP use of HttpSession

If a JSP does not need to use the `HttpSession` — which is created by default — some overhead can be saved by disabling it with the following code:

```
<%@ page session="false"%>
```

JSP include

Files can be included in JSP pages in the following two ways:

- **Directive**: The content of the specified file is included when the main page is converted to a servlet (during the translation phase). For example: `<%@ include file="me.jsp" %>`.

- **Action**: The content of the specified file is included when the page is requested (during the request processing phase). For example: `<jsp:include page="me.jsp" />`.

If the included file does not change, the *Directive* variant will be faster. If it does change (in the case of an exploded artifact — WAR — and with the container in development mode — which isn't recommended in production), the directive will require a recompilation of the main page, which will affect performance.

The *Action* variant is a more dynamic solution, should you need to change included pages.

Compression

By using compression, the physical amount of a set of data that travels over the network will be minimized. Communication will, thus, be less susceptible to network latency. This will naturally come at the computational and CPU-intensive cost of compressing/decompressing data. Performing compression is most often worth the trouble and cost but this should, as usual, be validated per environment, platform, and use case.

Compression in a servlet is conveniently performed by the use of streams. The `java.util.zip.GZIPOutputStream` / `java.util.zip.GZIPInputStream` class will perform GZIP-format-based compression/decompression. Similar standard implementations exist for the ZIP and deflate formats.

In order to properly recognize a compressed request or response, the proper *content type* must be interpreted for incoming, or a set for outgoing, communications, for example, `application/x-gzip` for GZIPed transmissions.

Asynchronous servlets

To meet the needs in terms of increased traffic from applications that use, for example, AJAX to create rich and responsive graphical user interfaces, servlets and filters can be made asynchronous. These servlets accept a call and immediately spawn a new thread in which execution is continued. The initial servlet thread will be non-blocking and can return immediately without having to wait for resources or responses from other events. Instead, it will be free to handle new incoming requests. The response to the original client will be made from the newly spawned thread whenever it is ready.

An asynchronous servlet is marked as shown in the following code, with the `asyncSupported` attribute in the `@WebServlet` annotation:

```
@WebServlet(urlPatterns={"/asyncservlet"}, asyncSupported=true)
```

Within a service method (here for a GET operation), an implementation of the `javax.servlet.AsyncContext` interface is then used to spawn a new thread by executing code like the following:

```
public void doGet(HttpServletRequest req,
    HttpServletResponse resp) {
    AsyncContext actx = req.startAsync();
    // start and execute new thread
    actx.start(new Runnable() {
        public void run() {
            String param = actx.getRequest().getParameter("p");
            /* perform processing HERE */
            HttpServletResponse response = actx.getResponse();
            /* output to response HERE */
            actx.complete();
        }
    }
}
```

The `req.startAsync()` method call tells the servlet to release, but not return a response to the client after the method has finalized the execution. Instead, the newly spawned thread will commit the response and send it to the client as the `complete()` method of `AsyncContext` is executed.

Undertow's proprietary solutions

To achieve extreme speeds in the Undertow web container and server, it is recommended that you look into the usage of its own non-blocking servlets and native handlers. These are realized by implementing the `io.undertow.servlet.ServletExtension` and `io.undertow.server.HttpHandler` interfaces, respectively.

Note that these handlers are completely proprietary to Undertow!

We mentioned the Undertow handlers briefly in the previous chapter, and more information can be found in the Undertow online documentation at: (`http://undertow.io/documentation/servlet/using-non-blocking-handlers-with-servlet.html`).

Tuning JSF-based applications

WildFly ships with the *Mojorra* JSF 2.2 implementation, but it also comes with a feature called *Multi-JSF* that allows it to utilize any type or version of JSF implementation. Here, we will only look at features and configurations of the Mojorra implementation, however.

We previously got to taste one of the most common web components (the data table) that is part of almost every web application. Unfortunately, there is no magic switch that can dramatically improve the performance of a single JSF component. However, some general best practices do exist to accelerate the JSF life cycle. We can group them roughly into three areas:

- Configuring JSF state saving efficiency
- Using the Ajax support in JSF to reduce the cost of page rendering and data transmission
- Loading (JavaScript/CSS) files efficiently

Configuring JSF state saving efficiently

One of the most important settings that affect the performance and the memory used by the JSF user interface components is where to save the session state. You can opt between saving the state in the server (the default), which normally provides better performance but has high memory usage, or saving it in the client, which reduces the server memory footprint, at the cost of performance loss.

Besides this, by using the server-session state, you can have control over the serialization process, which is mandated by the JSF specification, to keep the application state consistent through the JSF life cycle. Thus, the suggested guideline is to leave it to the default (server) session-state saving, or explicitly configured with the following context parameter setting in your applications `web.xml` file:

```
<context-param>
    <param-name>javax.faces.STATE_SAVING_METHOD</param-name>
```

```
    <param-value>server</param-value>
</context-param>
```

Looking at our data table example, saving the state on the server gave us about 15 percent higher throughput compared to saving it on the client. As always, you should test and see how this and any other change affects your specific application.

The state saving method in server mode

When using the server-based state saving method, we have at least four major configurations that can affect performance.

First, as memory usage can become excessive in the server mode, we can limit the number of views stored in a session by the following two context parameters:

- `com.sun.faces.numberOfViewsInSession`: This has a default value of 15. This setting limits the number of JSF views per logical view in a session for both client and server modes of the state saving method. The **Least Recently Used (LRU)** algorithm is used to maintain the limit.

- `com.sun.faces.numberOfLogicalViews`: This has a default value of 15. The LRU algorithm is used here as well to maintain the limit.

A value that is too low on either of these parameters will throw a `javax.faces.application.ViewExpiredException` error during the *restore view* phase, but a low enough number will save memory, thereby leaving room for more sessions per server.

Another way of conserving memory is by compression. When setting both of the following context parameters to `true`, the state for the view will be serialized and compressed before being *Base64* encoded:

- `com.sun.faces.serializeServerState`: This has a default value of false.

- `com.sun.faces.compressViewState`: This has a default value of true.

Doing this will however require the use of more CPU resources (mainly from serialization), which normally affects performance negatively. Bandwidth and memory usage, on the other hand, will benefit.

The state saving method in client mode

In the client-based state saving method, there are three major configurations that can affect performance.

First, like in the server mode, enabling (setting it to its default `true` value) the `com.sun.faces.compressViewState` parameter will make the application use GZIP compression. This will reduce the memory and bandwidth usage but will require more CPU resources.

Secondly, the size of the client buffer is set to 8192 bytes per request by default. Depending on the complexity of the views of the application, this value can be adjusted using the `com.sun.faces.clientStateWriteBufferSize` parameter. A higher value will naturally use more bandwidth and memory. Should compression be turned on, the CPU usage will also go up.

Finally, we have the configuration parameter that lets you stipulate the implementation (class) to be used for serialization: `com.sun.faces.serializationProvider`. Using this parameter, you can define an implementation that satisfies your specific needs. You can even provide your own implementation by implementing the `com.sun.faces.spi.SerializationProvider` **Service Provider Interface (SPI)**.

A summary of state saving method configurations

The most important configurations of the state saving methods and their effects, which were discussed in the preceding section, have been summarized in the following table. The values (**Small**, **Medium**, and **Large**) are merely relative and are used to indicate the configurations' general effect to each other. Hence, they do not, for example, directly indicate an actual low (small) or high (large) amount of resource utilization.

State saving method	Compression	Server side memory usage	CPU usage	Bandwidth usage
Server	False	Large	Small	Small
Server	True	Small to Medium	Large	Small
Client	True	Small	Large	Medium
Client	False	Small	Medium	Large

The project stage

When you develop a JSF-2-based application, it would be wise to have your development project configured, in its `web.xml` file, to use the `Development` mode, as shown in the following configuration:

```
<context-param>
    <param-name>javax.faces.PROJECT_STAGE</param-name>
    <param-value>Development</param-value>
</context-param>
```

At the cost of some performance, this will give you better error messages, even from the client-side JavaScript. As the application is moved into production (or during performance tests), the value should naturally be changed into `Production` to regain performance.

JSF Immediate

The `immediate` attribute is a standard JSF UI component attribute and is also available on most command and input components in both the PrimeFaces and RichFaces component libraries.

For components that have the value of `immediate` set to `true`, validation, conversion, and events associated with these components will be processed directly in the *Apply Request Values* phase rather than a later phase. The component values will also be directly associated with their corresponding backing bean attributes. This can, for example, be used for performance enhancing flows, where one quickly wants to short-circuit the JSF life cycle while still performing some tasks on incoming values.

Using AJAX support in JSF

One of the major upgrades of the JSF 2 release was the addition of the AJAX support for user interface components. By using AJAX development techniques, web applications can retrieve data from the server asynchronously in the background, without interfering with the display and behavior of the existing page. This leads to an increase in the network interactivity with the website but also a potential boost in the overall performance. Since only a portion of the webpage can now be updated as a consequence of users' actions, the user interfaces can get a better feel of the flow and responsiveness in comparison to when the entire page needed re-rendering. In this section, we will show you, with examples, how AJAX can improve its performance by using features of the RichFaces and PrimeFaces component libraries.

Partial DOM updates by a component and attribute

The modern JSF component library has many benefits. The AJAX support for their various UI components is arguably one of the major ones. For example, if you need to limit the part of the web page that needs to be updated, you can, in most components, do it by means of a special component or a single component attribute.

Based on the `f:ajax` tag of JSF 2 *Facelets*, RichFaces supports partial updates using the similar `a4j:ajax` tag (the convention changed from `a4j:ajax` in RichFaces 4 to `r:ajax` in RichFaces 5) to update a part of the DOM tree.

The following code sample shows you how RichFaces puts AJAX in action using a4j:ajax:

```
<h:inputText value="#{userBean.name}">
  <a4j:ajax event="keyup" render="out" />
</h:inputText>
<h:outputText value="#{userBean.name}" id="out" />
```

As seen in the following figure, an input text field, "senses" each keystroke and echoes every char to an output text field with the "out" ID – all with the help of the a4j:ajax component, which actually handles all the "sensing" and echoing. The only part of the DOM tree that gets updated is the branch with the outputText component.

A RichFaces sample of the a4j:ajax component performing partial updates to the DOM tree. Each character typed into the inputText component to the left is echoed in the outputText on the right.

 More RichFaces examples are available in its online showcase at http://showcase.richfaces.org/.

In other component libraries such as PrimeFaces, the AJAX support is available in both specialized and similar (p:ajax) components/tags. AJAX support can also be available within other components using specific attributes. In the following PrimeFaces example, the update attribute of the p:commandButton component points to the ID of another component (outputText). This component will be updated with the value of the userBean.name, which was earlier populated in the inputText component:

```
<h:outputLabel for="name" value="Name:"/>
<p:inputText id="name" value="#{userBean.name}" />
<p:commandButton value="Submit" update="display"/>
<h:outputText value="#{userBean.name}" id="display" />
```

The preceding code will display the following:

When the button labeled Submit is pressed, the text in the inputText component is copied to the rightmost outputText component

 More PrimeFaces examples are available in its online showcase at http://www.primefaces.org/showcase/.

Updating a single component in the DOM tree by AJAX is naturally very efficient. Often more or larger sets of components need to be updated though. You might need to update a row in a table, an entire table, a submenu, and so on. You will normally see the most performance gains when the tree's least needed amount is updated.

When several areas of a page needs to be updated at the same time, however, the choice lies between updating each branch of components individually or the smallest common parent component (such as a common panel) that covers them all. If you have identified a view like this to be in need of tuning, then here you must test which direction is best for your particular use case.

Single partial AJAX async (form) requests

The previous examples will submit all data in the form in which the components are organized. Sometimes, you might only have the need to send data from a specific component and any optional parameters. This will normally reduce the network traffic volume even more (in the request at least, but often, also in response). RichFaces supports this by setting the `ajaxSingle` attribute—which is available on some components—to `true`, as shown in the following example:

```
<a4j:commandButton action="#{bean.save}"
  value="Submit" ajaxSingle="true"/>
```

In PrimeFaces, a similar attribute is available on command components (such as `commandButton` and `commandLink`) and is named `partialSubmit`. Here it is, however, defined to handle only *values related to partially processed components*.

The command components in PrimeFaces also have an attribute named `ajax`. With that enabled (and set to `true`, which also is the default value) the submit type of the component will be handled by AJAX.

Also, in PrimeFaces, by enabling (setting to `true`) the `async` attribute on the command components will prevent the AJAX requests to be queued.

All of these three PrimeFaces attributes can potentially improve the performance of your application.

> As an observant reader might have noticed, different component libraries have many features that are similar, if not the same. Although they sometimes use the same names for components and attributes, it does not mean that they have the same functionality or perform the same actions. This makes quick transitions and comparisons between libraries tedious and the usage hazardous. It is, therefore, important to always verify the real and exact meaning of every attribute in the documentation of the respective library.

Filters

In the now relatively old, but still used RichFaces 3 library, you can use an AJAX filter (`org.ajax4jsf.Filter`) and its related initialization parameters to handle code correction for AJAX requests and optimizations of XML parsing. The filter is actually a standard servlet filter defined in the `web.xml` file of a web application as follows:

```
<filter>
  <display-name>RichFaces Filter</display-name>
  <filter-name>richfaces</filter-name>
  <filter-class>org.ajax4jsf.Filter</filter-class>
</filter>
```

The filter has a few initialization parameters that can affect performance, which are as follows:

- `enable-cache`
- `forcenotrf` (also known as `forceparser`)

The `enable-cache` initialization parameter, which is set to `true` by default, enables the caching of framework-generated resources (such as JavaScript, CSS, and images). During development and debugging, this parameter could be set to `false` in order to ensure that caching won't affect results. In production, it should be set to `true` to ensure best performance.

Using the default `true` value of the `forcenotrf` parameter will force parsing by an HTML syntax checker as well as conversion to well-formed XML on any JSF page. Setting it to `false` only parses AJAX responses. This will improve performance, but might cause visual side-effects during AJAX updates.

As parsing and correcting text, such as HTML, is a both a time and CPU-consuming operation, it is important to use an efficient parser. In RichFaces 3, the available options are as follows:

- NONE: No corrections are made.
- TIDY: Recommended for applications with complicated or non-standard markup. This parser is often very slow.
- NEKO: Accelerates AJAX requests a lot but also requires the markup to be completely strict, or errors might occur.

The parsers are configured as follows (the path value of each parser is normally defined to handle files that contain whatever each parser needs or specializes in, but here, they are all just marked with an asterisk, *):

```
<context-param>
   param-name>org.ajax4jsf.xmlparser.ORDER</param-name>
   <param-value>NONE,NEKO</param-value>
</context-param>
<context-param>
   <param-name>org.ajax4jsf.xmlparser.NONE</param-name>
   <param-value>*</param-value>
</context-param>
<context-param>
   <param-name>org.ajax4jsf.xmlparser.NEKO</param-name>
   <param-value>*</param-value>
</context-param>
```

Loading resource files efficiently

When inspecting a webpage with a rich UI, such as the ones using a JSF component library, you will see a lot of resources such as CSS, Javascript, and image files being used. These are vital in creating the intriguing experience of the page, but they come with a cost. Each new file will need to be retrieved over the network in a new request. Both the number of requests as well as the size of the files requested affect the performance negatively as their numbers rise.

In RichFaces, you can enable *resource optimization*, which will aggregate all possible requests into one by adding the following configurations to your web.xml file (the resourceOptimization parameter actually has different names in different versions, so it is wise to verify this with the documentation of the version you use; this is for RichFaces 4.2 and above):

```
<servlet>
  <servlet-name>Resource Servlet</servlet-name>
  <servlet-class>
    org.richfaces.webapp.ResourceServlet
  </servlet-class>
  <load-on-startup>1</load-on-startup>
</servlet>

<context-param>
  <param-name>
    org.richfaces.resourceOptimization.enabled
  </param-name>
  <param-value>true</param-value>
</context-param>
```

RichFaces also optimizes packaging and compression on the fly when the `javax.faces.PROJECT_STAGE` context parameter, discussed earlier, is set to `Production`. When this parameter is set to `Development`, resources are still packaged but no compression will be used, which is great for debugging.

From *PrimeFaces extensions* (`http://primefaces-extensions.github.io/`), another strategy for resource optimization is provided. Here, compression, aggregation, and image loading by *Data URIs* (roughly a type of aggregation where files are embedded in CSS) is performed during the artifact creation using the following Maven plugin:

```
<groupId>org.primefaces.extensions</groupId>
<artifactId>resources-optimizer-maven-plugin</artifactId>
```

For applications where many resources are used often both per page and in separate pages, the combination of resource optimization and client-side caching is likely to give the overall performance a significant boost. The first request will, however, normally be a bit slow as this is required to retrieve the big files.

WebSockets

WebSockets is a relatively new technology in which the API is specified by the W3C. It provides *full-duplex* communications between two peers over the TCP protocol. It normally runs over an HTTP where an initial client-server handshake will include an *HTTP upgrade* to the less verbose WebSocket protocol (specified by the IETF), before moving on to sending actual messages. A single thread per client-server connection will be used, and that connection is kept open until either party closes it.

WebSockets support in Java comes from the *Java API for WebSockets* specification. Here, WebSocket endpoints can be created using classes with the `@ClientEndpoint` and `@ServerEndpoint` annotations.

Modern web browsers support the WebSocket protocol, and JavaScript is regularly used on the client side.

From the given description, it should be clear that WebSockets in itself is a technology that has been built for performance. Tuning is mainly a design issue. Things such as the size and complexity of messages will always matter, but in equal comparison to all other technologies listed in this chapter (possibly except for the Undertow proprietary solutions that have not been compared), WebSockets has constantly proven to be the fastest. As the message size and/or number of requests increases, the superiority of WebSockets also becomes increasingly clearer.

Services

In Java EE, there is support for two major types of services:

- Web Services
- RESTful Services

We will talk more about each of these shortly, but first, we will discuss services in general.

Both of the server types mentioned enable *loose coupling* between two parties acting in the client-server mode. The two parties can be different systems in separate organizations, which are located at different geographical locations. They can also be two different modules within a local system or application stack.

Not only are the service types available in numerous implementations of different languages and operating systems, but they can also communicate with each other no matter what the platforms are. This platform independence will, for example, let a client written in C# and running on Windows, communicate with services implemented in Java, deployed in WildFly, and running on a Linux server. All it takes is an agreed convention.

Services were originally thought of and designed to be stateless. There are however projects and even specifications that can make services stateful and enable transactional integrity. Before jumping on that train, however, we would like to urge everyone to think about it at least twice. Services were originally created to be stateless. Adding session synchronization, object serialization, passivation, and transactional support will not be good for the performance and some features will go against basic design principles (in for example SOA).

Web services

In Java EE, support for Web Services comes in the shape of the **Java API for XML Web Services (JAX-WS)** specification. In WildFly, this is realized by *JBossWS* and the integration with *Apache CXF* (JBossWS-CXF).

In general terms, Web services allow clients to communicate with service endpoints on a server by the use of XML. The client-server communication uses the XML-based **Simple Object Access Protocol (SOAP)** protocol that defines an envelope structure and regularly runs over HTTP. It could, however, really use any underlying protocol (such as SMTP, JMS, or basic TCP).

In Java EE, a modern web service is normally realized by a `@WebService` annotated servlet or EJB (POJOs are also possible), with web service operations being implemented by `@WebMetod` annotated methods.

In the service endpoint, or *port* as it is also commonly known, the payload of a message can be handled in many ways. It can be parsed, transformed, and converted into something else, such as a new document or a (set or graph of) Java object(s). Converting an XML message to Java objects is very common, and it is supported by the **Java Architecture for XML Binding (JAXB)** specification.

Specifically, JAXB *binds* web service operations and messages with the Java method and allows you to customize the mapping while automatically handling the runtime conversion. This makes it easy for you to incorporate the XML data and processing functions in applications based on the Java technology, without having to know much about XML. A generic view on how SOAP and JAXB operates with an XML message is presented in the following diagram:

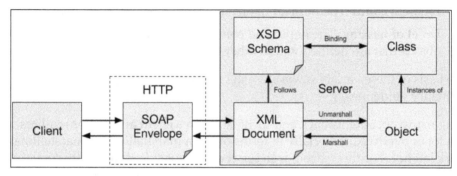

Binding and marshalling/unmarshalling of an XML document using JAXB and transferred by SOAP

The core process, which allows the translation of Java objects into XML, and vice versa, is known as *marshalling* and *unmarshalling* respectively. As with all things that deal with strings and XML, they are CPU-intensive operations, which can easily become bottlenecks of performance. Thus, most of your tuning efforts with web services should be directed at reducing the conversion complexity between the XML and Java object graphs.

Marshalling and serialization are two similar processes that are often confused with the other. They are are loosely synonymous but semantically different:

- Marshalling involves the transformation of the memory representation of an object (its data) into a format that is suitable for storage or transmission, a format that often is XML or JSON.
- Serialization transforms the actual objects with state into a format for persistent storage or transmission. The format is normally a byte stream; text-based formats work as well but normally with an increased overhead in storage and performance.

Performance factors

With web services, there are not many configuration parameters available for tuning. If you choose to implement your web service endpoint as a servlet or EJB, the tuning parameters available for the EJB and servlet container (Undertow), respectively, will apply. These were addressed in the previous chapters, but in short, mainly pools can be tuned.

Instead, the design of web services and the characteristics of the XML-based documents sent between client and server become the predominantly important factors. The following are three major variables that affect the documents:

- **Document size**: The total length of the XML document
- **Element count**: The number of elements that the XML document contains
- **Level of nesting**: The depth and complexity of objects or collections of objects that are defined within other objects in the XML document

On the basis of these variables, we can elaborate the following performance guidelines.

Sending many documents back and forth between a client and server requires quite a lot of overhead, especially in terms of extra marshalling/unmarshalling and network latency. For this reason, web services are not suited for chatty conversations. Similarly, it is not a good idea to fragment a message into many different fine-grained chunks even if this will minimize the message complexity and not increase the total size of the actual message payload (the business information).

 More messages will always mean more overhead for managing and sending the actual data over the network.

In harmony with general SOA recommendations, you should design *coarse-grained* web services instead. To be effective, these services should also perform a relatively large amount of work on the server and acknowledge the client with just a response code or a minimal set of attributes.

Minimizing the size of a message that will be sent over the wire (or whatever medium your network operates in) is an important performance-related aspect. The same set of data can be sent in many ways.

One way is to serialize the message and transmit it as a byte sequence within a SOAP message. This, however, does not always create smaller messages and is often impractical both in terms of performance and handling. The serialization and deserialization is a very expensive operation that can easily cost more than the intended gains. Handling the data of the serialized chunk will also be ineffective, as it will always need deserialization before anything can be done with it. This becomes especially obvious in situations where you initially only need to access a small set of data of a large message in order to make decisions about how to handle the rest.

Instead of basic serialization, the message could be compressed using more effective algorithms. These could, for example, be implemented by JAX-WS handlers using the `@HandlerChain` annotation. These handlers operate much like interceptors. They execute before (or after) an incoming (or outgoing) call reaches the service endpoint (or the client); they can be chained, and they operate on both the client and server side. With handlers handling the compression/decompression, the work is transparent to any business layer, but it should be verified by performance tests that the overall performance will actually benefit.

With the introduction of the `javax.jws.WebService` annotation in Java EE 5, it became easy and very tempting to simply enable POJOs as web services. As POJO evolves over time in a model, it might come to include collections of other objects. The size of the message retrieved can then grow in size and expense in more or less complex and uncontrollable ways. Also, bloating a content-carrying object with, for example, transport logic, does not rime well with sound architectural guidelines like *separation of concerns*.

Looking at how an XML document can be structured in terms of nodes and attributes tells us that there are several ways to include the same set of information. Using (short named) attributes over nodes (there will always be two tags in a node: one "start" and one "end") will save you quite a lot of bytes per message.

We could do this more or less *manually* by creating an XML document into which we copy relevant data from a source, such as a Java object. We can also do this in a more automated way using JAXB.

Let's say we have simple `Person` POJO, as shown in the following code:

```
public class Person {
    String name;
    String address;
    String city;
    String postcode;
    String country;
    // ...
}
```

Using JAXB, this will (approximately) translate into the following SOAP envelope:

```
<env:Envelope
  xmlns:env='http://schemas.xmlsoap.org/soap/envelope/'>
  <env:Header />
  <env:Body>
    <ns2:getListResponse xmlns:ns2='http://packtpub.com/'>
    <return>
    <person>
      <name>John Doe</name>
      <address>Storgatan 1</street>
      <city>Stockholm</city>
      <postcode>12345</postcode>
      <country>SE</country>
    </person>
    <!-- other persons -->
    </return>
    </ns2:getListResponse>
  </env:Body>
</env:Envelope>
```

As you can see, lots of characters are wasted in XML node elements that could conveniently be replaced by attributes, thus saving a good quantity of bytes. Annotating the `Person` POJO with relevant JAXB annotations as shown in the following code will instruct the JAXB parser to create a message with the same information, but at the same time, it will be more optimized in size:

```
@XmlRootElement
public class Person {
    @XmlAttribute
    String name;
    @XmlAttribute
    String address;
    @XmlAttribute
    String city;
    @XmlAttribute
    String postcode;
    @XmlAttribute
    String country;
    // ...
}
```

The corresponding XML code is in this case is about 20 percent smaller:

```
<env:Envelope
  xmlns:env='http://schemas.xmlsoap.org/soap/envelope/'>
  <env:Header />
  <env:Body>
```

```
<ns2:getListResponse xmlns:ns2='http://packtpub.com/'>
<return>
<person name="John and Jane Doe"
  address="100" city="Anytown"
  postcode="12345" country="USA"/>
<!-- other persons -->
</return>
</ns2:getListResponse>
</env:Body>
</env:Envelope>
```

Another important factor, which can improve the performance of your web services, is caching. You could consider caching responses at the price of additional memory requirements or potential stale data issues. Caching should also be accomplished on web services documents such as **Web Service Definition Language (WSDL)**, which contains the specifications of the web service contract (endpoints and operations). It's advisable to refer to a local backup copy of your WSDL when you are rolling your service in to production, as shown in the following example:

```
@WebServiceClient(name = "ExampleWS",
  targetNamespace = http://packtpub.com/",
  wsdlLocation = "http://127.0.0.1:8080/ExampleWS/hello?wsdl")
```

At the same time, you should consider caching the instance that contains the web service port. Its `name` attribute provides a unique identifier among all port types defined within the enclosing WSDL document.

 In short, a port contains an abstract view of the web service, but acquiring a copy of it is an expensive operation, which should be avoided every time you need to access your web service.

The potential threat of this approach is that you might introduce objects (the proxy port) in your client code, that are not thread safe. You should instead synchronize their access or use a pool of instances. An exception to this rule is the Apache CXF implementation, which documents that "CXF proxies are thread safe for MANY use cases" These cases are described in the project FAQs at http://cxf.apache.org/faq.html.

RESTful services

REpresentational State Transfer (REST) is an architectural style that, like web services, is independent of language implementation, platform, and underlying transport mechanism. In practice, it (almost always) uses HTTP and URIs for transport and communication.

Java EE supports REST by the **Java API for RESTful Web Services (JAX-RS)** specification. In WildFly, JAX-RS and several extensions come from the *RESTeasy* project.

REST services are simpler in many ways and, when well designed, they are arguably more logical than web services. As addressing, accessing, and controlling are done by the use of URIs, the necessary tool support on the client side can often be minimal. A browser is often enough for raw access.

The stateless features of REST and it being closely related to HTTP methods and URIs makes it ideal for platforms where high performance is of importance. For example, will farms of fast web servers (and/or application servers) with (thin) REST services be able to effectively serve magnitudes of clients. Thanks to the nature of the RESTful services, these farms will also be extremely scalable and can adapt to the demand in traffic. This adaptability is important in the world of today where the efficient use of elastic and virtual servers is an important business factor

REST services are good for many use cases where the state is not required. It can also be more chatty, fine, and granular than web services without loosing much performance, as headers are normally smaller and marshalling is not (always) needed.

How the URI is constructed has minimal impact on performance. The use of the URI path and/or the key-value attributes matters more in design perspectives where the same information can be modeled in several ways — as in the following two URIs:

```
http://mysite/animal/monkey/tooth
http://mysite?animal=monkey&part=tooth
```

Should the message size of a RESTful service become a concern, it is possible to cache results just as you would for an ordinary web application.

By compressing data, it is also possible to minimize the amount of bytes traveling over the network. This will, however, put extra requirements of functionality on the client and might make several, less ordinary browsers unable to use the services.

Apart from caching and compression, designing what data to use and how it should be structured during transmission is really the only way to limit network packages.

Using the structure of a URI to carve out, or drill down to, the related business level of information that you are interested in is a powerful feature where design efforts should be allowed to focus.

Making RESTful services as "thin" and responsive as possible is also a design goal.

Summary

In this chapter, we have discussed various web application and web service technologies with a focus on how to tune them.

We started out with what to look for when selecting a web framework and talked about the evolution of web frameworks. To demonstrate a very common GUI component, we looked at the data table and how it behaved using different web technologies. Although servlets/JSPs were faster for a simple use case, factors such as productivity and maintainability were low, while complexity quickly got (too) high as the need for enhancements and alteration came into the picture. JSF with a component library (PrimeFaces) supported by AJAX can be a better solution.

As we went through a few tuning hints, solutions, and technologies related to both servlets/JSPs and JavaScript, we also mentioned proprietary solutions in Undertow and talked about WebSockets as the best performing and arguably the most promising technology in web application development today.

Moving on to services, we made a point that web services should be coarse grained as they are good at handling XML documents of a significant size. RESTful services can do this as well, but they are even more apt at handling more fine-granular queries and commands.

The inherent stateless nature of REST services also makes for extremely scalable and high-performing platforms that can easily adapt to a varying number of clients.

For web applications as well as RESTful and web services, minimizing the amount of data sent between client and server over the network can be an important performance enhancement. This can be done by the following:

- Caching
- Compression
- Minimizing the actual message content by design

It is essential that you correctly test which factors are the most important for your use case. Negative results in performance might occur for some tuning options.

After talking about applications and services using the classic client-server paradigm, we will now turn our attention to the tuning of message-oriented middleware.

9
JMS and HornetQ

Being able to connect and share information between two or more, often heterogeneous and most commonly distributed, systems (or applications or components) is a very common challenge in IT management. Historically, solving this involved binding the systems together with proprietary hard-coded connections. Consequently, the systems became *tightly coupled* as they had to be highly aware of each other. In practice, it became impossible to change one system without making changes to any other.

With the advent and use of **Message-oriented Middleware** (**MOM**) and the inherent message broker component, the systems became more *loosely coupled*. The terms "MOM" and "message broker" are often used interchangeably, and they normally denote the software (or hardware) component responsible for actual message transportation. Loose coupling means that the systems no longer need to directly know about, and depend on, each other's API interfaces or inner workings. Changes to one system—or even a complete system exchange—now becomes irrelevant for all other systems. All that matters is that the messages that are exchanged between the systems stay the same, and they are exchanged by an intermediary message broker located at some agreed address.

Introducing JMS

MOMs are not very well defined and their implementations sometimes tend to touch integration platforms by, for example, including data transformation. Here, we will only care about, and focus on, the messages and the broker that facilitates transportation of these messages.

In Java EE, the **Java Messaging Service** (**JMS**) specification (Version 2.0 is currently used in Java EE 7 and WildFly 8.0.0.Final) defines the API for how Java code can interact with the MOM message brokers. In WildFly, the broker component is realized by *HornetQ* (http://hornetq.jboss.org/), currently in Version 2.4.1.Final.

In JMS, and in general, the message broker supports the following two major communication models, or destination types, as they are also called:

- **Queue**: As seen in the following diagram, a message is sent from a client called **Producer** to a given **Queue**. The message is then distributed to another receiving client named **Consumer**. The **Consumer** has registered itself as a recipient with the same **Queue**. A queue often uses **Point-to-Point** (**PTP**) communication. This is true, but only really per message! Should several consumers register themselves to the queue, a message will reach one and only one of them. The one it will reach is defined by a given distribution algorithm that selects among the available consumers. Should no consumer be available, the queue will store the message (in memory or in persistent storage) until a consumer becomes available. When a consumer has received a message, it will acknowledge this to the queue.

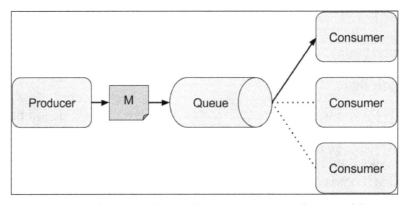

A conceptual model of a Queue with a Producer, a Message M, and registered Consumers

- **Topic**: A message is sent from a client called **Publisher** to a given **Topic**. This message is then distributed to all receiving clients, called **Subscribers**. The Subscribers subscribe to the **Topic** and expect to get all messages on the subscription. This model is often also called *publish-subscribe*, or *pub-sub* for short. As a subscriber receives its copy of the message, it will acknowledge this to the **Topic**. A message must be delivered to all connected subscribers. For an unconnected subscriber to receive any missed messages on reconnection, it needs to have a *durable* subscription.

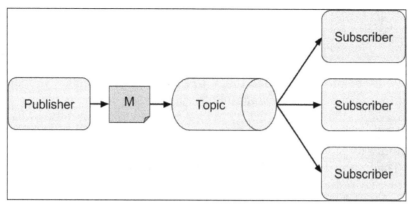

A conceptual model of a Topic with a Publisher, a Message M and registered Subscribers

At the core of MOMs and JMS is the rule of *guaranteed delivery* of messages as the descriptions of both the Queue and Topic above notes. If the broker is configured to rely on storing messages in-memory only, they will naturally be lost if the broker, for some reason, has a complete production failure. It is, therefore, common to store messages in persistent storage as soon as they enter the broker. This will increase stability and guarantee message delivery, but it will also come with the price of increased use of resources and slower throughput.

The message and its optimizations

In JMS, a message, `javax.jms.Message`, consists of a header, some properties, and a body. In the body, the actual payload of business data is located. As for most payloads, the less the data transferred, the less I/O will occur, which in turn infers increased throughput. Keeping a JMS message as small as possible puts less strain on both the network and the persistence layer of the JMS provider.

The following are the five types of messages available in JMS, each defining what the message body can contain:

- `javax.jms.TextMessage`: It holds a Java string object.

- `javax.jms.ObjectMessage`: It holds a serialized Java object.

- `javax.jms.MapMessage`: It holds a message constructed by a set of key-value pairs. The keys are String objects, and the values are Java primitive data types.

- `javax.jms.StreamMessage`: It holds a stream of Java primitive data types.

- `javax.jms.BytesMessage`: It holds a message constructed by uninterpreted bytes.

For all JMS message types, the *keep-it-small* principle applies to provide the best preparation for good performance.

One of the most commonly utilized types is `javax.jms.TextMessage`. Today, it is often used to transport XML messages. Reducing the size of the message is not only good for the performance of the JMS provider, but also minimizes the XML parsing process, and thus, it contributes to improve overall performance. It is important to not just blindly use an existing (and often ambitious in coverage) XML document standard. The removal of unneeded information should always be considered as considerable size reductions may be possible.

It can be easy, and therefore tempting, to use the `ObjectMessage` type as it is convenient to pass already constructed and structured Java objects between producers and consumers. The cost of serialization can, however, be very expensive. Sending just the required information of an object by, for example, excluding non-required information using `transient` attributes can improve performance at varying levels, depending on what is excluded.

The type that offers the best possibility for constructing compact and effective messages is `BytesMessage`. Here, you have total control of the exact number of bytes the message will consist of.

As for the content of the body, the size, amount, and structure of properties in a message should also be considered during the tuning process.

Tuning the session

When connecting to a JMS session, you should strive to reuse an existing session as it can be quite expensive and time-consuming to create a new. Note that reusing an existing session is only fully acceptable within a thread as the session in not thread-safe.

In order to realize the requirements of guaranteed delivery, JMS defines an acknowledgement mechanism that is used in the communication between the clients. The behavior of this mechanism can be controlled by selecting an appropriate acknowledgement mode. The JMS specification provides the following three modes:

- `CLIENT_ACKNOWLEDGE`: Any client code must acknowledge the message by calling one of its acknowledge methods. Failing to do this may lead to a serious buildup of resources on the server.

- `AUTO_ACKNOWLEDGE`: A client's consumption of a message will be automatically acknowledged immediately when it's received, either returning from the `receive` method or calling the `process` method on a message listener.

- `DUPS_OK_ACKNOWLEDGE`: Acknowledgment is done lazily, which can lead to duplicate messages being sent if the JMS provider fails in the process.

Using the `AUTO_ACKNOWLEDGE` mode will generate an acknowledgement to be sent for each message received, leading to more network traffic. If the application can handle duplicate messages without any problems, selecting `DUPS_OK_ACKNOWLEDGE` will provide the best performance by providing the possibility of sending acknowledgments in batches. The default size of these batches is 1 MB, it is specified by the `dups-ok-batch-size` parameter, and it can be changed with the following CLI commands:

```
/subsystem=messaging/hornetq-server=default/connection-factory=InVmConnec
tionFactory:write-attribute(name=dups-ok-batch-size, value=2097152)
```

```
/subsystem=messaging/hornetq-server=default/connection-factory=RemoteConn
ectionFactory:write-attribute(name=dups-ok-batch-size, value=2097152)
```

There are three different methods available in the JMS `Connection` object to create a JMS session:

- `createSession()`
- `createSession(boolean transacted, int acknowledgeMode)`
- `createSession(int sessionMode)`

The behavior of the `createSession()` method is described in the following table:

Environment	Acknowledging behavior
Java SE	`AUTO_ACKNOWLEDGE`
Java EE with active JTA transaction	The session will participate with the transaction (and either commit or rollback as controlled by the transaction)
Java EE without active JTA transaction	`AUTO_ACKNOWLEDGE`

Similarly, the behavior of the `createSession(boolean transacted, int acknowledgeMode)` method is described in the following table:

Environment	transacted=false	transacted=true
Java SE	The provided `acknowledgeMode` will be used.	The session will participate with a local transaction (and either commit or rollback as controlled by the transaction). The argument `acknowledgeMode` is ignored.

Environment	transacted=false	transacted=true
Java EE with active JTA transaction	Both parameters are ignored. The session will participate with the transaction (and either commit or rollback as controlled by the transaction).	Both parameters are ignored. The session will participate with the transaction (and either commit or rollback as controlled by the transaction).
	It is recommended to use `createSession()` instead.	It is recommended to use `createSession()` instead.
Java EE without active JTA transaction	The argument transacted is ignored, and only `AUTO_ACKNOWLEDGE` or `DUPS_OK_ACKNOWLEDGE` is allowed.	The argument transacted is ignored, and only `AUTO_ACKNOWLEDGE` or `DUPS_OK_ACKNOWLEDGE` is allowed.

Finally, the behavior of the `createSession(int sessionMode)` method is described, based on the four available session modes, in the following two tables:

Environment	sessionMode=SESSION_TRANSACTED	sessionMode=CLIENT_ACKNOWLEDGE
Java SE	Will use a local transaction controlled by the sessions and the *commit* or *rollback* methods	`CLIENT_ACKNOWLEDGE`
Java EE with active JTA transaction	The `sessionMode` parameter is ignored and the session will participate with the transaction (either commit or rollback, as controlled by the transaction)	`sessionMode` is ignored and the session will participate with the transaction (either commit or rollback, as controlled by the transaction)
Java EE without active JTA transaction	Not allowed	Not allowed

Environment	SessionMode=AUTO_ACKNOWLEDGE	SessionMode=DUPS_OK_ACKNOWLEDGE
Java SE	`AUTO_ACKNOWLEDGE`	`DUPS_OK_ACKNOWLEDGE`
Java EE with active JTA transaction	`sessionMode` is ignored and the session will participate with the transaction (either commit or rollback, as controlled by the transaction)	`sessionMode` is ignored and the session will participate with the transaction (either commit or rollback, as controlled by the transaction)
Java EE without active JTA transaction	`AUTO_ACKNOWLEDGE`	`DUPS_OK_ACKNOWLEDGE`

If the session participates in a JTA transaction, the actual acknowledgements will not be sent until the transaction either commits or rolls back. This has the side-effect of minimizing network calls which in turn has a positive impact on performance if several messages can be acknowledged in the same call.

As an addition to the three standard JMS acknowledgment modes, HornetQ also supports two vendor-specific variants:

- `PRE_ACKNOWLEDGE`: If it is okay to lose messages due to a failure; this mode can be used to send the acknowledgement to the server before it is even delivered to the client. This saves extra network calls and CPU resources, otherwise needed for handling message loss. The following scenario, taken from the HornetQ documentation, is a good example of when to use this mode:

  "An example of a use case for pre-acknowledgement is for stock price update messages. With these messages, it might be reasonable to lose a message in event of crash since the next price update message will arrive soon, overriding the previous price."

- `INDIVIDUAL_ACKNOWLEDGE`: If it's not known when a message will be acknowledged, there are scenarios where using one consumer per thread is not applicable. In these cases, `INDIVIDUAL_ACKNOWLEDGE` can be used in the same manner as `CLIENT_ACKNOWLEDGE`, with the exception that messages are acknowledged individually.

Tuning MessageProducer

Just as with the `Session` object, try to reuse a created `MessageProducer` (within the same thread). It is possible to even reuse a `MessageProducer` to send messages to different destinations. The trick is to create the producer with a `null` destination and specify the target destination in the `send` method instead.

As we briefly mentioned earlier, persisting each incoming message in order to guarantee that they will not be lost in the event of a broker restart or crash will not be positive for performance. It is arguably the most performance-degrading action in messaging. If guaranteed, message delivery is not a requirement for a given scenario; it can be disabled by setting the delivery mode on the relevant `MessageProducer` to `DeliveryMode.NON_PERSISTENT`.

It is possible to set the amount of time a message should be kept in the JMS provider by using the `setTimeToLive` method. Even if this functionality is intended to make sure that what is regarded as old messages isn't processed, it can also provide better performance by relieving message consumers from the sometimes unnecessary task of processing old messages by just dealing with the more actual ones.

Each message sent to a destination will get a unique `MessageID` that can be used for correlation, and so on. If this isn't needed, it is possible to disable the ID by calling the `setDisableMessageID` method. This will save both message size and total time for message generation.

The same thing applies to the *timestamp* that is put in the message when it is sent to the JMS provider. It can be disabled by using the `setDisableMessageTimeStamp` method.

In order to hint to the JMS provider about which messages should be delivered before others, the JMS specification implements ten levels of priority values, where 0 is the lowest and 9 the highest values. The priority can be set using the `setPriority` method.

> It's possible to set the delivery mode, priority, and time-to-live as settings on `MessageProducer`, but it is also possible to override these using the `send` method for individual messages—just as with the destination as previously described.

Optimizing HornetQ

Up to now, we mostly discussed optimizations that can be done using standard JMS functionalities. In the rest of the chapter, we will focus on HornetQ-specific optimizations that can be used in WildFly.

Persistence storage tuning

As HornetQ uses a journal (basically a set of binary files) located on disk for persistent storage of messages, the first thing is to make sure is that the files are placed on their own dedicated physical disk(s). Any other I/O to that disk may harm performance as it will compete with HornetQ to control the disk head. This is very important as the HornetQ journal is an *append-only* journal, and moving the disk head will have a serious impact on performance. The journaling directory can be changed by the following CLI command (exchange the path value for your absolute path):

```
/subsystem=messaging/hornetq-server=default/path=journal-directory:write-
attribute(name=path, value="/path/to/journal/files")
```

Whenever a journal file is created, it is created with a fixed size, and whenever the journal is filled, a new journal file will be created. HornetQ will detect when a journal file is not needed any longer (for example, when all its data has been deleted) and will either reuse it or delete it.

A compaction mechanism that helps reclaim file space is also active. Compaction will be triggered if the number of journal files is bigger than the value of the `journal-compact-min-files` parameter (the default value is `10`). Another setting, called `journal-compact-percentage` (the default is `30`), controls whether an individual journal file should be targeted for compaction by stating the minimal percentage of live data. A value of less than this number will trigger a compaction if the `journal-compact-min-files` criterion has been met. Changing the default settings may help in some cases. The settings can easily be managed by using the CLI—here, changing the values to `20` and `40` respectively:

```
/subsystem=messaging/hornetq-server=default:write-attribute(name=journal-
compact-min-files, value=20)
```

```
/subsystem=messaging/hornetq-server=default:write-attribute(name=journal-
compact-percentage, value=40)
```

The recommended optimal size setting for the journal file is to match the capacity of the cylinder on the disk used. The default value is 10 MB and can be changed with the CLI by stating the number of bytes, as follows:

```
/subsystem=messaging/hornetq-server=default:write-attribute(name=journal-
file-size, value=2048000)
```

This value needs to be larger than the maximum size of the messages, or HornetQ cannot persist all messages. Note that this is not true for *large messages* that will be discussed in detail later in this chapter.

The minimum number of journal files is set to `2` by default. Even if no data exists to persist, this minimal number of journal files will be created at startup. As an optimization, you may change the default setting to better match the number of files used by a given application during normal load. This will minimize unneeded creation of journal files as they will always be available. Changing the number of files is easily done using the CLI (here setting it to `5`), as follows:

```
/subsystem=messaging/hornetq-server=default:write-attribute
(name=journalmin-files, value=5)
```

Writes to the journal include a low-level buffer that can be tuned in terms of size (`journal-buffer-size`) and write-timeout (`journal-buffer-timeout`). Increasing the timeout can improve throughput at the cost of latency.

The actual writing to journals on disk is normally synchronized with the caller's JTA transaction lifecycle or blocking for non-transactional requests. These behaviors may be changed (set to `false`) to increase performance by the following CLI commands (note that doing so breaks the guarantee of data integrity in case of failures):

```
/subsystem=messaging/hornetq-server=default:write-attribute(name=journal-sync-transactional, value=false)
```

```
/subsystem=messaging/hornetq-server=default:write-attribute(name=journal-sync-non-transactional, value=false)
```

The actual interaction with the filesystem is either done using Java NIO or, if available, the Linux **Asynchronous IO (AIO)** library. Even though Java NIO delivers great performance, AIO will provide even better performance. When data is persisted using AIO, a callback acknowledgement will help HornetQ avoid waiting for synchronizations. The usage of AIO is only available on Linux and if the *libaio* is installed. The supported filesystems are `ext2`, `ext3`, `ext4`, `jfs`, and `xfs`.

 Warning: Locating journals on a **Network File System (NFS)** share will work, but it will fall back to a slower synchronized mechanism.

If AIO is used, increasing the default size (`500`) of an internal blocking-write requests queue, which is called `journal-max-io`, may increase performance even more. Using the CLI, the command for changing this value (here to set to `1000`) is as follows:

```
/subsystem=messaging/hornetq-server=default:write-attribute(name=journal-max-io, value=1000)
```

As mentioned earlier, the most rewarding performance-enhancing tuning feature of a messaging broker such as HornetQ is to disable the persisting of messages. If it is an acceptable scenario to disable persisting for all destinations in HornetQ, it can be done using the following CLI command:

```
/subsystem=messaging/hornetq-server=default:write-attribute(name=persistence-enabled, value=false)
```

Handling large messages

HornetQ supports special handling for really large messages by using input and output streams. The actual data will end up on disk, and the location can be changed by the following CLI command (exchange the path value for your absolute path):

```
/subsystem=messaging/hornetq-server=default/path=large-messages-
directory:write-attribute(name=path, value="/path/to/large/message/
files")
```

As previously described, it's not advisable to use the same disk for large messages as for the regular journal files.

The limit for what is considered a large message is set to 100 kB by default, but it may be reconfigured by the following CLI commands (for in-VM and remote ConnectionFactories respectively):

```
/subsystem=messaging/hornetq-server=default/connection-factory=InVmConnec
tionFactory:write-attribute(name=min-large-message-size, value=204800)
```

```
/subsystem=messaging/hornetq-server=default/connection-factory=RemoteConn
ectionFactory:write-attribute(name=min-large-message-size, value=204800)
```

This reflects the actual size of the stored message and not necessarily the size of the message in memory. A `TextMessage`, for example, is stored using a two-bytes encoding. This means that a `TextMessage`, larger than half the size of the defined value of a large message, will be considered a large message.

Large messages may also be compressed (at the cost of using CPU resources). To enable this, use the following CLI commands (for in-VM and remote ConnectionFactories respectively):

```
/subsystem=messaging/hornetq-server=default/connection-factory=InVmConnec
tionFactory:write-attribute(name=compress-large-messages, value=true)
```

```
/subsystem=messaging/hornetq-server=default/connection-factory=RemoteConn
ectionFactory:write-attribute(name=compress-large-messages, value=true)
```

Optimizing paging

To economize memory usage, HornetQ supports *paging* messages to disk instead of keeping them all in memory. This feature is enabled in WildFly by default, and the configuration for selected destinations is done using something called *addresses* in HornetQ. An address is a kind of matching pattern with support for the special wildcard character: #.

The default setup is that, whenever an address uses more that 10 MB of memory, it will start paging new messages to disk, and it will there use paging files, each 2 MB in size. These settings (for the address #, matching all destinations) can be managed with the following CLI commands:

```
/subsystem=messaging/hornetq-server=default/address-setting=#:read-
attribute(name=max-size-bytes)
{
  "outcome" => "success",
    "result" => 10485760L
}
/subsystem=messaging/hornetq-server=default/address-setting=#:write-
attribute(name=max-size-bytes, value=20971520L)
/subsystem=messaging/hornetq-server=default/address-setting=#:read-
attribute(name=page-size-bytes)
{
  "outcome" => "success",
    "result" => 2097152L
}
/subsystem=messaging/hornetq-server=default/address-setting=#:write-
attribute(name=page-size-bytes, value=4194304L)
```

 Warning: Whenever addresses are used to identify matching destinations, the actual setting will be used by all matched destinations. This means that the preceding example sets the page-size-bytes to 4194304 for each destination matched and not total for all of them.

The behavior when the page-size-bytes limit is hit depends on the address-full-policy address setting, which in turn supports the following policy settings:

- PAGE: It enables paging. It is the default setting in WildFly.
- BLOCK: It blocks message producers.
- DROP: It silently drop messages.
- FAIL: It returns an error to the producer.

It may be changed for an address by the following CLI command (here using the wildcard address #):

```
/subsystem=messaging/hornetq-server=default/address-setting=#:write-
attribute(name=address-full-policy, value=DROP)
```

So a good paging configuration has a considerable impact on performance as keeping more messages in memory, is better than paging and depaging them to and from a disk. Also, message selectors will only work on messages in memory, and any matching message will only be consumed when it is depaged from disk into memory. The same limitation exists for JMS browsers.

Another important factor is that a message needs to be in memory to be acknowledged. If a message is paged to a disk during consumption, the acknowledgment request will be blocked (if blocking acknowledgment is configured) until depaged. If there is no memory available for depaging, the consumption may appear to hang.

From a performance point of view, the paging files should, just as with large messages, be put on a separate disk with the regular journal files. The exact location of the paging files can be configured by the following CLI command (exchange the path value for your absolute path):

```
/subsystem=messaging/hornetq-server=default/path=paging-directory:write-
attribute(name=path, value="/path/for/paging/files")
```

Message deliverance optimizations

Whenever the HornetQ communication is a part of a JTA transaction, the actual commit (or rollback) request will not return until the persistence is done. If it is acceptable, in case of a failure, to lose the transactional integrity, it is possible to make the request return at once (for increased performance). HornetQ will handle the commit (or rollback) in the background when the `journal-sync-transactional` parameter is set to `false`. This parameter can be set by using the following CLI command:

```
/subsystem=messaging/hornetq-server=default:write-attribute(name=journal-
sync-transactional, value=false)
```

Acknowledgement for non-JTA scenarios will wait (block) until persistence is done for durable messages but return immediately for non-durable messages. This behavior is controlled by the `BlockOnDurableSend` and `BlockOnNonDurableSend` parameters, and these can be configured using the following CLI commands:

```
/subsystem=messaging/hornetq-server=default/connection-factory=InVmConnec
tionFactory:write-attribute(name=block-on-durable-send, value=false)
```

```
/subsystem=messaging/hornetq-server=default/connection-factory=InVmConnec
tionFactory:write-attribute(name=block-on-non-durable-send, value=false)
```

```
/subsystem=messaging/hornetq-server=default/connection-factory=RemoteConn
ectionFactory:write-attribute(name=block-on-durable-send, value=false)
```

```
/subsystem=messaging/hornetq-server=default/connection-factory=Remo
teConnectionFactory:write-attribute(name=block-on-non-durable-send,
value=false)
```

Using the blocking mode has an impact on performance as it results in extra requests to HornetQ. The recommendation, if possible, is to use JTA to control the sending of messages.

To remedy the blocking in non-JTA send acknowledgments, HornetQ can use a separate stream for *asynchronous send acknowledgments* for improved performance. This involves creating a handler that implements the `org.hornetq.api.core.client.SendAcknowledgementHandler` interface with the `sendAcknowledged(ClientMessage message)` method. A handler instance is set on `ClientSession` and a message is sent to the server as usual. When the server receives the message, it will send an asynchronous acknowledgement back to the client, which is picked up by the `sendAcknowledge` method mentioned earlier.

For this feature to be enabled, `confirmation-window-size` must be set to a positive integer value denoting the number of bytes. A non-JTA acknowledgement request will not block by default, until HornetQ has persisted to a disk. Even if this is good for performance, you should be aware that enabling blocking provides a more strict delivering policy. This is controlled by the `BlockOnAcknowledge` parameter and can be changed with the following CLI commands:

```
/subsystem=messaging/hornetq-server=default/connection-factory=InVmConnec
tionFactory:write-attribute(name=block-on-acknowledge, value=true)
```

```
/subsystem=messaging/hornetq-server=default/connection-factory=RemoteConn
ectionFactory:write-attribute(name=block-on-acknowledge, value=true)
```

Flow control

To prevent clients (and the server) from being overwhelmed with data, HornetQ uses flow control for both the consumer and the producer. By default, it is based on a *window-size* system, but it can. as we shall see, be changed to a configuration specifying the number of messages per seconds as an alternative.

For the producer, the default window size is set to 64 kb. For the consumer, the value is set to 10 MB, which limits the number of in-flight bytes. If you have very fast consumers, increasing the window may result in better performance. These settings can be administered by the following CLI commands:

```
/subsystem=messaging/hornetq-server=default/connection-factory=InVmConnec
tionFactory:write-attribute(name=producer-window-size, value=65536)
```

```
/subsystem=messaging/hornetq-server=default/connection-factory=InVmConnec
tionFactory:write-attribute(name=consumer-window-size, value=1048576)
```

```
/subsystem=messaging/hornetq-server=default/connection-factory=RemoteConn
ectionFactory:write-attribute(name=producer-window-size, value=65536)
```

```
/subsystem=messaging/hornetq-server=default/connection-factory=RemoteConn
ectionFactory:write-attribute(name=consumer-window-size, value=1048576)
```

An alternative solution is to control the flow based on the number of messages per second. This can be achieved by setting the `producer-max-rate` and `consumer-max-rate` parameters to a value other than the default (`1`, which means disabled), using the following CLI commands:

```
/subsystem=messaging/hornetq-server=default/connection-factory=InVmConnec
tionFactory:write-attribute(name=producer-max-rate, value=10)
```

```
/subsystem=messaging/hornetq-server=default/connection-factory=InVmConnec
tionFactory:write-attribute(name=consumer-max-rate, value=10)
```

```
/subsystem=messaging/hornetq-server=default/connection-factory=RemoteConn
ectionFactory:write-attribute(name=producer-max-rate, value=10)
```

```
/subsystem=messaging/hornetq-server=default/connection-factory=RemoteConn
ectionFactory:write-attribute(name=consumer-max-rate, value=10)
```

Miscellaneous tips and tricks

In many systems, no security settings are used and the destinations are free for everyone to use. In these cases, a small performance gain can be achieved by totally disabling the security check in HornetQ, using the following CLI command:

```
/subsystem=messaging/hornetq-server=default:write-
attribute(name=security-enabled, value=false)
```

Whenever redelivery is active, it has an impact on performance because these messages compete with the normal flow of messages. Setting the redelivery delay to a high value and the redelivery limit to a low value will minimize this impact.

A common pattern is to use temporary queues as response channels, and a really bad variant is to create a temporary queue for each request. If used, make instead sure that these queues are reused for as many requests as possible. If durable topics are used, remember to delete non-active subscribers so that HornetQ doesn't have to keep a lot of unneeded messages.

As an alternative to JMS, HornetQ also supports its own low-level API called the **Core API**. Using it can be good for performance, but it is of course bad for standard compliance and future migrations. Another variant of this that is worth investigating is the **Simple/Streaming Text Oriented Message Protocol (STOMP)**. Check more at `http://stomp.github.io`.

Just as with all TCP traffic, the TCP buffer sizes may be profitably tuned. Note that the recent versions of Linux include an auto-tuning mechanism for this, and overriding it may be counterproductive.

Monitoring

HornetQ as a separate project does not come shipped with any management tool, besides the MBean support. In WildFly, the CLI is integrated to both retrieve and set various settings on the part of the HornetQ system.

During optimization work and production monitoring, things such as queue size and the number of connected consumers are of interest.

Information about the in-VM and remote connection factories can be retrieved and set using CLI. The following commands provide a detailed list of the following options:

```
/subsystem=messaging/hornetq-server=default/connection-factory=InVmConnec
tionFactory:read-resource-description
```

```
/subsystem=messaging/hornetq-server=default/connection-factory=RemoteConn
ectionFactory:read-resource-description
```

The same information can be accessed using JMX through the following two MBeans:

- `jboss.as:subsystem=messaging,hornetq-server=default,connection-factory=InVmConnectionFactory`
- `jboss.as:subsystem=messaging,hornetq-server=default,connection-factory=RemoteConnectionFactory`

In the following screenshot, the JConsole shows the in-VM connection factory:

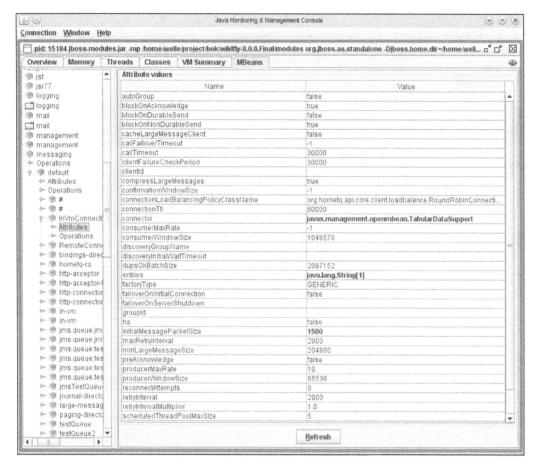

Information about a connection factory MBean

Some of these values can also be seen in the **Management Console**, as shown in the following screenshot:

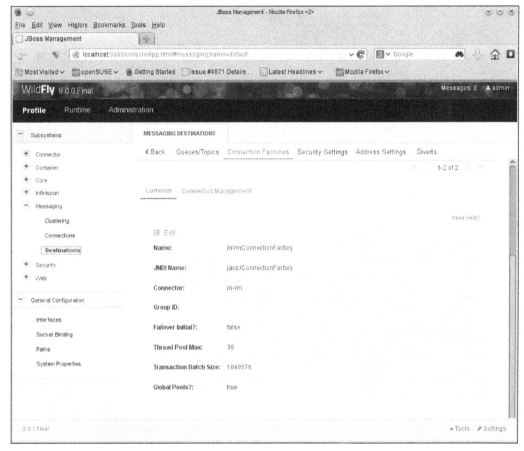

Figure: Information about a connection factory in the Management Console.

There is also information available for individual destinations. In this example, a sample queue named `jmsTestQueue` will be used.

From the CLI, a list of all available variables can be retrieved with the following command:

```
/subsystem=messaging/hornetq-server=default/jms-queue=jmsTestQueue:read-
resource-description
```

The matching MBean is called `jboss.as:subsystem=messaging,hornetq-server=default,runtime-queue=jms.queue.jmsTestQueue` and its attribute values are listed in the following JConsole screenshot:

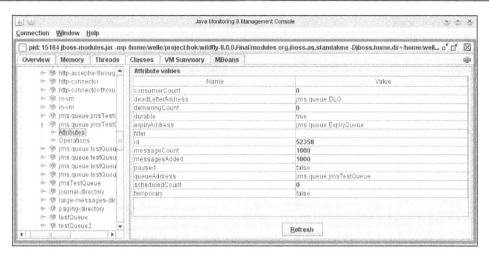

Information about a destination using JMX

The same queue is seen through the **Management Console** in the following screenshot:

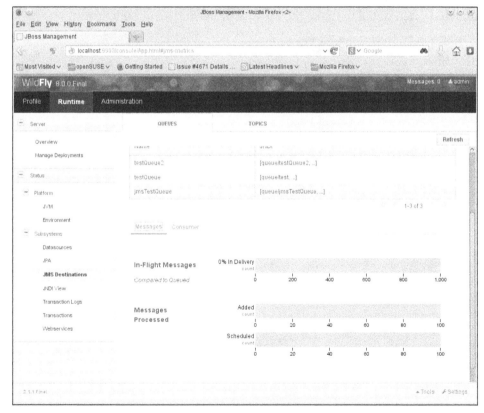

Information about a destination using the Management Console

Summary

In this chapter, we discussed various performance tuning features related to JMS and HornetQ—the JMS provider in WildFly. HornetQ is a very competent MOM that has high performance as one of its major design goals.

The following are some of the general rules for performance-tuning JMS:

- Keep messages as small as possible
- Avoid durable messages (if possible)
- Use JTA to be able to batch handling messages
- If losing messages due to failures is okay, then there are some optimizations available

Tuning HornetQ includes looking at the storage of persistent messages, where dedicated and separate disks should be used for journals and large messages. Paging sizes, flow control and message delivery options are also major factors that affect performance. As HornetQ is an advanced and large project, we urge you to read its documentation in detail to make the most of all its bells and whistles.

We will shortly look more into HornetQ as we now will engage a cluster of WildFly instances.

10
WildFly Clustering

In the initial chapter of this book, we mentioned that systems often need to be able to *scale* with the load exerted to them.

A system that scales up (vertically) with, for example, more memory and CPU cores in a single computer, has arguably several advantages. Upgrades of new hardware resources are almost always completely handled by the operating system and the JVM. Thus, administration, monitoring, and even applications will only need some to no alteration at all. Consequently, there is not much more to actually tune here, apart from what we've already discussed in previous chapters.

> Unfortunately, the *clustering monitoring* subsystem that was initially scheduled for WildFly 8 has for now been delayed until the release of WildFly 9. With it, you will be able to review statistics of the cluster red applications within the cluster according to the plan. You will also be able to integrate diagnostic tools by using the management API, however, this is subject to change at any time. Alas, for now, monitoring is limited to CLI and JMX.

On the other hand, on a system that scales out (horizontally) with the addition of more computer nodes, there will normally be a lot of new things to tune. For a large amount of enterprise solutions today, clustering has become the predominant scaling strategy. This is often due to cost but also because a single computer simply cannot scale to such a level or with such dynamicity as a distributed system. In this chapter, we will discuss tuning in the different realizations of horizontal scaling, in the different layers of a distributed Java enterprise stack and in a WildFly cluster. We will also discuss what clustering is all about.

A lot of misconceptions exist in the areas of distributed systems and clustering. It is, therefore, extremely important to define and describe what different terms mean in each context. Here, we will start out by defining the following core terms:

- Cluster
- Load balancing
- Replication
- Failover, failback, and session state
- High Availability

Cluster

A **cluster** is a collection of distributed computer nodes that are connected by a network in some way, often using **Local Area Network (LAN)**. The purpose of the connected nodes is to efficiently handle tasks by communicating with each other and sharing or dividing work and information among themselves. From an onlooker's perspective, the cluster acts like a single computer, as depicted in the following diagram:

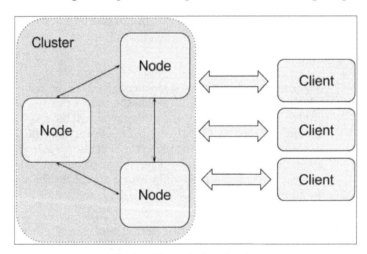

Clients calling a cluster of nodes

Its main purpose is, however, to be more (cost-) efficient in terms of, for example, handling more requests and performing more computations compared to a single machine. Extending this to Java EE means that one (or more) application server, such as WildFly, runs on each computer node and in each of these application servers, there are applications or other components (such as EJBs) that execute and work together in order to handle traffic and perform computations.

Load balancing

In a cluster, the nodes can often handle **load balancing** themselves. Busy nodes can communicate with others, and transfer work to nodes that are not so busy. A non-clustered topology of nodes that do not communicate with each other can also be load balanced, as seen in the following diagram:

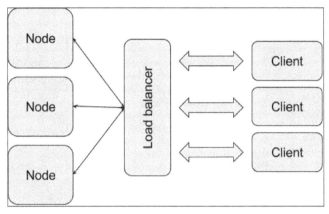

Clients calling non-clustered nodes through a load balancer that directs traffic to the nodes

The nodes will then have a common gateway, or load balancer, in front of them, which routes traffic to the available nodes. The routing is usually performed according to an algorithm (such as first-available, sticky-session, or round-robin) that may or may not adapt itself based on the traffic to, and load on, each node. Using Apache HTTPD with a mod_cluster module as a load balancing gateway in front of a farm of WildFly application servers is a very common setup. We mentioned this setup in *Chapter 7, Tuning the Web Container in WildFly*, and will look into it further in a little while.

Replication

Clustering also normally includes the **replication** of computation and/or data. Data replication involves moving the data from one node to one or more of the other nodes, as seen in the following diagram:

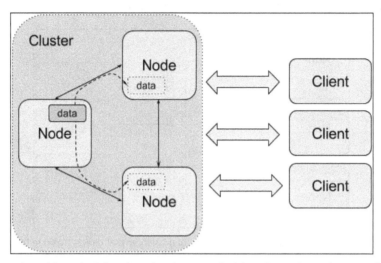

Data replicated from the left node in the cluster to all of the other nodes in the same cluster

Alternatively, data can be moved to a common storage from where others may reach it. This is, however, not considered to be true replication but *shared storage*. The result of replication is that no matter which node the communication is routed to, the integrity of the data is preserved at one or more locations.

Failover, failback, and session state

Should a node not be able to fulfill its duties for any reason, another mode could step in and take care of the work and data. This is called **failover** and is exemplified in the following diagram (true or silent failover is completely transparent to the client):

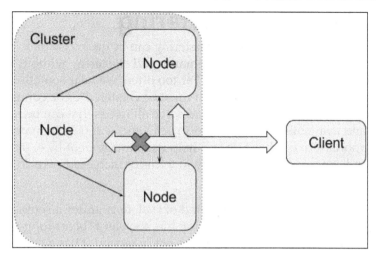

Failover: Should a node in a cluster leave the cluster for some reason
a client call can be handled by another node in the cluster

Should the failing node come back to work again after a period of time, work and data can be transferred back again by a **failback** procedure. This transfer often has some restrictions, for example, it can only happen during the next call from the client.

Data chosen for replication in Java EE solutions most often describes the **session state**. A session is a set of data that belongs to a particular communication flow. It can be persisted but more commonly resides in faster and more volatile memory (RAM). A common example is the HttpSession, where each instance with content is said to belong to, and be unique to, each end user.

High Availability

When talking about a cluster or a system with load balancing, **High Availability (HA)** is also often mentioned. A HA system is a system that, as a whole, is *available without interruption* at *almost* all times. The *almost* here is the fresh wind of reality kicking in. In practice, it can be enormously costly — if at all possible — to construct a system with 100 percent availability. It is, therefore, common to talk about the number of *nines* the system is available to. Four nines means 99.99 percent, five means 99.999, and so on. The number of nines is an often-recurring attribute in **Service Level Agreements (SLA)**.

In a HA system, the resilience to disturbances is imperative. Common solutions are to have more nodes alive than necessary or to have the possibility of quickly starting up new ones. A virtualized environment becomes increasingly utilized for these purposes and for quickly scaling up or down according to how the load changes over time (per hour, day, or month).

The real need of clustering

As previously described, the nature of clustering can be quite complex. From experience, management often blindly demands full clustering without knowing and taking the full implications into account. Far too often, we hear something similar to this: "the system is mission critical, so it must be clustered". The common belief is that clustering will save the business and solve all issues that can be related to performance and availability. Now, clustering can and will help in many cases, but it is always important to be objective and help the management by explaining the actual needs and consequences, especially in terms of increased costs in maintenance and complexity.

It is important to always consider what kind of system is under discussion. For instance, a system that deals with upholding life, such as a "heart-lung machine", is a system that has to operate without errors every second it has a connected client (the patient). This scenario is, of course, extremely important and requires both failover and full replication (and no, Java EE would probably not be an option for implementing such a thing in reality).

An "Internet book shop", on the other hand, might also be considered to be very important ("critical!") for business. It may need clustering in the form of load balancing in order to handle load and failover to guarantee uptime in the case of failure or maintenance downtime. If it's okay that a few clients might lose their "shopping list" and have to log in again on the rare occasion of a failover, then no replication will be needed at all. Thus, it will be easy to scale horizontally. This basic level is actually all that many organizations need and accept, especially when the total cost and other implications of clustering becomes clear.

There are some common tricks to replication that may lower its cost for some resources (such as memory and network bandwidth). These tricks might, however, come at the expense and risk of possibly losing some data in some very special situations.

One example is where replication is performed to only some, and not all, nodes in a cluster, as shown in the following diagram (the risk of all nodes carrying a particular set of data failing is probably very low):

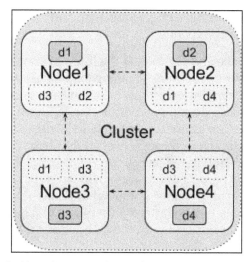

Buddy replication involves replicating the data of one
node to only some of the other nodes in the cluster

Another trick is to send replication data to other nodes asynchronously. This makes the response to the client independent, more loosely coupled, and possibly faster, as it doesn't need to wait for the replication transfer and acknowledgments from the other nodes. Implicitly, this also provides an improved possibility for the server to send batches of replicated data between nodes. Asynchronous replication is exemplified in the following diagram:

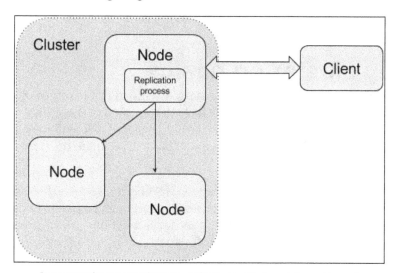

In an asynchronous replication, a client request does not need to wait
for replication to finish before a response is returned to the client

Setups such as these can provide a very stable platform that still meets business requirements related to both functionality and availability.

As an example, we can take another look at the Internet book shop. Let's say that we have a minimal cluster of two nodes that are load balanced. If we have 100 simultaneous perfectly balanced users, this would mean that we have 50 users on each node. When using asynchronous replication with a timeout of 30 seconds, we implicitly say that we can afford loosing the last 30 seconds of session data. In reality, we estimate how many of these 50 users might have clicked on a book to buy (putting it in the session data) in the last 30 seconds. Here, let's say two users clicked on a book. In this case, 98 percent of our users will not notice a failure on one of the nodes (with the exception of, perhaps, a somewhat longer response time when the failover occurs). The two percent of affected users will still have their list of earlier selected books in the shopping card with the exception of the very last selection.

A single point of failure

Even if the different Java EE layers of an application are clustered, there are still other parts of the infrastructure that may be single points of failures. Examples are network hardware (switches and so on), load balancers, and database systems. These need to be investigated further to minimize the impact of a failure.

Another important consideration during risk analysis is to divide the available cluster nodes between several data centers when possible. This ensures that the application will run even if one of the data centers is unavailable.

WildFly clustering basics

When two or more WildFly instances are started with an HA configuration (such as `standalone-ha.xml`), they form a cluster. In each of these instances, the selected web applications and EJBs can be easily clustered. We will look at these later on in this chapter. First, however, we will have investigate the foundations of clustering in WildFly.

The low-level parts of cluster communications in WildFly, such as discovery and group handling, are handled by technologies from an open source project called **JGroups** (http://www.jgroups.org). Higher-level functions, such as replication and data handling are performed using **Infinispan** (http://infinispan.org).

JGroups

The following text taken from the JGroups website provides us with a good introduction to JGroups:

> *JGroups is a toolkit for reliable messaging. It can be used to create clusters whose nodes can send messages to each other. The main features include the following:*
>
> - *Cluster creation and deletion. Cluster nodes can be spread across LANs or WANs.*
> - *The joining and leaving of clusters.*
> - *Membership detection and notification about joined/left/crashed cluster nodes.*
> - *The detection and removal of crashed nodes.*
> - *The sending and receiving of node-to-cluster messages (point-to-multipoint).*
> - *The sending and receiving of node-to-node messages (point-to-point).*

The actual configuration of JGroups is done through a protocol stack where each layer can be configured to match the needed setup for matching specific network characteristics. These layers include infrastructural building blocks such as the following:

- Transport (UDP, TCP)
- The fragmentation of large messages
- Reliable message transmission (and retransmission in case of errors) using unicast and multicast
- The failure detection of crashed nodes
- The flow control

Additional support for message ordering, encryption, compression, and so on also exists. Additionally, it is possible to implement your own protocol. Communication with JGroups is performed through a *channel* that acts as the frontend for the complete stack, as seen in the following diagram:

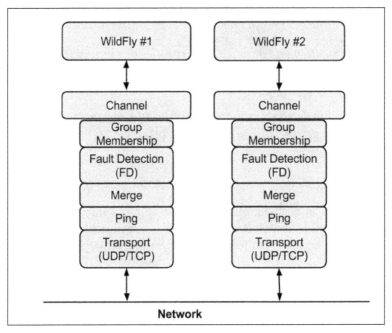

Two JGroups stacks communicating through a network

In WildFly, the JGroup setup is located in the JGroups subsystem. This subsystem is activated in the included configurations called `standalone-ha.xml` and `standalone-full-ha.xml` by default.

Here, there are two stacks that are configured, one for UDP and one for TCP. The actual underlying native JGroups stacks can be retrieved using the following CLI commands for UDP and TCP, respectively:

```
/subsystem=jgroups/stack=udp:export-native-configuration
```

```
/subsystem=jgroups/stack=tcp:export-native-configuration
```

Describing these setups in detail is out of the scope of this book, but we urge you to investigate the JGroups documentation to get a good understanding of how it works.

Using the default UDP or TCP setup often depends on the size of your cluster. From experience, we have noted that TCP is normally faster for a cluster with just two to three nodes, whereas UDP is better suited for larger clusters. To change the configuration to use TCP, the following CLI command can be executed:

```
/subsystem=jgroups:write-attribute(name=default-stack,value="tcp")
```

As UDP is using multicasting for communication, every node that listens to the specified multicast address and port will get the message. The default socket-binding group used by JGroups is `jgroups-udp` and is configured to use the `230.0.0.4` IP address with the `45688` port.

The TCP stack actually also uses multicast. In this case, it is used for the automatic discovery of other nodes. The socket-binding group used in this case is `jgroups-mping`, which specifies the multicast `230.0.0.4` IP address with the `45700` port. As an alternative, it is possible to change the discovery unit from *MPING* to *TCPPING*. This allows a node to connect to a specified list of nodes without relying on auto discovery.

If you run several clusters on the same network, you have to make sure that they use different multicast setups in order to avoid interference. This can be accomplished using the CLI.

For a UDP stack, run the following command:

```
/socket-binding-group=standard-sockets/socket-
binding=jgroups-udp:write-attribute(name=
multicast-address, value="230.0.0.4")
```

For a TCP stack, use the following command:

```
/socket-binding-group=standard-sockets/socket-
binding=jgroups-mping:write-attribute(name
=multicast-address, value="230.0.0.4")
```

Alternatively, WildFly can be started with the `jboss.default.multicast.address=230.0.0.4` VM- parameter.

Changing the group name will also work but this means that messages will be handled by all node's JGroups stack and then ignored if they do not belong to the correct group. This involves unnecessary work, and it is better to change the multicast address instead.

Another thing that can contribute to the efficiency of the UDP stack in large clusters is that it utilizes the *MERGE3* implementation to control merges. This is a more efficient implementation than *MERGE2*, which is utilized by the TCP stack. It is also important to remember that multicast will normally only work when the nodes are located in the same subnet.

WildFly creates the following channels when it starts a cluster:

- `server`
- `web`
- `ejb`

In WildFly, a lot of information and statistics are available using the CLI or from MBeans. This information not only includes the channels, but also the different building blocks in the stack. As an example, the following CLI commands can be used to get the number of messages and bytes that pass through the `web` channel:

`/subsystem=jgroups/channel=web:read-attribute(name=sent-messages)`

`/subsystem=jgroups/channel=web:read-attribute(name=received-messages)`

`/subsystem=jgroups/channel=web:read-attribute(name=sent-bytes)`

`/subsystem=jgroups/channel=web:read-attribute(name=received-bytes)`

A corresponding MBean can be found with the `jgroups:type=channel,cluster="web"."."` name, as seen in the following screenshot of JConsole:

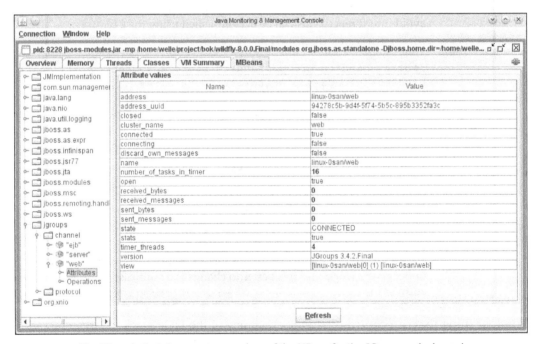

The JConsole that shows us some values of the MBean for the JGroups web channel

By using the CLI, it is possible to ask the channels which nodes are part of the cluster. This list of nodes is called a *view* in JGroups. The following is an example command to get the view for the `web` channel:

```
/subsystem=jgroups/channel=web:read-attribute(name=view)
```

In the same manner, information can be gathered about the individual building blocks under `/subsystem=jgroups/channel=web/protocol=XXX`.

No matter if you add your own stack or start off using one of the distributed ones (which is recommended) for your tuning, we also strongly recommend that every change be tested individually to tune the setup that fits your scenario in the best manner.

Tuning UDP transport

As JGroups guarantees reliable delivery, any lost UDP datagrams will be bad for performance, as JGroups then need to retransmit messages. A common reason for this is the undersized socket that receives buffers on the UDP protocol. These are controlled by `mcast_recv_buf_size` and `ucast_recv_buf_size` and can be configured by the following commands in the CLI for the `web` channel:

```
/subsystem=jgroups/channel=web/protocol=UDP:read-attribute(name=mcast_
recv_buf_size)
{
   "outcome" => "success",
     "result" => 25000000
}
/subsystem=jgroups/channel=web/protocol=UDP:write-attribute(name=mcast_
recv_buf_size, value=50000000)
/subsystem=jgroups/channel=web/protocol=UDP:read-attribute(name=ucast_
recv_buf_size)
{
   "outcome" => "success",
     "result" => 20000000
}
/subsystem=jgroups/channel=web/protocol=UDP:write-attribute(name=ucast_
recv_buf_size, value=40000000);
```

By monitoring the number of dropped UDP datagrams using the `netstat -su` command, these values might need adjustment, especially if the cluster consists of more than just a few nodes.

Even if these settings are tuned, the underlying OS might very well impose a limitation on the UDP buffer size that can't be exceeded.

Tuning node fault detection

Whenever a new node appears, it needs to be discovered and merged into the existing cluster. This merger can be more costly than expected, as there might be a lot of data that needs to be transferred before the node is ready to execute.

This data transfer will naturally occur when a new node is started, but it may also happen if a node is regarded as unusable by the fault-detection protocol (and the following extra checks) in JGroups. If the node is totally unresponsive for a long time due to, for example, a really large GC or lack of CPU resources, it might be removed from the cluster. When the node comes "alive" again, it will try to merge into the cluster and the transfer costs might very well trigger the causes for why it was expelled the first time. This may lead to a "bad cycle" consuming a lot of resources that could be used elsewhere in a better manner. If this occurs often, you might need to tune the fault-detection protocol to be somewhat slower to suspect nodes, or even better, fix the real problem that has made it unresponsive.

Tuning flow control

To prevent fast senders from filling the buffers of overwhelming slow readers, JGroups implements ticket-based **flow control** (**FC**). The tickets are used to prevent packet loss and are defined as the number of bytes that are allowed to be sent but not acknowledged.

Some switches and network cards also implement the flow control (IEEE 802.3x) to slow down fast senders (please refer to your hardware documentation). This is a good low-level performance feature that can be used if the UDP stack is used in JGroups, even if the functionality is somewhat duplicated by the JGroups stack.

Infinispan

Support for caching is mainly handled by the Infinispan subsystem in WildFly. It can handle various data types and is utilized by for example HTTP sessions and SFSBs. It also uses JGroups for low-level communication.

Infinispan is a key-value data grid with support for high-end functions such as cluster distribution, transaction isolation, eviction, expiration, state transfers, and persistent storage (cache loaders/stores). It is often used as a replicated cache, which is exactly how it is used in WildFly.

Infinispan supports the following cache types:

- `local-cache`: This is a local cache that does not replicate anything. If several caches exist, they are completely isolated from each other.

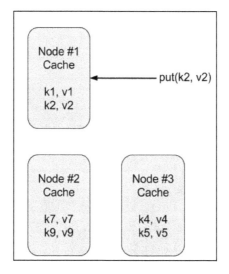

- `invalidation cache`: Cache data is stored in a shared cache store (such as a database) and invalidated from all nodes when changed, which means that they will need to retrieve the data again.

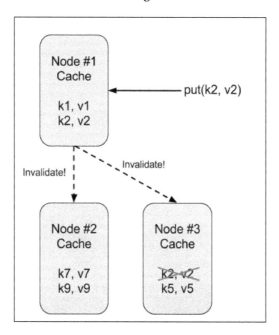

- `replicated cache`: All data is replicated to all nodes, making the caches identical.

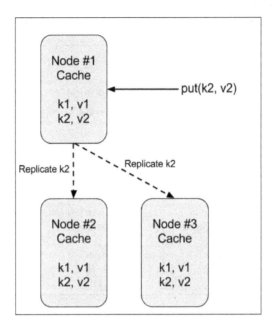

- `distributed-cache`: Instead of replicating the data to all nodes in the cluster, a hashing algorithm is used to specify where in the cluster the data should be stored. Together with a number that specifies the number of nodes that should keep a copy of the data, huge yet fail-tolerant clusters can be built.

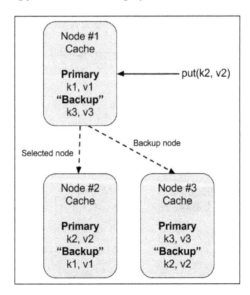

Note that even if we ask **Node #3** about the **k1** key, it will work, as this node will fetch the data from **Node #1**, and act just as we'd use **Node #1** directly. All this is based on the hashing algorithm.

It is possible to give Infinispan a "hint" of the location of a node. This hint provides information needed for the system to make sure that the selected backup nodes are located in, for example, another rack or even data center. Available settings exist for *machine*, *rack*, and *site*.

To limit the number of remote calls of multiple GET requests that are issued, Infinispan can use a L1 (level 1) cache to temporarily store values fetched from other nodes, for a short time. Enabling L1 will improve the performance of repeated reads of non-local keys. This will, however, come at the expense of memory and the fact that invalidation messages need to be issued whenever data is updated. We suggest that you test the application both with and without this enabled before blindly trusting it to provide improved performance.

Configuration-wise, Infinispan uses *cache containers* to group caches for different purposes. The following table lists the available cache containers and their caches, as distributed with a clustered WildFly:

Cache-Container	Default type	Description
Server	Replicated	-
Web	Distributed	Stores the HTTP sessions
EJB	Distributed	Handles SFSBs
Hibernate	Local	Local query cache
Entity	Invalidation	Entity cache
Timestamps	Replicated	Entity timestamp cache

Which one of the existing caches that is defined in a cache-container is specified by the default-cache attribute. Here, the value of this setup is retrieved by using the CLI for the web cache container:

```
/subsystem=infinispan/cache-container=web:read-attribute(name=default-cache) {
  "outcome" => "success",
    "result" => "dist"
}
```

The `dist` value in this case points to a cache in the cache group with a corresponding name. All kinds of cache information can be retrieved and managed using CLI commands such as the ones that follow. These retrieve and set the total number of nodes that can store a value for a specific key name (here, `owners`):

```
/subsystem=infinispan/cache-container=web/distributed-cache=dist:read-
attribute(name=owners)
{
   "outcome" => "success",
     "result" => 4
}
/subsystem=infinispan/cache-container=web/distributed-cache=dist:write-
attribute(name=owners, value=5)
```

In WildFly, the timeout for the L1 can be changed using the following CLI command for the `web` cache (the time is in milliseconds):

```
/subsystem=infinispan/cache-container=web/distributed-cache=dist:read-
attribute(name=l1-lifespan)
{
   "outcome" => "success",
     "result" => 60000L
}
```

Similarly, in the following command, we set the time to two minutes (120,000 ms):

```
/subsystem=infinispan/cache-container=web/distributed-cache=dist:read-
attribute(name=l1-lifespan, value=120000L)
```

All replication in Infinispan can either be executed synchronously or asynchronously, as visualized in following two diagrams:

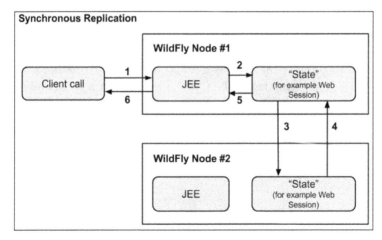

The synchronous replication of State between WildFly nodes

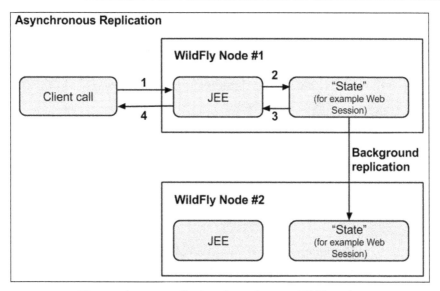

The asynchronous replication of **State** between WildFly nodes

By utilizing asynchronous replication, performance will normally increase at the risk of loosing data in the case of failures. Asynchronous replication is the default behavior in WildFly and is set to an interval of 10 ms. These settings can naturally be changed using CLI. The following steps show us how the web cache can be adjusted:

1. First, we set the replication interval (here to 5000 ms):

   ```
   /subsystem=infinispan/cache-container=web/distributed-
   cache=dist:write-attribute(name=queue-flush-interval, value=5000)
   ```

2. We then continue by setting the maximum number of replication events (here, 10) to be queued before the replication, even if the interval hasn't been reached:

   ```
   /subsystem=infinispan/cache-container=web/distributed-
   cache=dist:write-attribute(name=queue-size, value=10)
   ```

3. Finally, we switch to the SYNC (from the default ASYNC) mode:

   ```
   /subsystem=infinispan/cache-container=web/distributed-
   cache=dist:write-attribute(name=mode, value=SYNC)
   ```

The Admin Console in WildFly has a lot of information about the setup of these caches under the **Profile** tab. Unfortunately, it lacks the runtime information. Luckily, this can be retrieved using the CLI.

Starting a clustered WildFly (using a HA profile) will not start the cluster initialization process until a clustered application is deployed. The node will then either join a cluster or start a new one. This is not optimal from a management and/or performance point of view, as a redeploy or undeploy operation will make the node leave the cluster (if no other deployed application keeps it in the cluster). When the application is redeployed again, the node will need to join, and possibly create, the cluster again. This default lazy behavior can be changed so that WildFly always starts up the cluster during the normal startup and keeps it up and running until shutdown. Issue the following CLI command for each of the caches in a node that you want to start the clustering for (in this case, the distributed web cache):

```
/subsystem=infinispan/cache-container=web/distributed-cache=dist:write-
attribute(name=start, value=EAGER)
```

> More information on Infinispan can be found in the book titled *Infinispan – the Data Grid Platform* by Packt Publishing, at http://www.packtpub.com/infinispan-data-grid-platform/book.

Clustering in Java EE and WildFly

WildFly supports clustering for all major Java EE components. For some components, this support is mandated by specification, and for others, WildFly has proprietary support like many other application servers.

In the upcoming sections, we will discuss clustering and related performance tuning as they exist in the different layers of the Java EE stack and relevant subsystems of WildFly.

Clustered EJBs

As we will see, WildFly, like most other application servers, provides support for clustering of the relevant types of EJBs. It is, however, important to remember that clustering of EJBs is still proprietary and not a part of the Java EE specification.

> The @org.jboss.ejb3.annotation.Clustered annotation and its XML counterpart is unique to the WildFly (and JBoss AS and JBoss EAP) application server and not a part of the Java EE APIs.

This type of heterogeneity sometimes makes the work of migrating clustered applications quite complicated. It also makes it hard to do fair and comparable performance measurements between different platforms.

MDB

Message Driven Beans (**MDB**) cannot be clustered by themselves. An MDB is always merely a client that accepts incoming messages from, for example, a queue or a topic in a messaging system such as HornetQ. Instead, it is the messaging system that might be clustered. Alone or as a cluster, from a queue's perspective, it will choose one registered MDB as a recipient and send a message to it. When talking about topics, all (possibly available, depending on configuration) subscribing MDBs will have the message sent to them. The relevant tuning related to the messaging is located in HornetQ and will be discussed later on in this chapter.

SLSB

With the `@Clustered` annotation **Stateless Session Beans** (**SLSB**) can be clustered and EJB clients will have a dynamic view of the EJBs topology. The clustering of SLSBs only involves load balancing. No replication exists, which is natural as SLSBs have no state.

> According to the WildFly 8 clustering documentation, the `@Clustered` annotation is arguably needed for clustered SLSBs in WildFly 8.0.0.Final (as described previously). In our tests, however, SLSBs becomes clustered without the annotation when WildFly is started with a HA profile.

SFSB

Stateful Session Beans (**SFSB**) are by default, and without the `@Clustered` annotation, clustered when WildFly is started with an HA configuration profile. Just as with SLSBs, with the `@Clustered` annotation, EJB clients will have a dynamic view of the SFSBs' topology.

The passivation of SFSBs in WildFly is handled by the subsystem of Infinispan. In a basic configuration (such as `standalone.xml`) without HA support, a local cache with file-based storage is used. When WildFly is changed to use an HA configuration profile (for example `standalone-ha.xml`), the replication is changed to use a clustered cache. As noted in *Chapter 5, EJB Tuning in WildFly*, it can be beneficial for performance in terms of response times to disable passivation by setting the `passivationCapable` attribute to `false` on the SFSB. This has the logical (in the way Infinispan is used) but rather nasty side effect of also turning replication off. Thus, the state will not be replicated to other nodes as one of them, for whatever reason, leaves the cluster.

A client that calls a clustered SFSB with the passivation turned off like this will receive an exception in return as the call will no longer be handled with integrity when the node has left the cluster. In many ways, this will cause more loss in performance enhancements than gains.

> Turning passivation off on a *clustered* SFSB (`passivationCapable=false`) also turns off the replication for that SFSB. This type of tuning in a clustered environment is not recommended without very good reasons. Strategies to handle the side effects are vital. Technically, these can be experienced in the way of lost session states and exceptions being thrown to clients. Business-related side effects may vary in the degree of seriousness but should be treated as severe until proven otherwise.

Load balancing

How the calls from a remote client to a clustered EJB are distributed depends on the type of EJB and the type of load balancing algorithm that is defined. Choosing an algorithm that suits the needs of your specific application and environment will normally affect performance significantly.

By default, calls from a client to a cluster of **Stateless EJBs** (**SLSB**) will be distributed among the SLSBs in a round-robin/random like behavior. For a clustered **Stateful EJBs** (**SFSB**), the calls are *sticky* by default, which means that the same instance in the cluster will be called from a specific client as long as the EJB instance is available. Should the selected node disappear from the cluster, the replication transfers the session to other instances that can handle subsequent calls.

The load balancing algorithm is realized by a **cluster node selector**, which in turn, is a Java class that implements the `org.jboss.ejb.client.ClusterNodeSelector` interface with the `selectNode` method implemented. WildFly ships with `RandomClusterNodeSelector`, which is a cluster node selector that, just as its name suggests, randomly selects a node in the cluster. Using this selector in a production environment that has demands of high performance and predictability is not recommended. Instead, it is highly recommended that you use a selector that is more predictable in its behavior and/or can make more intelligent decisions in selecting a node to direct calls to. This does, however, require you to create your own selector.

> Rigorous testing is vital before putting a custom cluster node selector into production, as faulty behavior can be costly and sometimes, hard to resolve.

The following example implements a custom cluster node selector using the simple but often effective **round robin (RR)** algorithm:

```
public class RRSelector implements ClusterNodeSelector {
  private AtomicInteger nodeIndex;
  public RoundRobinClusterNodeSelector() {
    LOGGER.info("RoundRobinClusterNodeSelector created");
    nodeIndex = new AtomicInteger(0);
  }
  @Override
  public String selectNode(String clusterName,
    String[] connectedNodes, String[] availableNodes) {
    if (availableNodes.length < 2) {
      return availableNodes[0];
    }
    return availableNodes[nodeIndex.getAndIncrement() %
      availableNodes.length];
  }
}
```

This class then needs to be defined in the configuration on the client side. If the client is a server-side container-based component, such as an EJB, the configuration is placed in a file named `jboss-ejb-client.xml` (note the `.xml` extension used here!). This file is in turn located in the topmost deployment artifact, for example, in the `META-INF` directory of an EAR. The configuration of the XML file with the mentioned selector is shown in the following code:

```
<jboss-ejb-client xmlns="urn:jboss:ejb-client:1.1">
  <client-context>
...
    <clusters>
      <cluster cluster-node-selector="RRSelector">
...
      </cluster>
    </clusters>
  </client-context>
</jboss-ejb-client>
```

If the client is a standalone Java application, the corresponding configuration needs to be placed in the `jboss-ejb-client.properties` file (note the `.properties` extension used here!). This file will then need to be located in the classpath of the application. In this file, the selector is defined as shown in the following property for a remote cluster named `ejb`:

```
remote.cluster.ejb.clusternode.selector=RRSelector
```

The `ejb` name corresponds to the cache container that backs the clustered EJB. The `ejb` name is also default, as configured in the Infinispan subsystem in WildFly. This subsystem is then referred to from the `cache-container` attribute of the `cluster-passivation-store` element of the EJB3 subsystem.

Clustered Persistence (JPA) layer

As described in an earlier chapter, the JPA provider in WildFly, which is Hibernate, can use caches for both data and query cache. This is also true for a clustered WildFly server.

If the application specifies the use of a query cache, WildFly will use a local Infinispan cache called `local-query` by default, with a replicated timestamp cache (named `timestamps`) that keeps track of all the most recent changes made to the queried tables. As this cache is replicated, all nodes will know whether their local query cache is out of date.

These caches are accessible from the CLI under `/subsystem=infinispan/cache-container=hibernate/replicated-cache=timestamps` and `/subsystem=infinispan/cache-container=hibernate/local-cache=local-query`.

The actual entity is cached by default if it is enabled for the application in an invalidation cache called `entity`. This entity is located in the CLI under `/subsystem=infinispan/cache-container=hibernate/invalidation-cache=entity`.

Even if a second-level-cache has proven itself effective in a non-clustered environment, it has to be tested again and re-verified as it moves into a clustered environment. The relatively small overhead of the invalidation cache can often affect performance more than anticipated. Similarly, the timestamp cache can cause performance issues in large clusters.

Clustered web applications

A web application that is deployed to nodes in a cluster becomes available for clustering when the `<distributable/>` element is added at the top level in the `web.xml` file of the application.

 Converse to EJBs, the servlet specification does stipulate clustering with replication of session data for web applications.

In web applications, the data attributes of the *web sessions* (`HttpSession` instances) as used in servlets and JSPs, is what is actually replicated between nodes.

By default, the entire HttpSession (with all attributes) will be replicated to each node each time an attribute in the session is altered during a request. If the session is large in size due to many and/or large attributes, replication can become a serious bottleneck.

By setting the `replication-granularity` element in `jboss-web.xml` to `ATTRIBUTE` (the default is `SESSION`) as shown in the following code, only the changed attributes in a request are replicated between the nodes of the cluster:

```
<replication-config>
  <replication-granularity>ATTRIBUTE</replication-granularity>
</replication-config>
```

Keeping the data of the HttpSession as small as possible benefits performance. Few and small attributes also minimize memory usage, keeps down CPU usage during the required serialization/deserialization process, and holds down the use of network resources.

 A lot of enhancements of clustering and performance have been incorporated in WildFly 8. See more at `https://community.jboss.org/wiki/ClusteringChangesInWildFly8`.

Load balancing with mod_cluster

HTTP-based load balancing can, as we have previously mentioned in *Chapter 7, Tuning the Web Container in WildFly*, (where we also talked about the basic installation and configuration), be set up by installing the **mod_cluster** module in the Apache HTTPD web server and enabling the mod_cluster subsystem in WildFly. With mod_cluster, we get a very effective and adaptive software-based load balancer that can direct traffic to a dynamic farm of WildFly server instances. Load balancing with mod_cluster is based on *load factors* communicated from the connected servers. Thus, mod_cluster can make its traffic-directing decisions based on the actual and individual load on the nodes instead of just relying on an internal algorithm. Naturally, classic load-balancing features, such as, static per node load and sticky session can be used as well. A conceptual example of HTTPD and mod_cluster using using load factors (f) of WildFly instances to direct traffic is shown in the following diagram:

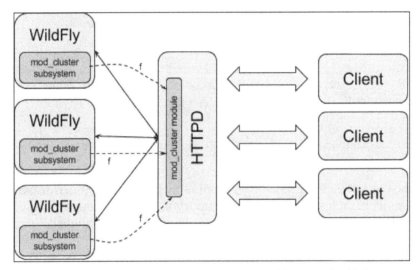

An Apache HTTPD web server with a mod_cluster module acts as load balancer in front of some WildFly instances with the mod_cluster subsystem enabled

The load factor that decides how mod_cluster directs traffic is communicated from each WildFly instance to the load balancer. How the load factor is calculated on each server is decided by a load provider. The following are the two types of load providers that exist:

- simple-load-provider
- dynamic-load-provider

With the **simple-load-provider**, a *static* load factor is set for each server. The given load factor will never change (unless it's manually done), and the load balancer will always make the (same) decision based on this factor. The static load configuration can be useful, for example, in farms where the different servers have the same or known diverging hardware capacity and where traffic is quite constant and similar in terms of the computation need. A server with low capacity can have a lower load number than a server with a higher capacity. The configuration of the simple-load-provider is located within the mod_cluster subsystem configuration of a WildFly server, as shown in the following configuration snippet. The value of the load `factor` attribute (which accepts any integer and has the default value of 1) should be higher for servers with more capacity:

```
<mod-cluster-config ...>
  <simple-load-provider factor="1"/>
</mod-cluster-config>
```

Switching to a simple-load-provider setup, such as the preceding one, from the default dynamic-load-provider requires the following steps to be followed:

- Remove the default dynamic load provider setup by using the following command:

  ```
  /subsystem=modcluster/mod-cluster-config=configuration/dynamic-load-provider=configuration:remove
  ```

- Add a simple load provider by using the following command:

  ```
  /subsystem=modcluster/mod-cluster-config=configuration:write-attribute(name=simple-load-provider, value=1)
  ```

Getting the right number for the load attribute is not always easy and few systems will have a traffic flow even enough for the simple-load-provider to be optimal.

With the default **dynamic-load-provider**, a WildFly instance will communicate a load factor to the load balancer that can be based on several performance-related load metrics. These *load-metric* types include measurements from connection pools, the web container (sessions, connector, traffic load, and more), the JVM (such as heap usage), the operating system and underlying hardware (for example, the CPU and memory usage), as well as your own custom load-metric type. A sample configuration of the dynamic-load-provider with a few load-metric types is shown in the following configuration:

```
<mod-cluster-config advertise-socket="mod_cluster">
  <dynamic-load-provider history="5" decay="2">
    <load-metric type="cpu" weight="5" capacity="1"/>
    <load-metric type="sessions" weight="2" capacity="256"/>
    <custom-load-metric class="myclass"
```

```
        weight="1" capacity="64">
        <property name="mykey1" value="value1" />
        <property name="mykey2" value="value2" />
      </custom-load-metric>
    </dynamic-load-provider>
  </mod-cluster-config>
```

With all these possibilities of tuning, it will certainly be possible to have a setup as close to perfect as it can be. Finding this perfect setup is, however, something completely different. We would advice you to start with a relatively easy and basic setup. Beginning with just one load-metric type, such as the CPU usage (which is the default) or number of sessions, and get its values to work well in representative traffic conditions. After this, you can slowly add more types, tune values, and add possible weighting to each type as you learn more about how the system responds to alternating conditions and values. Having a homogenous system with equal hardware and services/applications running on all WildFly instances will simplify this work enormously.

> More information about mod_cluster, its load providers, and types is available at http://mod-cluster.jboss.org and http://docs.jboss.org/mod_cluster/1.2.0/html/.

Clustering the HornetQ messaging system

In a cluster of HornetQ instances, each node (standalone or as a subsystem in WildFly) handles its own messages. Message sharing and processing uses *core bridges* (a proprietary low-level communication channel in HornetQ) which are enabled by default and uses UDP multicast in WildFly. With these bridges, connections between nodes make it possible for messages to be consumed by clients that are registered to a node that doesn't have the message stored locally but on another node.

The choice of the cluster topology can affect the performance in many ways, especially when the number of nodes exceeds two. In, a *symmetric cluster*, for example, all nodes know about each other's existence, and each node also knows about all available queues and consumers on the other nodes. Consequently, a node is a maximum of one hop away from another. Having a minimal number of hops is naturally good for performance. This topology is exemplified in the following diagram. Here, the Master nodes (Node #1-3) are connected by core bridges, and each node has its own Journal for (persistent – if durable) storage of messages. A client may, for example, connect to one node, say Node #1, and help consume messages from Node #2 or Node #3 to support good load balancing.

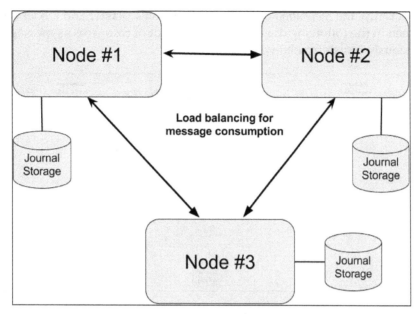

A symmetric HornetQ cluster

In a *chain cluster*, on the other hand, a node only knows about the node (and its queues and consumers) ahead of and behind itself. For a three-node chain cluster, a message can, therefore, potentially be two hops away. This could impose worse performance (in waiting for a message) but it may be required due to a structural need within the organization or the setup of the physical network.

For all the mentioned types of cluster topologies, only load balancing is involved.

Clustered HornetQ nodes can either be of *Master* (also known as *Live*) or *Backup* types. By default, clustered WildFly nodes are all of the Master type and use their own private journals for persistent storage. This means that even if the consumption of messages is spread over the cluster, the messages stored on one node will not be available for others in case of a node failure. So, only Master nodes will handle the JMS traffic, and Backup nodes are more of a hot standby.

In terms of HA and failover (with optional failback), HornetQ provides the following two setups:

- Message replication between Master and Backup nodes
- Shared persistent storage of messages for Master and Backup nodes

For the first setup, the *replication* of messages between a Master and a Backup node, as seen in the following diagram, can take a lot of resources as messages are continuously transferred between the nodes:

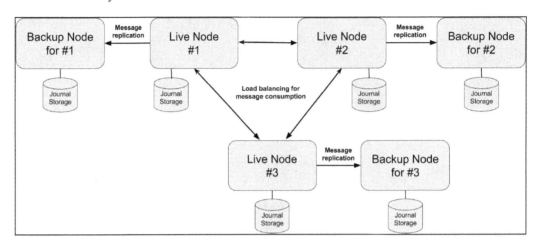

Regular clients are however, not directly blocked by normal replication. There is also often a relatively high-time delay as the Backup node starts up and synchronizes itself and its messages before it can serve clients. Knowing which node has the most correct and current set of messages can, under some situations of failover and failback, also be unclear.

On the other hand, and as given in the second setup, and as seen in the following diagram, a *shared persistence storage* of a Master and one or more Backup nodes, is a good way to ensure that all messages can be consumed without the hesitation of missing any. One should, however, note that shared storage is also where a typical bottleneck might occur. Both network and disk latency will heavily influence performance in this location. Using a SAN with a fast controller and disks is recommended for this setup, whereas a NAS should be avoided at all costs.

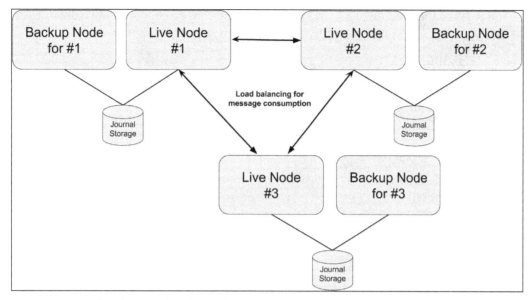

In a cluster with replication between a Live (Master) and its Backup nodes, each node has its own Journal for persistent storage of messages

From experience, we have seen that it is advantageous to have a separate HornetQ cluster (built using HornetQ embedded in WildFly or standalone HornetQ servers) serving WildFly instances (clustered or not) with application logic.

In a HornetQ cluster realized by WildFly servers with embedded HornetQ and where deployment artifacts (such as MDBs) use JMS resources (such as factories and queues), problems are very likely to occur. These problems include poor stability (especially for the Backup nodes) and synchronization issues of artifacts and resources during deployment.

Summary

In this chapter, we talked about the importance of knowing the terminology related to clustering, including load balancing, high availability, failover, and replication. While each feature has its benefits, there may also be drawbacks, especially in terms of maintenance and complexity. The two foundations of clustering in WildFly are as follows:

- The cluster node communication by JGroups
- Data distribution and caching with Infinispan

Large parts of the Java EE stack and its components can be clustered and tuned. In WildFly, these components include the following:

- The different EJBs
- Web applications
- Load balancing of HTTP traffic using mod_cluster
- The persistence layer
- HornetQ

The golden rule for whenever replication is involved is to make sure that the dataset is as small as possible.

Now you can tune WildFly. Get out there and test its wings!

Index

P

periodic-rotating-file-handler 122
PermGen (permanent generation) 64, 78
persistence storage tuning 252-254
pessimistic locking 178
PhaseTracker class 220
Point-to-Point (PTP) communication 246
POJO (Plain-Old-Java-Object) 127
Postgres Query Cache (PQC) 188
PRE_ACKNOWLEDGE mode 251
prepared statements 172-174
PrimeFaces
    URL 221
    URL, for examples 231
    URL, for extensions 235
PrintGCDetails parameter 93, 94
PrintTenuringDistribution parameter 94, 95
Process Validations phase 219
Producer 246
production environment
    availability, ensuring of relevant
        information 92
profiler 31
profiling
    about 28, 30
    in production environment 29
    versus sampling 30
program counter (pc) Register 64
properties, blocking-bounded-queue-
        thread-pool
    allow-core-timeout 106
    keepalive-time 106
    thread-factory 106
properties, second-level cache (L2C or 2LC)
    BYPASS 186
    REFRESH 186
    USE 186
proprietary solutions, Undertow 226
Publisher 246

Q

quality assurance (QA) 13
query cache 184, 187, 188
query caching
    data synchronization, optimizing 189
    versus entity caching 189

query hints
    about 187
    javax.persistence.cache.retrieveMode 188
    javax.persistence.cache.storeMode 188
    org.hibernate.cacheable 188
    org.hibernate.cacheMode 188
    org.hibernate.cacheRegion 188
    org.hibernate.comment 188
    org.hibernate.fetchSize 188
    org.hibernate.flushMode 188
    org.hibernate.readOnly 188
    org.hibernate.timeout 188
Queue 246
queueless-thread-pool executor
    about 106
    configuration properties 106

R

Remark phase 89
Remembered Sets (RSet) 90
remote EJB calls
    overview 137-140
remote JVM
    about 33
    on monitoring host 34
    on remote host 33
    VisualVM, connecting to 33
Remote Method Invocation (RMI) 33
remote WildFly server
    JMX, connecting to 37
remoting-jmx protocol 40
Remoting subsystem 116, 117
Render Response phase 219
replicated cache 280
replication 268
REpresentational State Transfer. See REST
Resource Adaptor (RA) 110, 152
Resource Archive (RAR) file 110
response time
    about 8
    factors, affecting 9
    measuring 8, 9
REST 241
RESTful services 241, 242
Return of investment (ROI) 22

RichFaces
    URL 221
    URL, for examples 231
round robin (RR) algorithm 287
roundtrip 8

S

sampler 32
sampling
    about 30
    versus profiling 30
scalability
    about 11, 12
    horizontal scaling 11
    vertical scaling 11
scheduled-thread-poolA pool executor
    about 107
    configuration properties 107
second-level cache (L2C or 2LC)
    about 183-185
    properties 186
serial collector 86, 87, 90
serialization 237
server configuration file 101
Server VM
    versus Client VM 70
Service Level Agreements (SLA) 9, 269
Service Oriented Architecture (SOA) 215
Service Provider Interface (SPI) 229
servlet container, and JSP compilation
    tuning 203
    tuning hints, for Jastow 205, 206
servlet/JSP applications
    tuning 223
servlet/JSP applications tuning
    asynchronous servlets 226
    compression, using 225
    JSP include 225
    JSP use of HttpSession 225
    scope, selecting 223
    session timeout, setting 224
session 269
session state 269
SFSB
    about 129, 285, 286
    optimizing 147, 148

passivation, disabling for 148, 149
Simple Data Writer 58
simple-load-provider 291
Simple Object Access Protocol (SOAP) 236
Simple/Streaming Text Oriented Message
        Protocol. *See* STOMP
single point of failure 272
Singleton Session Beans
    about 129
    monitoring, CLI used 152
    optimizing 149
Singleton Session Beans optimization
    CMC versus BMC 151
    lock mechanisms, adjusting 150, 151
    time-outs, adjusting 150, 151
size-rotating-file-handler 122
SLSB
    about 128, 285
    optimizing 140-143
SLSB pool
    tuning 144-147
snapshots, VisualVM
    application snapshot 36
    CPU snapshot 36
    memory snapshot 36
software development
    and quality assurance 14
software development, performance focus
    design 16
    implementation phase 16
    performance testing 17
    performance tuning 17
    requirement analysis 15, 16
software life cycle
    about 21
    metrics 22
    upgrades 22
stack 70
Stateful EJB (SFSB) 286
Stateful Session Beans. *See* SFSB
Stateless EJB (SLSB) 286
Stateless Session Beans. *See* SLSB
STOMP
    URL 260
Subscriber 246
subsystem configurations
    about 103

Thank you for buying
WildFly Performance Tuning

About Packt Publishing

Packt, pronounced 'packed', published its first book "*Mastering phpMyAdmin for Effective MySQL Management*" in April 2004 and subsequently continued to specialize in publishing highly focused books on specific technologies and solutions.

Our books and publications share the experiences of your fellow IT professionals in adapting and customizing today's systems, applications, and frameworks. Our solution based books give you the knowledge and power to customize the software and technologies you're using to get the job done. Packt books are more specific and less general than the IT books you have seen in the past. Our unique business model allows us to bring you more focused information, giving you more of what you need to know, and less of what you don't.

Packt is a modern, yet unique publishing company, which focuses on producing quality, cutting-edge books for communities of developers, administrators, and newbies alike. For more information, please visit our website: www.packtpub.com.

About Packt Open Source

In 2010, Packt launched two new brands, Packt Open Source and Packt Enterprise, in order to continue its focus on specialization. This book is part of the Packt Open Source brand, home to books published on software built around Open Source licenses, and offering information to anybody from advanced developers to budding web designers. The Open Source brand also runs Packt's Open Source Royalty Scheme, by which Packt gives a royalty to each Open Source project about whose software a book is sold.

Writing for Packt

We welcome all inquiries from people who are interested in authoring. Book proposals should be sent to author@packtpub.com. If your book idea is still at an early stage and you would like to discuss it first before writing a formal book proposal, contact us; one of our commissioning editors will get in touch with you.

We're not just looking for published authors; if you have strong technical skills but no writing experience, our experienced editors can help you develop a writing career, or simply get some additional reward for your expertise.

JBoss EAP6 High Availability

ISBN: 978-1-78328-243-2   Paperback: 166 pages

Leverage the power of JBoss EAP6 to successfully build high-availability clusters quickly and efficiently

1. A thorough introduction to the new domain mode provided by JBoss EAP6.

2. Use mod_jk and mod_cluster with JBoss EAP6.

3. Learn how to apply SSL in a clustering environment.

JBoss Weld CDI for Java Platform

ISBN: 978-1-78216-018-2   Paperback: 122 pages

Learn CDI concepts and develop modern web applications using JBoss Weld

1. Learn about dependency injection with CDI.

2. Install JBoss Weld in your favorite container.

3. Develop your own extension to CDI.

4. Decouple code with CDI events.

Please check **www.PacktPub.com** for information on our titles

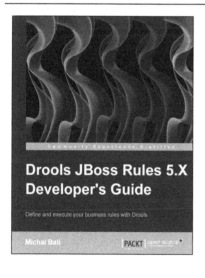

www.ingramcontent.com/pod-product-compliance
Lightning Source LLC
Chambersburg PA
CBHW062103050326
40690CB00016B/3183